TRANSIENT ANCHORS

From Refugee Tents to Research Towers

A MEMOIR

LIBERE J. NDACAYISABA

CONTENTS

Content Warning   v

Author's Note   vii

Part One
MAPS AWAY FROM THE SELF

1. At the Crossroads Between Hemispheres   3
2. First Steps in the Land of Liberty   11
3. Mà Vlast: Beauty of a Thousand Hills   19
4. The Embassy at Avenue des États-Unis   30

Part Two
THE WEIGHT OF SHADOWS

5. At the Gates of Death   47
6. The Stinky Smell of Survival   59
7. Schoolchildren in Warfare   66
8. The Altar Boy Returns to the Shadows   77

Part Three
NOT CALLED FOR PRIESTHOOD

9. Adolescence Away from Home   93
10. Science Was Not the Sin   108

Part Four
THE COLD START PROBLEM

11. Footings Through the Fog   123
12. Sanctuary at Last   135
13. The Parable of the Secular Son   150

Part Five
ECHOES OF THE OPEN ROAD

14. The Scientist in the Mirror   167
15. Seasons of the Cold Snow   183
16. Knowledge Crowns Those Who Seek Her   192
17. Called for Biomedicine   201

Part Six
TRANSCENDENT HORIZONS

18. The Hypothesis of a Lifetime   215
19. Citizen of Many Worlds   227
20. The Improbable Doctor   244
     Epilogue   256
     Acknowledgments   260
     About the Author   262

CONTENT WARNING

Transient Anchors depicts content that may be sensitive to some readers, including, but not limited to, scenes and depictions of death, genocide, childhood trauma, loss, and warfare.

DEDICATION

To those who looked for me,
To those who looked after me,
To those who looked up to me,
To those who looked out for me,
To those who looked down on me,
To those who looked forward to seeing me,
Thank you for being my anchors in the turbulence of life.

For all the loss and all the love,
For all the hurt and all the heart,
For all the sins and all the science,
For all the pain and all the prayers,
For all the hustling and all the healing,
For all the aches and all the anchors,
For all the silence and all the songs,
For all the suns and all the moons,
For all the souls that left soon,
For all the stories that made me.

AUTHOR'S NOTE

In *Kirundi*, the author's mother tongue, *impunzi* is the word used for both internally and internationally displaced people. In this book, the author uses *refugee(s)* to describe both categories of displacement. Some chapters describe internal displacement, while others involve crossing international borders.

The author has not, now or in the past, belonged to any particular political party in Burundi, and the stories told in this book are not intended to take sides in the country's sociopolitical conflicts.

While the author made every effort to verify facts, he acknowledges that memories are fallible and that human recollection is only as accurate as what the neocortex allows. The main characters were consulted to fact-check the authenticity of key events.

In alphabetical order, the following names are pseudonyms: Alexander, Professor Anderson, Andrew, Angelo, Sister Bernadette, Father Bernard, Butoyi, Carlos, Mademoiselle Catherine, Clarisse, Claude, Claudette, Sister Claudine, Mr. Claver, Daniel, Dave, Dr. David, Don, Donna, Elena, Emelyne, François, Grace, Dr. Harrison, Jane, Dr. Jason, Jeff, Jessica, Jonathan, Superintendent Joseph, Josephine, Kendrick, Dr. Lee, Linda, Madison, Marcus, Sister Marie, Marie, Medina, Mena,

Professor Mitchell, Mukasa, Natasha, Nathan, Pascal, Mr. Pascal, Paul, Rachel, Robert, Ryan, Sam, Samuel, Sarah, Severin, Steve, Thomas, Dr. William. Any resemblance to actual persons, living or dead, not related to the author's stories, is purely coincidental and unintended.

Part One

MAPS AWAY FROM THE SELF

"A smooth sea never made a skilled sailor."

— FRANKLIN D. ROOSEVELT

Chapter 1

AT THE CROSSROADS
BETWEEN HEMISPHERES

The blonde flight attendant made her way down the aisle and stopped at my seat in the Brussels Airlines aircraft cabin. It was a cold Sunday evening on January 27, 2008, at Brussels Airport in Belgium.

"Pardon me, can you please come to the front of the aircraft with me?" asked the flight attendant, tapping my shoulder as she motioned for me to follow her toward the front.

The surrounding passengers were staring, wondering what was going on.

With my hands sweaty, I hastily blinked, my eyes darting left and right as I looked for any context clues. The boarding process was complete, but the airplane door stayed open. *Why am I being singled out?* I wondered. Perplexed, I stood and followed the airline steward through the cabin toward the front of the airplane. I felt the passengers' gazes as we walked.

Two more flight attendants joined us as we exited the airplane. I had already experienced multiple stops—Entebbe, Uganda, then Brussels, Belgium—before boarding the third leg heading to Chicago's O'Hare Airport. The first two parts of the trip went without a hitch.

Perhaps there are different procedures for passengers from my country departing for the U.S. through Brussels, I contemplated. My mind flashed to September 11. *Was I being kicked off the airplane? Would they detain me? Were passengers worried this was a terrorist incident?* As this was my first flight, I had prepared for the experience. To look clean, I showered twice that day, wore brand-new shoes and clothes, and packed both my old and new identity documents. To be perfectly prepared, I had preprinted and arranged my boarding passes in order. The prospect of being chosen to leave the plane hadn't crossed my mind. *Did I break some unwritten flying etiquette? Was being a Black passenger a problem? Was this a normal process in air travel?* We stopped just outside the plane on the jet bridge. The three flight attendants made a semicircle in front of me; they looked uncomfortable. The young flight attendant spoke.

"Do you prefer to speak English or French?"

"Français, s'il vous plaît," I replied.

She was petite, with long, straight blonde hair. I tried not to stare. I had never met people with such glowing white skin and hair, a stark contrast to my own dark complexion and curly hair. This flight's passengers and crew made up the largest group of white people I had encountered. I heard many languages spoken. I was uncertain what manners dictated in this situation.

"We received a complaint from a fellow passenger that there is a strong smell, and, um..."

"Pardon, mais quoi?" I exclaimed, in full disbelief.

She repeated my offense and handed me a small bottle of what looked like perfume, kindly asking me to spray myself. My shoulders slumped as humiliation and embarrassment ran down my spine.

Where I'm from, calling out someone's smell in a public place would be considered insolent. In my culture, people would handle such matters more discreetly. If a report were necessary, passengers would subtly inform the air hostess of their concern in a whisper. The steward would whisper the situation to me and hand me the spray bottle. Or better yet, leave me a note along with the spray bottle to keep the process tactful and respectful.

As I pressed the top of the little bottle for a few more applications around my neck, many questions crossed my mind. I did not know that

I carried a distinctive smell. *Had I smelled my whole life and no one ever told me? Are all my people foul-smelling, and now that I'm not with them, the smell becomes clear?* I sprayed myself several times, both under and over my jacket. The smell was terrible; it reminded me of the antiseptic hospital sheets from a clinic where I'd once been hospitalized. I had to ignore the smell and apply it to myself. *Was it just from perspiring during the previous flights? Does flying cause unpleasant smells? If so, what will I do in the future when I need to fly between continents again?*

As I returned to my seat, passengers' eyes peeked up at me, wondering what had transpired. I wished I were confident enough in my spoken English to look at them and say, "I'm sorry for the trouble." The flight attendant asked if I would mind moving to another seat at the back of the aircraft. I gathered my belongings and walked toward the last row.

From the faces I glanced at while walking down the aisle, people didn't look repulsed. It was one individual who had complained; it must have been some asshole. I sat down, and they closed the aircraft door to proceed with flight preparation. We pulled from the gate and prepared for the next nine hours of flight.

My older brother, Isidore, was in California on an R-1 visa, a religious visa that enabled him to train for priesthood in an American deaf congregation. He had talked about the abundant, welcoming, and exciting life in America. This incident was my first glimpse of the new life ahead, and it was not as pleasant as advertised. The language barrier was strong, even while I was still in Belgium, and the cultural norms had already clashed. I was sure it was not the land of milk and honey, and I would have to adapt as I left my old life behind. The incident marked the beginning of such duality, of future paradoxes in which I would have to weigh what I knew growing up against my new reality.

Growing up, I didn't use deodorant or fragrances; I showered, and that was enough. *Will I have to spray myself and my clothing and smell like a hospital bed for the rest of my life? Will I be able to make friends to play soccer with?* The homesickness had already kicked in. I had just left my family, friends, and the only life I'd known for a new one I knew nothing about. I was all alone. On another continent. Halfway from home. Halfway to my destination. Between three hemispheres.

But this was all part of the adventure. *Let's get to the United States first, and I will figure out the rest once I'm on American soil*, I told myself.

Half an hour before landing in Brussels, I woke up as we approached Belgium. I glanced outside at what looked like castles on a winter morning through the window. *That looks freezing.* European winter looked nothing like the rainy tropics of East Africa. There were no more hills, no red dusty roads, no visible green vegetation. I had crossed hemispheres.

Upon landing, I checked the clock on the airport screens and realized it was Monday already. It was 6 a.m. in Bujumbura. My family and friends must now be waking up to the reality of my departure. I checked the small red LG flip phone. No signal. I could no longer access the African wireless networks. I didn't have international roaming. I already missed home, wanting to send "good morning" texts to the family and friends I had left behind. As I walked toward my gate for the Chicago flight, I longed to let everyone know I was doing okay. That's when I realized I was not reachable to anyone who knew me. I was all alone. On another continent. Halfway from home. Halfway to my destination. Between three hemispheres. At the crossroads between a new life ahead of me and the life I once knew.

Thinking back, the potent smell was likely a result of my profusely perspiring during the pre-boarding commotion of finding my gate and figuring out immigration paperwork. Before boarding started, a loud voice came over the airport PA intercom:

"Ladies and gentlemen, to all passengers traveling to Chicago: Federal law requires foreign nationals entering the United States of America to present valid immigration paperwork before boarding. Please have your Form I-94 and supporting documents ready for inspection. Thank you!"

They repeated the announcement in French.

"Mesdames et messieurs, à tous les passagers à destination de Chicago: La loi fédérale exige que les ressortissants étrangers entrant aux États-Unis d'Amérique présentent des documents d'immigration valides avant l'embarquement du vol. Veuillez présenter votre formulaire I-94 et d'autres papiers justificatifs pour inspection. Merci!"

My heart pounded. Heavy perspiration. I looked at my papers a few more times. Among all the applications and documents I had dealt with over the past six months, this was the one everyone had mentioned was the most critical. I was told not to make a mistake on this official form as it could hinder my entry into the United States. It was my first time completing Port of Entry documents while in a foreign country.

The United States had a unique document, one that asked about affiliations with various international political organizations. Officials at Brussels Airport distributed the forms in the terminal for U.S.-bound flights. While navigating the airport and finding my gate, I encountered plenty of French signage and customer service.

However, the U.S. Customs and Border Protection forms were in English, and, out of an abundance of caution, or perhaps fear of making a mistake, I grabbed both the I-94 and I-94W. On the second page of the I-94W (2007–2008 version), there was a set of questions I had to answer, some more complex than others.

Question B:

"Have you ever been arrested or convicted for an offense or crime involving moral turpitude or a violation related to a controlled substance; or been arrested or convicted for two or more offenses for which the aggregate sentence to confinement was five years or more; or been a controlled substance trafficker, or are you seeking entry to engage in criminal or immoral activities?"

I read it multiple times, attempting to understand everything.

Offense, crime, criminal, immoral activities. Okay, the question asked if I have done those things. I had not. *But what did "turpitude" mean?* It could be a critical keyword.

Question C:

"Have you ever been or are you now involved in espionage or sabotage, or in terrorist activities, or genocide; or between 1933 and 1945 were you involved, in any way, in persecutions associated with Nazi Germany or its allies?"

I knew I had never been associated with Nazi Germany in 1945. Even my parents were not born then. As a result of the 1884 Berlin

Conference, my country became part of *Deutsch-Ostafrika*, or German East Africa, between 1885 and 1918, before the takeover by the armies of *Belgisch Congo*, or Belgian Congo, under the colonial rule of King Leopold II. This was long before Nazi Germany.

I had not engaged in espionage or terrorist activities, but genocide raised questions. *What qualified as involvement?* I had been involved in one as a victim. *Should I check the box and explain later?*

The weight of global ideological divisions and geopolitics became part of my welcome. I wondered if this was something U.S. nationals worried about on a day-to-day basis.

Panicking, as I sat alone in a chair, I looked around for help. I tried to ask the family behind me, but they looked away, likely because of language barriers. A few seats to my right, someone around my age came over and introduced himself in Swahili. It seemed he had noticed my distress with the immigration forms.

"Habari gani?"

He probably noticed the Burundian flag necklace I wore and knew I understood Swahili.

"Nzuri."

"My name is Mukasa. I'm from Uganda. Where are you going?"

He switched to English, perhaps knowing well that I'd need to get used to the language as soon as possible.

"I'm Libère. Going to San Francisco for school."

"Oh, cool. I'm going to Los Angeles. I'm starting my junior year in college."

I wanted to ask more about Los Angeles, his school, and college life in California. *What does "junior year" mean?* I did not have time for small talk. I would later learn it meant the third year of a four-year university degree. At that moment, I needed to ensure the accuracy of my I-94 forms. I could not make a mistake "under penalty of perjury," because the mighty U.S. federal law would come after me. He noticed my panic, took my card to check whether I had entered the names and information correctly, and verified that I had checked the right boxes.

"Here you go, brother. All looks good."

I sighed with relief. My paperwork was ready. I could enter the United States.

"Asante sana, kaka," I replied.

Boarding was only minutes away. He asked if we could exchange numbers. I told him I did not have a U.S. number.

"How about Facebook?" he asked.

"I don't know what that is," I replied.

"Email?"

"I have one." I smiled, and we exchanged email addresses.

Mukasa spoke clear English and Swahili, switching effortlessly between the two. His confidence was noticeable, almost as though he were American, despite the long forehead and dark skin characteristic of an East African. I wondered how long it would take me to become as confident in my English. I also wondered if I would meet people in California who spoke my languages. His poise gave me hope, hope that someday I would adapt as well as he had.

These two events marked the introduction to my adventure in the Western Hemisphere. The discomfort at this crossroads symbolized what happens when one changes shores. We took off for Chicago O'Hare International Airport and as the plane left the runway, the antiseptic smell and weight of the forms briefly faded. Ahead, there were nine hours of flight, and beyond that, a life I had not yet conceived.

January 26, 2008. Bujumbura, Burundi. The flight ticket and itinerary from Bujumbura to San Francisco. (Entebbe is not a formal stop, since passengers heading to Europe do not exit the aircraft. The BJM to BRU flight stops there only to refuel and take in additional passengers)

Chapter 2

FIRST STEPS IN THE LAND OF LIBERTY

I approached the desk in front of the large-shouldered TSA officer at Chicago O'Hare's Customs and Border Protection.

"Good afternoon," I greeted him as I handed over my passport, boarding passes, and immigration forms.

"What's the purpose of your visit?" he replied in a deep, almost menacing voice.

"Education, sir. I'm going to school in California."

He looked at the I-94 forms and, after a glance at me, tossed one form to the side.

"What school will you attend?"

"Ohlone College."

"What will you study there?"

"Engineering."

Racing thoughts were hidden behind my measured responses. Each word carried the weight of my future. He rotated between looking through my papers, then at his screen, then back at my face. He stamped three times on different forms, folded them back together and handed them back.

"Welcome to the United States of America, and good luck in College."

"Thank you very much."

I double-checked my passport, I-20 form, and the I-94 card had all been stamped accordingly. I would later learn that the I-94W form was tossed because it is for nonimmigrant passengers requiring a visa waiver upon entry, while the I-94 is for nonimmigrant passengers entering with a visa. I only needed the I-94 and did not need to worry about the sociopolitical questions. If I had known enough English to make that distinction beforehand and had not been so nervous. I could have even asked Mukasa whether he knew the difference.

After clearing Customs and Border Protection, my next hurdle was to locate my gate for the next leg. I looked at the monitor screens. They were large, with so many flights to scan through. That was when I realized there was no French signage. After tracing the numbers, I realized the flight was now operated by American Airlines, and all customer service was in English. Just as the loss of the accent on my French first name, removed during the visa application process, symbolized the transition from a Kirundi- and French-centric life to American English, this moment marked the complete physical shift to a new life.

Now that I was cleared for California, I could relax and observe. It was like in *The Wizard of Oz* when Dorothy first lands in Oz. The fear and curiosity of the unknown, the need to explore. Everyone seemed to be in such a hurry. There were no goodbyes or good mornings. *Was it because no one knew anyone? How was that possible with so many people?* I knew everyone in my village, even their distant relatives, and I would be punished for failing to greet someone I knew.

At close range, a giant Black man passed me. I had only seen such tall people in movies and music videos. He had long strides and a distinctive walking rhythm. In the high ceilings of Chicago O'Hare International Terminal, a large US flag hung. The Star-Spangled Banner, in its majestically distinctive red, white, and blue, was much bigger than the one I had seen a week earlier at the US Embassy in Bujumbura.

I looked through the window. Airplanes were coming in and out of the runway and gates, with airport crew members busy deicing the planes. The heavy winter gear made it look unsafe. *Perhaps I would experience that feeling soon*, I thought. The white powder was so thick that I could barely see the landscape beyond the airport. I had seen snow only in photos. The real thing was even more mesmerizing up close. My eyes went back to the monitors. I had a connection to catch. I checked my flight number on the printed ticket, checked the screens, and confirmed the gate and flight. It was not in this terminal. I asked one of the customer service agents. The neon jackets gave it away. He spoke to me in English. Fast English. When he noticed I was not understanding, he pointed toward an exit where people were heading. I noticed one or two people from my previous flight, so I ran after them. I kept following the people I recognized and looked up and down, left and right, to make sure I was following the signs. I had never had to rely entirely on strangers to find my way, but everything was different. At some point, one woman from the previous flight, noticing that I was probably going to get lost, came over to look at my ticket and said, in a gentle tone, "It's okay, I will show you when we get there."

"Thank you very much," I softly responded.

She was blonde, Midwestern, Anglo-Saxon-looking, and had a baby in a stroller. It was the first white baby I had seen. His blond hair and hazel eyes peeked out, but his heavy winter gear mostly covered him, and I tried hard not to stare uncomfortably. Every few minutes, I discreetly smelled around myself to make sure I was not stinking up the whole place. When we exited the terminal connection bus, the woman signaled for me to follow her. We entered a different terminal, went up the escalator, and she walked me toward the gate.

As we moved through the terminal, I experienced the American "fake" smile. A woman in a navy business suit approached from the opposite direction, her heels clicking efficiently on the polished floor. At precisely six feet away, her eyes flicked up from her BlackBerry phone to meet mine. Her lips pulled back in a swift, horizontal motion. To me, it was not the slow bloom of a genuine smile, but something more mechanical. The corners of her mouth lifted exactly halfway, creating perfect symmetry without warmth. Her cheeks engaged just enough to avoid seeming rude, but not sufficient to create the little creases that mark genuine joy. The expression lasted perhaps two seconds before dissolving as quickly as it had appeared. Her eyes had already moved past me before her mouth finished the gesture, as if her face were operating on a different timeline. This strange ritual was repeated with nearly every American I passed. A businessman rolling his suitcase offered the same calibrated expression: lips stretched, eyes vacant, the whole performance lasting no longer than a camera flash. Each smile appeared at the same distance, held for the same duration, then vanished with the same efficiency. From my perspective, it felt like watching a social algorithm execute itself over and over. In Burundi, a smile, rarely shared with a stranger, was more of an invitation. It started in the eyes, spread naturally across the face, and lingered while you exchanged greetings, asked about family, and shared a moment of human connection. These American smiles felt like facial transactions completed at walking speed, acknowledgments without engagement, courtesy without contact. I found myself studying the physics of these expressions: the way the zygomatic muscles pulled was just enough force to be socially acceptable but not enough to be memorable. How the muscles around the eyes remained completely uninvolved, leaving the upper face static while the lower face performed its brief duty. It was like watching people's faces split in half, the bottom saying "hello" while the top said "keep moving." *Do I smell, and are they laughing at me? It looked positive. Are they welcoming me to America? Why not just speak and say hello?* At least twenty people had smiled by the time I reached my gate, but I felt lonelier than before.

"Gate for San Francisco." She pointed to the gate screen. I checked the flight number on the screen to see if it matched the number on my boarding pass. It did.

"Thank you very much," I responded, nodding to communicate that I understood, but perhaps more so to express relief.

She and the little boy walked away, disappearing into the distant crowd. I never knew her name. I did not know her destination. I hated myself for being unable to engage in conversation and get to know her. In Burundi, I would have gotten in trouble for lack of courtesy. In a matter of minutes, she had kindly shepherded me to the shore of my next destination and vanished before I could start a conversation. I spent days thinking about the encounter. Where I am from, you show gratitude. When someone helps you like that, you are supposed to pack goodies and send a gift bag to their house, or write them a letter. I had no way to thank her. I felt indebted; my ancestors would be disappointed. *But then again, was it the right thing to do in this culture? What was the protocol?*

Dear kind lady at Chicago O'Hare, wherever you are, I hope your kindness has been returned a thousand times over, and I surely pray that a pleasant seat is eternally reserved for you in heaven—or wherever we go in the afterlife.

When it was time to board for San Francisco, a mix of anxiety and excitement kicked in. It was the last leg to my final destination and my new home. I was used to moving and living in unfamiliar places, but this would be the farthest from my family and roots I had ever been. I knew it would be different; I just did not know how much. I watched the flight monitor, closely memorizing the names of the states we were crossing, trying to make sense of how the airplane could fly at such a high speed, yet it still took so long to cross from one state to another. In Burundi, you could go from end to end, crossing seven states by car at 40 to 50 mph maximum, in four to six hours. The physical scale of the United States made me ponder my place within it. I was used to a country the size of the Chicago Metropolitan Area. *How would I ever fit into such a vast country?*

THE PLANE TOUCHED DOWN at San Francisco International Airport, or SFO, just as the horizon softened into twilight on Sunday evening. The airport was a sprawling, gleaming world of polished floors and endless corridors. It pulsed with the rhythm of arrivals and departures, a symphony of languages and footsteps echoing off the walls. For a moment, I lingered near a large window in the terminal, watching the planes glide in and out like restless birds. This was not Bujumbura's airport, where the hum of activity was gentler and less hurried. Here, everything felt fast, bright, and impossibly grand. Customs was a blur of questions, lines, and official gazes. I clutched my passport tightly, carefully answering every query, my Kirundi-accented English steady but deliberate.

"Welcome to San Francisco," a large sign read above me.

I still had no signal on my phone. I had no way of knowing where my brother would be waiting. I kept scanning the crowd in the arrival exit hall until I saw him. He was there, with the same easy smile. We hugged, and for a moment, I thought of home and how our family embraced each other when one of us returned from boarding school for Christmas, Easter, or summer holidays. It was grounding.

We took the elevator up to the airport train station, my suitcase rolling unevenly behind us. I had seen American trains in the movies, but nothing had prepared me for the way it felt: sleek, metallic, and fast. This was nothing like the black smoke of old engine trains I had seen a few times in Western movies. Nothing like the loud noises made by trains stopping at old saloons, with cowboys in Amish and Cattleman hats and trench coats riding horses in dusty towns with no electricity. It was a silent and smooth serpent piercing through a contemporary city. The signs read BART, for Bay Area Rapid Transit, the interconnected network of a train railway system that connects the city of San Francisco to the neighboring East Bay, toward Fremont and Pleasanton through Oakland, and to the North Bay toward Richmond and Antioch through Berkeley. As we made our way between stops, I looked through the window, watching the city reveal itself in fragments. As we emerged above ground, the Bay Area unfolded like a painting. The sky was a palette of oranges and purples, blending into the bay's shimmering waters. Bridges arched gracefully in the distance, their lights like pearls strung across the dusk. The hills, both in the city and far in the North and East Bay, though different from those of Burundi, stirred something familiar in me.

Houses clung to their slopes, painted in pastel shades of blue, yellow, and pink, their windows glowing with life. As the train swayed gently, warehouses turned into clusters of apartment buildings, and streets filled with cars unfurled beneath us. The graffiti along the train tracks was bold and defiant, a language I could not read but understood instinctively. It was art born from resilience, from the need to say, "I am here." The people on the train were as much a part of the scenery as the city itself. A woman in a business suit tapped away on her phone, her face drawn with the weariness of a long day. Across from her, a man cradled a bouquet, the petals bright against his dark jacket. A group of teenagers laughed loudly, their voices filling the train car with a kind of joy I had not expected. I realized how similar this was to the communal feel of Burundian shared minibuses, where conversations are also loud, and teenagers are causing a ruckus as usual.

We stepped off the train, and I felt the cool night air settle around us. It was a dry ocean breeze. Walking to the church on Octavia Street, where my brother was staying, I noticed the few trees that lined the street, their branches draped with tiny lights. They were not banana trees or avocado trees, but they carried the same quiet dignity, standing watch over the passersby. Taller houses stood closer together here, their porches adorned with plants in ceramic pots. In one window, a cat stretched lazily, and in another, the flicker of a television projected colored light through the window. As we entered the little room we were going to share on the third floor above the church, I could not help but think of Burundi.

"Is there any way I can call home?" I asked after I put down my bags.

"There is a landline phone you can use downstairs, but it is very expensive for international calls."

"I will call one person just so they know I made it here safely."

This was important. I had left them with fears, and I felt the weight of responsibility to reassure them I was okay. In the quiet room, I dialed the number for my uncle's home. I had calculated the time zones and knew it was morning in Bujumbura, and my uncle Jean-Berchmans, whom we call *Papa Chris*, and my aunt Françoise, whom we call *Mama Chris*—a common tradition in Burundi to call the elders by combining Papa or Mama with the first name of their firstborn—were getting ready to go to work at this hour.

"Allô," Mama Chris's voice came on the phone.

"Allô, it's Libère. I made it safely to San Francisco, and I am with Isidore now," I replied, full of relief and happiness at hearing a familiar voice.

"Praise the Lord. We were waiting for your call," she said, the echoed delay in her response from long-distance calling accentuating the physical distance between us.

"We are having breakfast and are about to head out for work, but I will put you on speaker so you can tell us about your trip."

"Allô, l'Américain!" Papa Chris and Cousin Lewis, Chris's younger brother, came on the phone, almost simultaneously calling me "the American." I could tell that, unlike the somber goodbyes forty-eight hours prior, they were ecstatic that I had made it safely.

I told them about the commotion in Brussels, the lengthy flight, the snow above Brussels and at O'Hare Airport, and my initial impressions of San Francisco. They informed me that my family had returned to Gasorwe early that morning so they could catch school. Mom and my siblings had cried inconsolably the night after the airport drop-off. I wondered about their feelings as they watched me fly away, uncertain of my destination and experiences. I thought about their bus ride home that morning; it must have been a long trip from Bujumbura. Their return north had mirrored my trip west. I wished they had a phone I could call to catch up. I instantly felt the physical and metaphorical distance expand. A lump in my throat formed as I asked Papa Chris to relay the news of my safe arrival to my family up in the Gasorwe refugee camp. I did not stay long on the call.

"I have class tomorrow morning. I will call as often as possible," I said.

"Good night, and good luck in college," concluded Papa Chris.

Chapter 3

MÀ VLAST: BEAUTY OF A THOUSAND HILLS

When I remember the Burundi I left behind, its landscape unfolds in my memory like the movements in Bedřich Smetana's classical composition "Má Vlast (My Fatherland): Vltava (The Moldau River)." More acutely, listening to the six-tone poem's musical description of old Bohemia's countryside in Smetana's memory maps to the landscape of Burundi, as laid out in my own memory. The flowing musical narrative parallels not just a river's journey, but my own path from the village to the Western world.

My fatherland is often overshadowed by its giant neighbors, Tanzania to the east and the Democratic Republic of Congo to the west. Yet, despite its modest size, roughly 27,830 square kilometers, about the size of Massachusetts, it is home to fourteen million souls today and contains a world of wonders. To those who take the time to look closely at the land, people, and culture, Burundi is a treasured gem.

In the east, vast savannas stretch under open skies, where the Ruvubu National Park is alive with the graceful strides of gazelles and antelopes and the slow, majestic movements of the African buffalo. In the northeast, the fluttering songs of native and migratory birds echo at Lake Rwihinda, where many avian species have found sanctuary. Further inland, the landscape climbs toward the central plateau.

Morning mist kisses the hillsides, and iron-rich soil colors the earth red. Here, the hills cradle banana groves and coffee plantations. In the plateau, coffee cherries, almost as if nurtured by the hands of the ancestors, spring in bright green beans from white flowers and turn bright cherry-red in early summer before they are harvested, depulped, fermented, and washed to obtain healthy coffee beans, which are then dried and packaged for export to distant lands across the globe.

When passing through villages in the spring, the smell of coffee flowers, transiently blossoming after heavy rainfalls, fills the air with a pleasantly sweet citrus fragrance that spreads into the wilderness like a natural perfume. They last for a week or two before disappearing to make way for tiny green cherries that will soon expand. The rhythmic sounds of the coffee harvest fill the farms in early summer. Families gather in the warming sun with large baskets to collect the red cherries from the trees and sort out the best beans, typically the sweetly fermented ones. Coffee harvesting was one of my favorite childhood activities, as I enjoyed eating a few of the freshly ripened red coffee cherries. The fresh pulp around the bean was sweet and tangy, offering a refreshing dessert in the summer sun. The collected bounty is taken and sold to local refineries, and after many rounds, payday late in the summer is a joyful day when families rejoice in the wealth from the coffee tree for the season.

As you move further westward, the hills rise, giving way to mountains cloaked in dense forests. Here, waterfalls carve their paths, and springs feed rivers that flow between villages, supplying water to lower lands and sustaining life in every corner of the country. In the central north, Kibira National Park extends from Rwanda's Nyungwe National Park, reminding us of our countries' shared history and identity. In the south, the lush mountains of Musenyi in Bururi province are home to *Source du Nil*, the southernmost point and true birthplace of the famed Nile River, which sustains billions of lives from Burundi across multiple East African countries, through the Sahara Desert in Sudan and Egypt, all the way to Alexandria and into the Mediterranean Sea. On the far west lies Lake Tanganyika, a body of water so vast and deep it feels like an ocean. Its shores bustle with fishermen, markets, and the hum of Bujumbura, the country's economic capital and former colonial and political capital. It is home to large hippopotamuses and the famed Gustave, one of the largest crocodiles in the world, known to have eaten over 200 people and nicknamed "King of the Nile." The lake is a lifeline, a source of food, commerce, and connection to the broader world. Fishermen in dugout canoes and catamarans drift like shadows across its surface, their nets shimmering with promise as they haul in gifts from its depths. Its waters hold secrets older than memory, and its shores are where I first saw the horizon and wondered what lay beyond. Just north, the Rusizi River twists and turns, marking the border between Burundi and the Democratic Republic of Congo. Across the land, agriculture is the heartbeat of daily life, with families like mine sowing and harvesting crops that sustain not just households, but entire communities.

Growing up on the farm in the North, one of my favorite memories was seeing families take turns working on each other's farms. We were lucky to have land and often had people who came to help. If a neighbor needed help, others would show up. Once, both my older brothers became sick; Isidore had meningitis, and Télesphore had an accident at school where he lost his front teeth. Mom needed to take care of them. Three families sent their older-born children to help till the soil and plant the land so that we wouldn't run out of time to sow for the season. Similarly, when one of Mom's regular workers was sick, Mom would mandate that we all go to her house to help with chores until she recovered.

Before the arrival of European powers, Burundi was an independent kingdom. Its people coexisted mostly peacefully, united under the Mwami, a king who ruled with both authority and spiritual significance. But colonialism came—first under German rule, then Belgian—leaving behind more than just borders, Catholicism, and new languages. It sowed divisions that erupted into conflicts and political upheaval, shaping much of our modern history. Independence from Belgium came in 1962, and with it, the burden of self-determination. Waves of ethnic conflict, a cycle of violence that tore at the fabric of the nation, marked the decades that followed.

My grandparents recounted stories of our ancestry, tracing our bloodline back to the Ntare royal family, one of the four royal lines of the Burundian Kingdom. The *Ntare* (or *Ntari* in old Kirundi) is the most prolific and influential royal lineage in the country, composed of both the first and the last kings of the Burundi Kingdom. On my father's side, we still call ourselves *"abatare,"* even though we have no documented evidence of our connection to that lineage. Most Burundians claim some self-proclaimed royal ancestry. To me, it always felt like a way for Burundians to stay anchored to pre-colonial times.

Yet, despite the colonial legacy of pain and wars, Burundians, in their ethnic groupings—Hutu, Tutsi, and Twa—remain a generally unified and resilient people. We are of Bantu origin, speaking Kirundi, a language not spoken anywhere else, as unique as the land it names.

Most ethno-social studies characterizing Burundians and the people of the Great Lakes Region of Africa argue that, although the population is mostly of Bantu origin, the Tutsi are likely descendants of Hamites, Cushites, and Ethiosemites. This characterization led to the attribution of distinct physical features to describe the Tutsi people: namely, taller stature, pointed noses, and the large foreheads characteristic of the people of the Horn of Africa. Hutus were described as shorter, with darker skin and flatter noses, characteristic of western and central African origins. Twa are descendants of hunter-gatherers, or Pygmies, indigenous to the Great Lakes Region. Among Burundians themselves, these physical characteristics are not easily defined, but they have been the basis of divisions and conflicts since colonization. The *abatare* were Tutsi, and consequently, my family is Tutsi by lineage and ethnic definition.

French, a relic of Belgian colonial rule, ties us to the world outside, while Swahili serves as the language of trade and connection with our neighbors in Tanzania and Congo. Though English is taught in schools, it is a quiet presence compared to the musical tones of French in academic halls and Kirundi and Swahili in bustling markets and village squares.

The people of Burundi are bound by a sense of community that transcends hardship. Traditional dancing and the rhythm of royal drums are the heartbeat of our culture. The *umuduri*, a traditional stringed instrument, sings the stories of our ancestors. The *ingoma*, or royal drum, roars like the voice of the earth itself. It is more than an instrument; it is a symbol of unity and power, its sound resonating deep within the soul of our nation. When the Royal Drummers perform, it is as if the land itself is alive, vibrating with the energy of all those who have walked it before. The Royal Drummers of Burundi are legendary, their performances an explosive symphony of rhythm and movement. Watching them, you feel the pulse of a thousand generations—a rhythm that transcends the individual and becomes collective, communal, eternal. Every July 1, the group performs at the large provincial stadium in celebration of Burundian Independence Day.

Family names, a tradition in many cultures, are not part of our heritage. Instead, parents choose their children's last names that reflect the circumstances of their birth or the hopes they carry for the future. This tradition roots us in the moment, reminding us of where we come from and what we hope to become. First names in Burundi are practically chosen by the Catholic Church because, ever since colonial and missionary times, first names are not in Kirundi. We trace family ancestry through knowledge passed down over generations, not through family names.

My mother, born Françoise Romaine Rivuzimana, did not take my father's name, Venant Manariyo, and my siblings and I have our own unique names, assigned independently based on the meanings our parents wanted them to convey. From oldest to youngest, our birth names are: Isidore Niyongabo, Télesphore Ntirandekura, Libère Ndacayisaba, Violette Muhayimana, and Elysé Mpawenimana. None of these last names has any relation to my mother's or father's names. Our grandparents also have their own names: Helène Minani and Mathias Gahutu (nicknamed Bigombo) on my father's side, Louis Ntahondereye and Sophie Nankware on my mother's side.

From *liber* ("free") + *-ē* (adverbial suffix), my first name etymologically means freedom. Most people pick up on that quickly. Here is the thing: my parents were not high-class aristocrats who knew Latin and wanted to name me "freedom." The names the Catholic Church selects are usually saints, Popes, or biblical figures. On my Catholic "birth card" (or rather baptism card), which is different from the government-issued birth certificate, my name reads "Liberius," after Pope Liberius, a fourth-century Catholic Pope known for starting the celebration of Christmas.

As for my last name, Ndacayisaba means "I am still praying to God," or "I'm still asking God for more." The story goes that my parents were deciding between two last names for me: Siyomvo, which directly translates to "it's not the reason," and Barandondera, which translates to "they are trying me," as a response to ongoing family conflicts over land ownership. Dad wanted to use those names as a jab against the uncles who were causing trouble. Mom didn't like either name, but she could only hope and wait for a better one. She would find out later that, on the way to register me at the civil municipality, my dad spoke with my godfather, who suggested naming me Ndacayisaba—and she was happy with it. When people in the US find out I don't have a family name, they often give me a confused look, as if it's a foreign concept. Someone once asked about my brother and me: "How do you know you are really brothers?"

Religion is another thread woven deeply into the fabric of Burundian life. Over seventy percent of us are Catholic, a legacy of German and Belgian missionaries, though people also practice Islam, various Christian denominations, and indigenous beliefs. Growing up, Sundays were sacred. Mass was not just a ritual but a community gathering, a moment when we came together to reflect, sing, and pray. In Burundi, faith extends beyond houses of worship; the ringing of church bells at the nearby cathedral often echoed at the same time as the *Adhan* from the local mosque, and people from the same community would head out to their respective religious practices. Education and faith are often intertwined. The Catholic Church runs many schools, their halls echoing with the voices of children reciting lessons in French and Kirundi. It was in one such school that I first dreamed of a world beyond the hills of my village.

I WAS BORN IN BIHOGO, a small village in the northern part of the country, the middle child of five in a regular family of farmers, with land to till and bounty to harvest. I was the heaviest baby Mom ever had, and on the day of my birth, she was on her way to a clinic in the nearby province of Karuzi. It became obvious they would not reach the distant maternity clinic before sundown. There were no other clinics nearby. She took a detour and went to stay with her mother (my grandmother), and I was born that sunny evening in Rusagara, a Karuzi village just across from Bihogo. A valley with a small river running through it separates the two villages. As the tale is told, I was born with a gigantic head and was already a pain in the neck for Mom's postpartum recovery, so we stayed in my grandparents' care for a few days before returning to Bihogo. In Burundi, births can occur anywhere, and parents have eight days to register them. I was already crossing rivers and provinces in the first eight days of my life, foreshadowing my eventual nomadic existence. Secular minds would call it fate; the religious may call it biblical predestination.

As a child, the rhythms of the land shaped our days. We planted beans, peas, bananas, sorghum, and sweet potatoes in the rich red soil. Coffee trees lined our fields, their cherries ripening under the sun, while a canopy of avocado trees shaded our home, their branches heavy with fruit. Pumpkins and cabbages, with large, lush leaves, covered our fields by the river.

In the village, life was simple but full. We cultivated under the sun, but we also laughed, danced, and gathered around the fire to share stories. We played with butterflies and listened to songs from colorful woodpeckers. They made our backyard avocado trees their playground. We watched dragonflies dance at night and admired the beauty of white doves and the majestic flight of ravens that toured above our farms. The land gave us not just sustenance but identity, grounding us in a world that often seemed to shift under the weight of history. My mother's hands were never still; they were always cooking, weaving, or cradling.

My father, like his father, *sokuru*, Gahutu Mathias, was an adventurer who worked in different provinces and was sometimes gone for months at a time. He worked as an environmentalist, planting trees to combat deforestation. He was also stubborn and a strict disciplinarian. Although he only had a fifth-grade education and my mom never even went to first grade, he made it a directive that every child of his must excel in school. I can still hear the commotion of Isidore and Télesphore being lectured about their homework. The stories of Télesphore crying that Isidore didn't help him with his primary school homework are still told today. Before I even started school, I had learned the expectations. Whenever my father came home, we all had to report on our daily duties before we could sit down for dinner. When he returned from a long stint in another province, the home felt extra celebratory. At dinner in the little living room, Mom and Dad danced as we ate and laughed at the stories he told of his adventures. I can still hear the music playing from the little cassette radio and the rhythm of their dancing feet echoing under the dim light, illuminated by the petrol gas lamps. Although there is no drinking age and most villagers feed beer to their kids, alcohol was prohibited for the children in our household. The rule was that if we ever craved or felt the need to taste or experiment with it, we would instead go to him and demand anything we desired. One day, I used that excuse to secure money for candy when freshly brewed banana beer was being served to neighbors who were visiting. I told my father it smelled good, and I wanted some.

"You know the rules. What are you asking for?"

"Can I have candy?"

With no hesitation, he handed me three coins, and I ran to Ndiror-eye's store to buy candy. In the village, neighbors were family, and family extended to anyone who crossed our threshold.

Nkurikiye, Mom's goddaughter, lived with us and helped around the house. A charismatic young lady with the most contagious laugh, she was like our big sister. She was the conflict resolution expert and the maintainer of peace. A natural protector in her demeanor, her pristine attention only outmatched her commanding presence over our well-being, serving as both disciplinarian and role model.

STORIES OF MY CHILDHOOD in the village before the war are a mixture of what my memory has preserved and stories from my mother and siblings about my curiosity and stubborn ambition. They say I wanted to do everything my way, apparently just like my paternal grand-father, *sokuru* Mathias, as we called him. My older siblings recount how, if anyone tried to get in my way, I would pick up a wooden stick and beat them, sometimes even chasing them if they tried to outrun me.

Mom still tells stories of a stubborn three- to six-year-old me. One recurring tale is of me commanding everyone to run home whenever dark clouds formed.

"Do you all not see the rain coming? My work is done here, and I won't wait," Mom recalls my commands, as if I was actually helping much on the farm anyway. I would outrun everyone to evade the tropical downpour.

There are stories of me, at three years old, saying, "Since Mom is sick, I will cook." That cooking is "so easy I can do it." I supposedly had clear instructions on how to light the firewood and prepare ugali, a thick porridge made by boiling water with flour. Making it is a task so physically demanding that only young adults could do it. We mostly boiled ingredients in water to prepare meals, with occasional sautéed dishes for holidays. We were land farmers, and since our diet was heavily vegetarian, we ate meat only on holidays.

As kids, we walked barefoot everywhere. The ground was kind to our feet, no matter the season—the cool mud, warm dust, and smooth paths worn by generations. During the summer months, we would rejoice on the dusty ground, playing in the dirt and annoying the elders who had to wash our clothes. The rainy season brought the joy of running in the rain and playing in puddles with bare feet. *sokuru* Mathias would visit and bring gifts. Once, he brought us shoes to wear for Sunday Mass and special occasions. The last pair I owned before the war was a set of brown Sperrys. Although they were too big, I was promised I would grow into them. My maternal uncles often came to visit us from the capital, Bujumbura. They were wealthier and had cars. My cousins' clothes were immaculately clean; I knew they did not play on the red-soiled playground we had in the North. These visits from urban relatives showed me a different way of life.

We lived in a traditional mud house, where builders used tree trunks as vertical pillars and added tree branches or bamboo horizontally to support the mud bricks made from local soil. Stones formed its foundation, and a durable aluminum roof covered the top to withstand the tropical rain. With four rooms, the house was cool in the summer and warm in the winter. Our beds were made of tree trunks and covered with *ikirago*, a woven mat made from dried papyrus trunks. Thick, woven mats topped with a blanket made the bed comfortable, and another blanket was used to cover ourselves when it was cold. A rear house extension housed the livestock. We owned goats, rabbits, and chickens. While my older brothers took the goats out for grazing, my responsibility was to watch over the chicken flock. Each morning, I released the chickens and chicks, spent the day watching for hawks that might steal chicks, and counted the flock at sunset to ensure all were present, reporting any missing chicks to Mom immediately. Otherwise, I would get in trouble when Dad came back.

In village life fashion, I was also responsible for taking care of Violette. The practice is that the oldest takes care of the next child and so on. As soon as a child could eat regular food, they were left in the care of the next older sibling, who was not yet working on the farm. My sister was demanding, or maybe just spoiled, for being the youngest and the only daughter. The stories of her being glued to me are still legendary today.

"*Ene, Libe, Ene*," she would call, asking me to carry her on my back. The same baby language was used to call for food or water. My mom and older siblings still use this to make fun of how spoiled she was, to the amusement of everyone who knows our childhood.

"I'm tired of carrying her everywhere. Can we have a brother next time?" I would say every time Mom came back home. Part of the challenge was that sometimes I would get in trouble with Dad for losing chicks while taking care of her.

Once, we had a hen who had just hatched chicks. Unlike her peers, this hen lacked the usual ferocious fighting spirit. It was her first time having chicks. That day, I was supposed to look after them, but my sister got hungry, and we went inside the house so I could feed her lunch. I heard loud clucking noises outside. By the time I ran out to the rescue, a hawk had already taken three chicks. I knew that was a major loss, and I would get in trouble. When my father came home that night and found out we had lost three chicks on the first day of hatching, I received the expected lecture to focus on my duties.

What makes growing up in Burundi unique is not just the land or its history, but the people's ability to hold beauty and pain in the same breath. It is the child who laughs as they chase a butterfly, unaware of the struggles their family faces. It is the old man who sits beneath a mango tree, recounting tales of the Mwami with a voice weathered by time but rich with wisdom. It is the mother who carries a jug of water on her head, her stride steady, her song unwavering. It is the taste of freshly roasted peanuts sold in paper cones by the roadside. It is the smell of rain on dry soil and the sight of jacaranda trees in bloom. It is the sound of laughter carried on the wind across the globe, creating an indelible memory of home. Even now, living thousands of miles away in a bustling American metropolitan city, I carry Burundi with me.

Chapter 4

THE EMBASSY AT AVENUE DES ÉTATS-UNIS

"Congratulations. Come back on Thursday to pick up your passport," the consulate officer said through the little window inside the U.S. Embassy in Bujumbura.

"Thank you very much," I replied, blinking profusely to confirm I had heard correctly.

"We open at 9 a.m., so come early. Your visa will be stamped. You have class on Monday, so you must enter the US before then."

"I understand," I responded, extending my arm to shake his hand.

That was on Tuesday, January 22, 2008, six days before the commotion at Brussels Airport. I had received an F-1 student visa for college in California. Ohlone College, located in Fremont in the San Francisco Bay Area, expected me in class on Monday, January 28. The two locations are some 9,460 miles (15,270 km) apart, with a social and cultural distance of even greater magnitude.

THE PREPARATIONS FOR THAT week had started one to two years earlier, at Lycée Don Bosco in Ngozi, Northern Burundi, where I had attended my high school graduation in July 2007. I spent that summer emailing colleges in the U.S. to determine the admission requirements. I had contacted admissions offices at Stanford University, Rochester Institute of Technology, and Johns Hopkins University. I found that major universities in the U.S. required the TOEFL (Test of English as a Foreign Language). This exam is used by American universities to determine whether an international applicant has sufficient English proficiency to match the level of American-born high school graduates entering university.

Burundi is a Francophone country and does not offer this standardized test. I would have needed to fly to Uganda or Kenya to take it. They also required SAT (Scholastic Assessment Test) scores or an International Baccalaureate certificate. Like most kids from the countryside, I had attended public schools, taken the national college entry exam, and done well. My placement at École Normale Supérieure, studying mathematics and physics, would have eventually led me to teach high school in Burundi. Through Isidore, I learned that California community colleges do not require TOEFL or SAT scores for students from certain countries. I asked him to connect me with people at Ohlone College. Isidore was a student at Ohlone College, earning credits toward a bachelor's degree to enter the convent's seminary for Theology.

One contact I emailed was Elena, a student activities coordinator at Ohlone, who was curious to learn more about what kind of student I was. In classic American fashion, she asked in one of her emails what my dreams were, what I wanted to study, and what I wanted to do with my life. This American approach to education, focused on one's personal dreams and goals, represented a profound shift from the Burundian way. In such a system, one does not choose what to study based on aspirations or inherent personal curiosity. For Burundians, students take national exams, and the Ministry of Education assigns study areas based on performance on those exams. This happens in grade six for middle school placement, grade ten for high school placement, and grade thirteen for college entrance.

These days, I reflect on the effect such a system has on individual pursuits. If one takes the exam on a bad day, that determines one's destiny. It is particularly troubling that the most critical test is in grade ten, during the peak teenage years. A single exam sets the direction of one's life. I attempted to bridge the gap between different education systems. I needed to imagine somehow a world of infinite possibilities and place my highest aspirations within the realm of what is achievable. There would be no boundaries. I could choose my path, my adventure.

When I read Elena's email at the internet café in Ngozi, I took a few days before responding. I knew I would have to switch my thinking somehow and try to think not like a Burundian but like an American, whatever that meant in my teenage brain. *What would such a choice look like in an optimistic society where everything seems possible?* I summoned as much English as I could muster, struggling to convey my aspirations to alleviate human suffering through mixing medicine and engineering:

> *"[...]*
>
> *I have been dreaming off becoming a medicine Doctor and/or an engineer.If only there would a mannar to mix the two opinions,it would have been my first choice. Technology mixed to health sciencesor something Biotechnology would then be the my needed and wished fields. To be a good scientist who builds the world, who saves the lives,who works with his hands to fight the the death;this what I have been dreaming off and what I aim at now.*
>
> *[...]*
>
> *Please let me know if there is any missing or ununderstood answer to any of your questions.*
>
> *I thank you above all.*
>
> *Libère."*

I continued to describe, with all the clumsy typos and grammatical errors, what my grades looked like, more about life in the village and the refugee camps, and how I ended up at my current high school.

Every so often, I reread this email. The awkward process of translating my thoughts back and forth between Kirundi, French and English is notable. Beyond the embarrassment, however, it reminds me of the complexity of being multilingual. I can almost feel my brain translating between languages, struggling to communicate with clarity and conviction.

Elena connected me with Jeff, an international student admissions officer who was unfazed by my broken English and corresponded with me extensively. He explained that, since I didn't have access to the TOEFL, I needed to take and pass an equivalent English proficiency exam offered by the English Learning Center in Bujumbura.

From summer to fall of 2007, I immersed myself in English: listening to BBC news, reading whatever English materials I could find, hogging the TV at my uncle's house to watch Western movies and MTV, and listening to English music. Don't judge me, but R. Kelly taught me more English than some ESL (English as a second language) teachers in America. By mid-fall, I had memorized the lyrics to "I Believe I Can Fly" and "The Storm Is Over Now." Well, maybe sixty percent of the lyrics. Many songs by Celine Dion, Phil Collins, and even Kanye West's *Graduation* album were also on my top listening list. I would carry a pen and a piece of paper, and when I was sitting on a bus, I would write down what I was hearing to practice English writing for unfamiliar words. I also had one of those pocket dictionaries to look up new words I didn't understand. Often, I could not find a word in the dictionary because I didn't hear it correctly or simply did not know the colloquial pronunciations, such as *sayin'* and *racin'* in "The Storm Is Over Now."

In late fall, I signed up for the English test at Bujumbura's English Learning Center. After about an hour of examination, I passed with a score of 82 percent; I needed 80 percent to pass for admissions. I rushed to the internet café and sent Jeff the certification. The test center had transmitted my scores accordingly, and I was told to wait a few days for a follow-up email. I frequented the internet cafés daily, checking my inbox.

In November, Ohlone College offered me admission, pending the visa interview at the US Embassy in Bujumbura. Celebrations. Anxiety. The preparations for the interview intensified, and the reality of potentially leaving my homeland was materializing. Excitement. Fear. Guilt. I did not know whether I was preparing for academic pursuits to pursue better education that would satisfy my scientific and intellectual curiosity, or if I was simply escaping Burundi in pursuit of the proverbial American dream.

Besides the option to join the École Normale Supérieure, I had registered, as plan C, at two other private universities in Bujumbura. At
Hope University, I planned to study medicine, and at Université du Lac
Tanganyika, I planned to study business administration, a popular
major at the time. As the fall progressed and the preparations for a
spring start at college in the US continued, I had requested a deferred
start for these backup options. In fact, besides a few close friends and a
handful of family members, I had told no one about these plans. I
focused entirely on securing the F-1 visa. In mid-December, I received
an appointment date and started preparing for the big day.

THAT MORNING OF JANUARY 22, twenty-five visa seekers lined up in
the U.S. Embassy in Bujumbura for various types of visas. I was one of
them. To the young northeastern villager in me, there was perhaps
nothing more intimidating than entering a U.S. embassy complex on
Avenue des États-Unis (yes, the street is called United States Avenue).
These marvels of civil engineering were familiar to me only from war
movies, complexes built to be the most secure structures in the neighborhood. Metal barriers and fortified concrete gates enclosed the buildings. Every inch appeared bulletproof. American soldiers, who looked
like the fiercest fighting force the world had ever known, stood guard.
And, of course, there was always the American flag flying high and
mighty in the corner, a warning to any rebels or hostile forces not to
approach the complex. The flag swayed against the winds of Lake
Tanganyika, serving as a reminder of the diplomatic mission and
consular activities conducted inside the sacred halls of the American
empire. Walking to the embassy with the proper paperwork and permis-
sions evoked an overwhelming sense of admiration, a strange mix of
deep fear and safety, but also pride in having the clearance and honor to
enter those gates. I thought about all the immigrant intellectuals who
had found refuge and success in America.

Of particular note was Einstein, the focus of Raymond Schaeffer's
Comprendre la Relativité d'Einstein (Understanding Einstein's Relativi-
ty), which I had been reading that year. During the spring of my final

year in high school, Isidore heard about what I was studying in physics and somehow ordered the book. He had it delivered to my room at Lycée Don Bosco in an Amazon package. The book became a favorite read. Although our school covered broad concepts of non-Newtonian physics that year, I did not understand most of the content; however, I was fascinated and reread it repeatedly. I still have that little book with me today, eighteen years later.

At the embassy's main gate, I presented my appointment documents and went through the metal detector. Once inside, there was one more security check. The smell of air conditioning, meant to combat the intense tropical humidity of Bujumbura, matched the intensity of the security. The sound of my footsteps on the polished floor echoed through the chatter in different languages. Even louder was the sound of my anxious heartbeat; it overpowered my ability to hear the voices around me and obscured my sensory processing. There were waiting chairs outside the interview rooms, with visa seekers seated by assigned numbers. One by one, they entered the consulate office. I was the second-to-last to be interviewed. I could observe the expressive faces of fellow Burundians and count how many people received visas that day as they left the interview room. Only one woman emerged in a positive mood.

My number was called on the screen. Deep breath. Neck stretch. I stood up and took measured steps toward the interview window. I handed over my folder of paperwork and greeted the officer.

"Good morning, sir."

"Good morning," he responded in a rather gentle tone.

Unlike my expectation of meeting a big, long-bearded, cowboy-looking officer, he was a young, skinny, friendly diplomat with nerdy glasses. He proceeded with the routine questions. I had practiced listening to English to ensure I would understand as much as possible of what I was being asked. He asked about my schooling in Burundi. He asked about my areas of interest and why I wanted to study in the U.S. rather than in Burundi or other African countries. It was one of the most brain-stretching five to ten minutes of my life as I dug up every vocabulary word, grammar rule, and contextual language lesson to convey my desire to combine biology and engineering. I emphasized that while Burundian and African universities offer engineering and biology degrees, none offer an interdisciplinary degree at the intersection of the two fields.

He asked a few more questions and ended with a smile.

"Congratulations. Come back Thursday to pick up your passport and visa."

"Thank you very much."

My consciousness seemed to pause. I probably made a few faces in disbelief at what had just happened. He grinned proudly, as though he were invested in my success. I slowly turned and walked away, fighting the urge to pinch myself or jump up and down to check whether my soul was still in my body.

As I walked out of the embassy that quiet afternoon, many thoughts rushed through my mind. *How would I get to California and be in class by Monday, January 28, 2008, the first day at Ohlone College? Did I have time to go north to say goodbye? Did I have everything for the rapid transition ahead?* I had six days to figure all of that out.

But first, I needed to contact California to let the school know to expect me.

The bells at the entrance jingled as I hurriedly pushed open the internet café door. Other patrons looked up from their screens to see what was happening.

"Sorry," I said, still sweaty from the fast walk from the embassy.

"Which machine is available?" I asked the front desk per usual procedure, who pointed to an empty desk, eyes wide with curiosity about what was so urgent that I had caused a disturbance. I sat down, pulled the keyboard closer, my fingers still trembling as I rushed to log in and type my message. Jeff had insisted that I email him as soon as I received a final decision from the embassy.

Before I could finish my message, my cousin Chris, Jean-Berchmans' firstborn, texted me. He was studying at the University of Buckingham in England and was the only family member who understood the foreign student visa application process. He was waiting for news and sent a simple text that read, "??" It was a request for an update, but also full of hesitation, just in case the outcome was not positive.

"The interviewer said they told me to come back Thursday to get my passport. He did say 'Congratulations.' I think that means I got it?" I replied, still unsure whether the visa had actually been granted.

"Congratulations!" Excitedly, he confirmed that I was approved and then messaged the entire family. I would not have dared announce such news myself without having the visa in my hand. News in Burundi ripples like street gossip. I sent the email, and as soon as I stood up to head to my uncle's house for lunch, texts and calls from all over the country started pouring in on my little Motorola phone, which I had received as a graduation gift. I tried to stay calm, telling everyone to wait until Thursday to be certain.

Papa Chris and Mama Chris greeted me with a flood of congratulatory messages when I arrived that afternoon. They were home for the usual midday siesta before returning to work. Since they were adults and experienced with visa matters, the reality of my success began to sink in.

"L'homme des sciences is going to America!" my aunt, Mama Chris, exclaimed, using the usual "man of science" nickname she used to tease me for being the nerdy and shy kid in the family.

"Well, not yet. I don't have a plane ticket," I responded. "How do I actually secure a ticket? I don't even have the money for it."

Reality sank in alongside the success as I realized I did not know how that process worked.

"We'll buy your ticket, and you'll pay us back when you're successful," she said, partially joking. I knew there was no expected interest when borrowing money, but I also knew I owed her more than the ticket price. I hoped I would someday pay her back many times over.

"Merci beaucoup," I replied.

We scheduled our visit to the Brussels Airlines office for Thursday afternoon, after I had picked up my visa-stamped passport.

THURSDAY MORNING, I returned to the embassy. I felt like one of them now, as if I were a recognized diplomat arriving to prepare for duty and discuss global affairs. Only the other woman from earlier that week and I were in the waiting area. I realized that only two out of twenty-five people had received visas that day. I could feel that this moment had changed not only my future but also my future self. I was already begin-ning to dissociate from my previous life in Burundi and imagine, spiri-tually, the new life ahead.

The other woman congratulated me and shared her story. She was a businesswoman and philanthropist visiting Texas for a conference, something she had done multiple times before. I picked up my passport and examined the freshly issued visa, my name and face stamped beside the U.S. seal, confirming that I was moving to California to study engi-neering in America. Goosebumps covered my skin as I passed my palm across the visa page one more time. I quickly placed my treasured docu-ments into the plastic folder, sealed it, and slipped it into my backpack, glancing left and right to make sure street pickpockets had not noticed what I was carrying.

As I walked to the Brussels Airlines office, I pictured the palm trees on California's coast as I had seen them in movies. The chill down my spine was eased only by the humid heat on the streets of Bujumbura. We secured a flight ticket departing Bujumbura on Sunday and landing at San Francisco International Airport on Sunday evening, California time, with stops in Entebbe, Uganda, Brussels, Belgium, and Chicago, USA. I had never left my country before, and I was about to cross three continents and three hemispheres within the next twenty-four hours. For the first time, the world felt smaller than I had previously imagined.

Preparations for my departure went into full swing. My mom and siblings needed to come down to Bujumbura to accompany me to the airport. I had not seen them for a few months, as I had hunkered down to work on the visa process. Télesphore, who was in his first year of nursing school in Ngozi, waited for Mom, Violette, and Elysé there, and they traveled together by bus to Bujumbura. When they arrived, the feeling of missing me disappeared as soon as we hugged. An air of concern replaced it.

Télesphore looked me up and down, almost as if checking that I was the same stubborn baby brother, now bound for university abroad. Violette and Elysé said little. They asked if I was joining Isidore, and that made them happy. Mom looked proud but, like Télesphore, took a few moments to study me closely.

"I wish your father were here to see this," she said quietly.

"Don't you always tell me to look in the mirror if I ever miss him? We can go see him in the mirror now," I replied, to everyone's laughter. Perhaps I was using humor to diffuse the semi-somber mood settling in.

Since Thursday, I had carefully packed my college admissions and immigration paperwork into a neat executive binder, as they were my most prized possessions. I had my new clothes folded and packed in a suitcase. Other than that, I left everything else behind. Papa Chris had advised that the practice was not to bring things to the West, but to bring things back when you return to visit. The advice went much deeper. It was not only about material possessions, but about knowledge and growth. That was also his way of counseling me to return home someday. For some reason, I packed the Einstein book, almost as emotional support to help me transition into the land where it came from.

On Sunday, we gathered for lunch, and, as custom dictates, the elders took turns giving me advice.

"Study hard and stay focused," Papa Chris said in his usual brief, direct, and precise manner.

"Those pretty white girls will distract him," Mama Chris interjected before I could respond. Laughter followed from everyone.

"Would you all like mixed children?" I joked in response, prompting more laughter.

I could see in my siblings' eyes and hear in my mom's brief laugh the hidden sorrow. The humor masked deeper fears and hopes on both sides. I had heard stories of people who go abroad and never return. I am sure they worried they were losing me. They were sending me off to a place they did not know. They worried about who I would meet, who I would become, and whether I would be safe.

Later, while we waited to head to the airport, my mom approached me with a concerned look.

"Are you okay, Mom?" I asked.

"Well, there is nothing I can do at this point. But please do not marry a foreign girl whom I will not understand," she said in a lower tone. My siblings, sitting next to me, burst out laughing again.

"Can you all let this go? You will not even have control over this," Violette said.

"Wait, Mom, would you prefer if Libère marries a white girl, or if he marries a Hutu?"

Mom paused for a minute.

"Okay, fine. Go marry whoever you like. As long as they are good to me, I will be happy," she replied with a somewhat defeated look.

In this exchange, an underlying fear rooted in Burundi's ethnic tensions emerged. I assured her I would find a good woman. It was clear this topic was a lighthearted way to avoid saying, "We will miss you," or bursting into tears. It is also a Burundian way of expressing love and care. I understood what they were wishing for me. Deep down, they worried I would be alone in a foreign land. They knew I would meet different people. This was their way of preparing me for the challenges ahead.

AFTER OUR GOODBYES, I entered the terminal and prepared for my very first flight. I had dressed well for the occasion in brand-new clothes: a black polo shirt with gold stripes, blue jeans, white sneakers, and a black winter puffer jacket for when I would arrive in the Northern and Western Hemispheres. Mama Chris, who had traveled to Europe many times, insisted on reminding me that January meant winter, with snow and extreme cold in the Western Hemisphere. She made sure I had appropriate outerwear.

I bought and wore a necklace with a Burundian flag, proudly displaying it as a "never forget your roots" symbol of remembrance, or perhaps as a signal to anyone I might encounter in foreign lands who would recognize the flag. In its bright red and green colors, divided into four triangles by a white saltire, the post-colonial flag features three green-contoured red stars that symbolize the national motto, *Unité, Travail, Progrès* (unity, work, progress), and represent the three ethnicities of Burundi: the Hutu, Tutsi, and Twa. Like every patriot, I wanted to represent my country across the world. Ah, patriotism, it runs deep and unites the diaspora. I carried the hopes and dreams of my ancestors. Beyond pride, the necklace also represented a symbol of protection.

Inside Bujumbura International Airport, I began to notice more foreigners than I was accustomed to seeing. People of all ages carried passports of different colors, spoke various languages, and came from all walks of life. The woman dressed in regal attire, speaking on her phone, had a West African French accent, Cameroon or Senegal, I guessed. I thought she must be a businesswoman, perhaps supervising important projects. Or she could be a politician on a UN mission. The white men in suits must be diplomats, or maybe NGO leaders. Perhaps they were here to resolve political conflicts or run philanthropic missions. The beer-bellied man speaking loudly on his phone mixed Swahili and Lingala, definitely Congolese. It sounded like he was going on vacation while leaving instructions about incoming shipments. He looked wealthy, undoubtedly a businessman.

Through the window, I could see the Brussels Airlines aircraft on the tarmac, massive and majestic, its engines roaring while men in neon safety jackets loaded luggage through a large door on its side. We lined up to board. I had my passport and boarding passes ready. The process went smoothly. Groups were called to the board. I followed the others, found my seat, and sat down. Once everyone was seated and the doors closed, I listened intently to the safety instructions, following along and memorizing the emergency procedures. The choreographed nature of the process eased my anxiety. I picked up the safety booklet as instructed by the flight attendants.

"Mesdames et messieurs, c'est le capitaine de vol. Bienvenue à bord de Brussels Airlines à destination de Bruxelles, Belgique. Notre trajet pour Bruxelles prendra environ dix heures de vol, avec un bref arrêt à l'aéroport international d'Entebbe en Ouganda pour ravitaillement. Nous sommes presque prêts pour décoller. Asseyez-vous et bon vol."

"Ladies and gentlemen, this is your captain speaking. Welcome aboard Brussels Airlines flight to Brussels, Belgium. Our trip to Brussels will take approximately ten hours, with a brief stop at Entebbe International Airport in Uganda for refueling. We are almost ready for takeoff, so please sit back and enjoy your flight."

As the aircraft accelerated down the taxiway, I looked through the window at the lights of Bujumbura, admiring Lake Tanganyika and the thousand hills one final time. San Francisco was my next home. I could feel the air changing as we took off. Nothing would ever be the same again. I was leaving *Má Vlast* behind. The English lessons, the dreams of a better life, the visa interview, the congratulatory messages, and the family coming together to send me off had all anchored me through the preparation process and the departure of a lifetime. Beneath the excitement for adventure, the young man on the airplane carried haunting scars of war and stories of survival.

January 24, 2008. Bujumbura, Burundi. The F-1 visa granted by the consulate at the U.S. Embassy in Bujumbura.

Part Two

THE WEIGHT OF SHADOWS

"The hour of departure has arrived, and we go our separate ways, I to die, and you to live. Which of these two is better only God knows."

— SOCRATES, FROM PLATO'S APOLOGY

Chapter 5

AT THE GATES OF DEATH

"Are you still feeling better this morning?" Mom whispered in Kirundi, her voice carrying an edge I had never heard before. Her hand trembled slightly as she checked my forehead for fever.

"Yes, I have no fever, and my stomach feels okay," I replied. I was still weak, but I noticed how her eyes kept darting toward the door.

"Don't tell Violette yet, but we have to go home today. Your dad is coming to pick us up later."

She looked unusually worried. This was not the familiar concern she showed when caring for us while sick. This fear felt deeper, more primal. I could tell something had happened.

"But she's not ready. She's still very sick," I said, looking at my sister. Her small body was curled on the makeshift bed on the cement floor, still burning with fever.

"I know, but we have no choice. Everyone is leaving, and we cannot stay. When your dad comes, we will all go home." Her voice dropped to a whisper, her expression intense. Violette and I had spent the past two weeks hospitalized in this quarantine. I was feeling better and was scheduled for discharge that day.

It was the morning of October 21, 1993. I was six years old.

THE BEAUTY OF MÁ VLAST exists alongside a dark past and present. Disease, war, loss, and conflict have shaped my homeland for generations, and I experienced some of its darkest moments in childhood. Many events over the previous three years had led to my sister and me being confined to this quarantine.

In late 1990, while I was still carrying Violette on my back and praying for a younger brother, a dysentery epidemic swept through Burundi. It lingered until 1994. Malaria continued its familiar cycle during the winter months. The rainy season was especially dangerous, as it created ideal conditions for the spread of viral and bacterial diseases. Modern clinics and medicines were scarce in the villages, so elders relied heavily on traditional remedies.

Whenever we woke up feeling unwell, my mother would consult Grandma, whom we called *nyokuru*, or a trusted local healer, asking what could stop the symptoms before they worsened.

One of the most common and powerful remedies was *umuravumba*, known scientifically as *Tetradenia riparia*. It was a plant so influential that it saved my life, my siblings' lives, and undoubtedly the lives of many children in Burundian villages and beyond. Its leaves were used to treat many illnesses, prepared in different forms and given through various methods. We drank it hot or cold, or rubbed it onto our skin, sometimes alone and sometimes mixed with other plants.

This aromatic shrub was our first line of defense. Despite its pungent, spicy, bitter, ginger-like scent, it worked wonders. One winter, my brothers and I developed a severe skin rash. Mom boiled *umuravumba* leaves and rubbed the mixture onto our bodies while we stood naked in the backyard. By the next day, the rash and the fever were gone.

Umuravumba was, of course, not a cure-all remedy, as it sometimes did not work, and devastating loss often followed. Such was the case in late 1991, when my brother Isidore caught meningitis and became severely ill. He was bedridden for many days. They tried all the village's medications on him, but he did not improve. One late afternoon, while we were sitting outside peeling potatoes to cook for dinner, he called my name. When I went inside, he asked for invuzo, extracts from sorghum beer that we used to eat. For some reason, he was craving it. When I asked whether he wanted it diluted with water, he did not respond. I asked repeatedly, progressively raising my voice, but he just stared at me, saying nothing. I suspected something was wrong. I ran outside, calling for Mom to come inside and check on him. We soon found out that he had lost his hearing. Meningitis is an inflammatory infection that, in its severe form, can lead to irreversible cochlear damage and total hearing loss. My brother had a severe case. For the next two years, multiple doctors and hospitals across the country examined him, but each time they said they could do nothing.

BEFORE ISIDORE FELL SICK in late 1991, and almost as if my prayers had been answered, my mom had a son in June that year. His name was Prosper Ntibazonkiza. I felt overjoyed, but only for a short time. He did not live to see his second birthday. In December of that year, while Mom was still breastfeeding Prosper, she caught dysentery, and by January 1992, she was so sick that she could no longer breastfeed him. Around the same time, doctors diagnosed Prosper with malaria. The local clinic, run by nuns, was already overburdened by the winter epidemic. They tried to treat both of them, but eventually had to ambulance them to the provincial hospital in Muyinga. Prosper did not recover and died that January. When the news reached us, I cried for several days in grief. I had to continue caring for my baby sister, despite my protests.

Amid the family grief, Mom was not getting any better, and Dad was still searching for doctors who could treat Isidore's hearing loss. Worried, my uncles took both her and Isidore to Bujumbura. As Mom recovered, Isidore caught dysentery while being treated for meningitis. He survived dysentery, received treatment for his hearing loss, and the doctor scheduled a follow-up appointment for January 1993. Papa Chris and his family moved to Mombasa, Kenya, for diplomatic work in February 1992, while Mom and Isidore returned to Bihogo that same month. The brief relief that they both survived was mixed with grief for Prosper and marred by the uncertainty of whether Isidore would regain his hearing. He eventually became completely deaf in late 1992. He remains deaf to this day.

We learned slowly how to communicate with him, with him reading our lips and regularly reminding us that shouting louder would not help. I knew this from the day he first lost his hearing, and I would remind visiting neighbors and family to speak normally to him.

I have always wondered if, like Bedřich composing most of *Má Vlast*'s symphonic poems while progressively turning deaf between 1874 and 1879, Isidore held a melodic symphony in his mind, a musical image of Burundi, our fatherland.

When the school year began in September, my dad took Isidore to continue fifth grade at the school for the deaf in Gitega. That same month, I started first grade, while my brother Télesphore began fifth grade at the same school. The joy of being a schoolboy anchored me through the grief and recent turmoil. I was learning my ABCs, showing off my writing skills by tracing numbers on trees after school, and entertaining Mom and those working on the farm. The jubilation, however, did not last long. By mid-October 1993, my sister and I had caught dysentery. The epidemic had returned that fall, raging through the province. They removed me from school and admitted us to the quarantine facilities.

WE HAD BEEN THERE for only two weeks when the events of October 21 unfolded. A heavy fog hung outside that morning, making the stench of disease in the primary school's backyard even more suffocating. The school had been converted into a quarantine for hundreds suffering from dysentery. The air was thick with the metallic smell of medicine mixed with human suffering. Through the dense mist, I could barely make out the shapes of people huddled around radios, their faces darkening with each news update. The atmosphere grew progressively more ominous as people began packing and leaving, even those still severely ill. Retching, moaning, hurried whispers, and crackling radio static filled the hall.

The night before, the newly elected president had been assassinated in a coup d'état. Word spread quickly that Hutu leaders, the same ethnicity as the deceased president, had issued orders to kill all Tutsis in revenge for the assassination of President Melchior Ndadaye. The air itself seemed to change as this news rippled through the clinic, the way an antelope senses a predator before seeing it.

We waited for my dad to pick us up that afternoon, but he never arrived. It had rained all day. The downpour had not stopped people from leaving the encampment, and we had to depart before it grew too dark. We packed everything and walked home—one bag on my head, another on Mom's. My little sister was on Mom's back, her fevered body radiating heat against our mother's spine. Unlike the farm days, when I could leave everyone behind and run home, I clutched my bag and steadily followed my mom.

The familiar path home felt different that day—threatening somehow. As we made our way down the old road that led to Mass on Sundays, we noticed that all roads had been blocked, trees cut down to prevent cars from passing. The rain intensified as we stopped to rest at a house by the road, owned by someone Mom knew from church. They were Hutu but had been family friends for many years. More people had gathered there, seeking shelter from the storm.

"Where are they even going?" one man whispered sardonically.

"Let them go home. Now we know where to find them," another responded, his tone even more sarcastic.

Both spoke aloud, their dark, menacing tones suggesting that going home was futile. I scanned the faces around me, trying to understand why they sounded so unfriendly this time. We had visited this house many times before; I had seen my parents share drinks with the owners and other locals, and I had played with their children. *Why were they suddenly so hostile?* On the far side of the living room, someone remarked that Dad had been stopped on his way to pick us up. The fear in my mom's eyes intensified.

"Let's go," Mom whispered.

"The rain is still pouring," I replied.

"Don't worry. It will clear soon, and we'll reach your dad shortly," she assured me.

I grabbed my things, and we set off, walking in the heavy rain. After about half a mile, the rain stopped, but the dark clouds mingling with the fading evening light made the walk colder than usual. The acrid scent of fresh dung and upturned soil lingered in the air—a smell I've never forgotten.

We found Dad at one of the intersections. He stood in front of a barricade, his bike parked at the side. It was around six o'clock, the daylight fading into night. A few feet away, a group of men holding machetes guarded the intersection. They were neighbors we knew—the men my father used to share beers with. This time, however, they were not laughing, cheering with drinks, or playing *urubuguzo* (also called *igisoro*), the local version of the mancala game typically played in neighborhood bars.

"There's your wife you've been waiting for," they shouted mockingly. "You can go home now."

Dad did not respond; he anxiously waited for us to reach him on the other side of the barricade. He hugged us, and together we walked back home. He explained that this group had been searching for a wealthy Tutsi family in the neighborhood who had already escaped. He also mentioned that another armed group was looking for my uncle Julien, the eldest of Dad's siblings, who lived next door.

We passed the old elementary school where I had started classes just five weeks earlier. All the classroom doors and windows were locked. No guard was in sight. No children played on the grounds. No birds sang in the nearby bushes where we once played hide-and-seek. Only the wind rustled the eucalyptus trees surrounding the schoolyard. A profound, heavy gloom filled the air that was once filled with happy laughs of pupils.

In the village, the streets were empty. The village was silent—not the peaceful quiet of an ordinary evening, but the heavy stillness that comes with a dark winter night.

Dad reassured us that everything would be okay. When we arrived home, he told us to rest. He planned to go on patrol, watch for intruders, and speak with his friends about the situation. We rejoined Télesphore, who had stayed behind with Nkurikiye. Some families from the neighborhood stopped by to check on us. Conversations circled the night ahead, and everyone insisted that nothing would happen to us.

For that brief hour, it was a relief to be surrounded by familiar, friendly faces. People came and went, promising to pray for my sister, who was still sick.

Within the hour, Grace, a Hutu neighbor, arrived at our house, nearly out of breath.

"They've taken him, and they're coming here," she warned. "Run—right now!"

The urgency in her voice made my recovering stomach tighten.

"Where will we go?" Mom asked, her voice unsteady.

"There's no time. Take Violette—let's go!" Grace shouted as she grabbed Télesphore's hand and ran. Mom quickly lifted my sister and followed.

"Close the doors and take Libère," Mom called to Nkurikiye as she rushed out. Nkurikiye grabbed me, and with no time to shut the door, we ran through the back of the house.

Before Nkurikiye and I could pass the tree fence and reach the road south of the house, we heard a large group of men on the main road chanting for "Hutu victory," approaching from the front yard. Some ran ahead, quickly surrounding the house. We hid behind a corner of the tree fence and stayed there all night. The thick fence of pencil cacti was dense on two sides, while a tall banana grove shielded the third. I curled into Nkurikiye's arms, the cool, slightly damp soil pressing against my feet. We could hear my father's faint voice answering their shouts as they struck out in frustration, angry that they had not found us at home. They searched the house and backyard thoroughly, calling out and looking between the banana trees and along the fences.

Footsteps coming from the left side sounded like a giant man pushing through the banana leaves. I could see his shadow under the bright moonlight as he approached the corner where Nkurikiye and I were hiding. Holding a long machete in one hand and a spear in the other, he stood directly behind the tree fence facing us. The moonlight caught the blade's edge, making it gleam, as if it had been sharpened or recently bought. He was tall, his shadow extending far through the green bean vegetation. At one point, the man tapped the fence with his machete as if to ruffle anyone who may be hiding there. Worried that I might make noise, Nkurikiye covered and pressed my mouth with her hand. I could feel her own heart pounding against my back as we huddled together.

In the distance, we could hear my father being beaten, screaming, asking them to stop. Each cry seemed to echo forever in the still night air. The optimism, trust, and hope he had shown earlier, reassuring us before he left, had vanished. Eventually, we heard my dad's last scream followed by a heavy thud that seemed to shake the earth itself. Nkurikiye held me tighter, her arms trembling around me. Even at that age, I knew what it meant; it was his last breath, and his soul had joined the angels. leaving us to navigate this earthly existence alone. The silence that followed was deafening, broken only by the continued chants of victory and the sound of our house being ransacked. A few minutes later, the big man standing guard above us rejoined his group. The sound of their footsteps and voices eventually faded, replaced by the chirping of crickets, as if nothing had happened. At some point, I fell asleep.

I WOKE UP IN the early hours of the morning, my feet cold and my body still held in Nkurikiye's arms. With gentle but urgent hands, she checked my fever, asked if I felt okay, and said we needed to move as soon as possible to go find my mom and my siblings. It was before sunrise, probably 4 or 5 a.m. The air was sharp with cold, and wisps of fog clung to the ground. She checked the empty streets, and we ran. On the way, we passed by my grandma's house, and we could hear her crying, lamenting that they had killed all her children. Nkurikiye kept running to our neighbor, Domitila's house. She was one of our favorite neighbors. She was the kindest old lady, a grandmother to all the village kids. She used to feed and care for any kid whose parents were busy on the farm. Nkurikiye probably had a sense that if Mom was to go anywhere, this would be the place. She knocked softly on the door.

"Who's there?" Domitila asked.

"It's Nkurikiye. Do you know where Libère's mom is?" she asked, her voice almost breaking.

"No, I do not know where they are," she responded, absolutely not trusting anyone without verifying intentions.

"I have Libère with me," Nkurikiye replied, almost as though to assure her that her intentions were good.

The door opened slowly, her eyes peeking through the narrow gap. She glanced around, then quickly ushered us inside and shut the door behind us. Inside, we found Mom, Violette, and Télesphore hiding in one of her bedrooms, along with several of my cousins. Everyone sat in complete silence.

Mom and Violette had not reached Domitila's house until early that morning. When they left the night before, they did not get far and spent the night hiding in different corners of the neighborhood. They listened to Grandma cry throughout the night as she tried to return in search of us, but without success. Télesphore, who had left with the woman who warned us, was not found until morning. A neighbor discovered him abandoned in a ground pit and reported it to Domitila. When she brought him back, the neighbor was subjected to the same investigative questioning as Nkurikiye.

The Hutu neighbors sheltering us sent their children to watch for any approaching danger and report back. They also shared any news they heard about our missing fathers. From nearby hills and surrounding neighborhoods, we could hear chants and screams, and we knew lives were being taken. The tension of waiting for news, combined with whispered reports from the children acting as lookouts, deepened the fear on everyone's faces.

On Friday, around midday, Mom decided we should return to the house to eat and pack a few belongings. Only minutes after we entered, a group of killers arrived and ambushed us. A man we knew well was leading them. Ndiroreye had been a friend of our family. We once exchanged food items with his household. Many times, Mom had sent me to his house to borrow salt, and his children often came to ours to ask for cooking oil. That day, he was no longer the man I recognized. His eyes were red, as if he were under the influence. He raised his bow and arrows and prepared to shoot at us. Mom dropped to her knees in front of him, praying and begging, placing herself between his arrows and us as we hid in the corner of the room.

"Get up and go," he shouted, lowering his bow. "You and your husband were good to me. Leave now and run away, or someone else will kill you."

We ran out of the house, grabbing whatever we could carry.

Ndiroreye would later confess to this moment. He described how, like a final meal, Dad had gone to a local bar the night before and bought drinks for him and the other killers, which they shared before the violence began. The court found him guilty, and he later died in prison.

After he ordered us to leave, some men ran after us, and we scattered into different hiding places. We ended up about a kilometer away, down in the valley where tall trees grew. I was wedged inside a thick bush with my cousin Eric, Uncle Julien's third-born. He was Télesphore's age.

I knew this part of the land, but Eric was even more familiar with the bushes because he and my brothers used to herd goats in this valley. We squatted with our heads lowered. The leaves were wet and cold against our skin, and thorns snagged our clothes, but we did not dare move. We knew how close the roads were, and we could hear everything.

The usual afternoon calls of doves echoed in the distance. I looked west toward the hillside where we used to harvest beans and wondered if we would ever return there in a few months. Prairie birds sang their familiar songs, but this time their voices sounded louder and more somber, mixed with the distant cries of children and adults.

Uncertain whether it was safe to move, we stayed there for hours, from morning until evening. The silence was so complete that footsteps could be heard from far away. Hutu men were searching for us. Each time someone passed, we pressed ourselves lower, the earthy scent of sorghum plants filling our nostrils. Several groups passed by before someone finally came looking for us. The neighbors had sent their children to search for us. When they found us, the feeling was a mixture of relief and worry. We were safe for the moment, but we did not know whether everyone else was.

Once it became clear that Domitila's hiding place had been discovered, she decided we could no longer stay at her house. After the children signaled that the path to the next hiding place was safe, she called us out. We moved slowly toward one of her plots of land that held a small, untouched forest. Tall trees towered overhead, and the ground was carpeted with dry, fallen leaves. I hated that place. The tree trunks in that forest were known for harboring some of the most enormous spiders. That night, spiders were the last thing on our minds. We chose a spot far from the roads where no one would hear us and settled there. The broad leaves offered some cover, but every rustle sounded like danger. We spent the night there until Saturday morning, when rumors of military vehicles began to spread, and the possibility of a safe escape stirred cautious hope.

The presence of the military in the area further increased tension in the neighborhood, as Hutu families began fleeing in fear that soldiers might persecute them for the killings. That Saturday morning, as we sat inside Domitila's house, we could hear the sound of running feet. The heavy thudding resembled cows charging toward the river on a summer day. Soon after, the village fell silent as people left.

We remained at Domitila's house until nightfall, when news from nearby villages began to arrive. The first military vehicle bypassed us and went to Rusagara, where I was born and where Grandma Sophia lived. There, they found my aunt, Mama Gede, injured by machetes, and transported her for medical care. Mama Gede survived and still bears multiple machete scars to this day. That vehicle did not return for us, as it had been reassigned to Karuzi. The hope of rescue that day disappeared. News of my aunt's injury deepened the fear that we had lost others on my mother's side. That afternoon, Mom tried to leave us at Domitila's house so she could go to Rusagara to look for her family. When she attempted to say goodbye, we all broke down in tears. Domitila refused to let her go and insisted she stay with us. Late that night, we returned to the hiding place. One family had a persistent cough and could not remain quiet. As the coughing continued, we feared we would be discovered, so we were moved to another location. We shifted again to a different corner as an added precaution. Thankfully, everyone in hiding survived until morning.

EARLY SUNDAY MORNING, the twenty-fourth, a neighbor briefly took us into their home for a meal. The food had been prepared for a wedding that was planned for that weekend. Everyone was starving, so we ate quickly before running back to Domitila's house. While fetching water, she encountered a group of Hutu men armed with machetes, celebrating and dividing their rewards.

She returned in tears, reporting that they had decided to kill all Tutsi males. The intent was clear. They sought to eliminate any trace of the "Tutsi gene," believing the most effective way was to kill every Tutsi man, while forcing the women to become wives of Hutu men. The mothers broke down, some clutching us in despair, others praying, and some urgently discussing new plans to hide and save the boys.

Amid the weeping and lamentations, we heard the sound of another military vehicle approaching from a distance. Domitila sent two girls to the roadside to raise their arms and signal that people were hiding there. When the soldiers noticed the raised arms, they were told that civilians were present and that the killers were only an hour away.

As the military vehicle drew closer and began to slow, we grabbed what little we had. Before it came to a complete stop, one of the girls who had run ahead was already back at the house, urging us to come out immediately. We had packed our uniforms, pens, and school notebooks. Those were the only belongings we had gathered that Friday afternoon, before Ndiroreye and his men arrived. We valued those pens and notebooks more than anything, but when we realized the military was there, we ran with everyone else hiding at Domitila's house and left our treasured possessions behind.

When we saw the vehicle, we waved frantically, our hearts pounding. It stopped, and we climbed in with others, packed tightly into the back of the small military jeep. The vehicle drove away toward safety, along the same road Mom and I had walked on Thursday evening. The metal floor was hard, and bodies were pressed together as we bounced along the road, yet no one complained.

It was silent.

We were alive.

Chapter 6

THE STINKY SMELL OF SURVIVAL

The military jeep delivered us to the Catholic Church, about 500 meters from the dysentery quarantine station and about a mile from the Gasorwe town center.

"Everyone, please proceed up the main road to the administrator's office, where everyone is assembled. Soldiers are patrolling the area. You are safe now. Another vehicle will take you to your next destination."

The car had to return to rescue more survivors.

We walked in a group, in stunned silence, looking around to make sure no hostile men followed us. We passed the old market; it was empty. Sundays used to be the busiest days of the week, with bustling people dressed neatly, stopping to buy a few things to take home to their villages. I had only been there once, and the joy from the smiles of buyers and sellers felt like a distant memory. My godfather, a Hutu, had bought me candy. As we walked past, I peeked inside. *What had happened to the camaraderie I once experienced here?*

As we approached the courthouse, the voices of people searching for their loved ones, children crying, and military cars arriving and departing created a commotion that felt both frightening and reassuring. Larger military trucks and passenger vehicles moved through the area. Smoke from makeshift outdoor cooking fires mixed with the smell of food filled the air around the administrative building.

"Those who have not started cooking, board the next truck immediately!" shouted a military commander, blowing a loud whistle.

"Where are they taking us?" one mother from our group asked the young men standing by the roadside.

"Likely to the provincial capital. We hear all the other refugee camps are full."

Ikambi z'impunzi? Refugee camp. I knew what "camp" meant in military terms, but I had never heard it used to refer to a camp for refugees.

"Mom, are we refugees?"

Mom held my hand tighter. Without saying a word, she gave me a reassuring look, as if to say everything would be okay.

Without stopping, we boarded the next truck and left the town. We passed multiple military barricades around town centers, where thousands of people had gathered. The army guards consistently signaled that the camps were full or that the keys to the establishments were unavailable and told the driver to keep going.

They took us to the provincial capital, about thirty miles from Bihogo, and left us where many survivors had gathered from different parts of the province. We occupied the empty courthouse, located in front of the prison and behind the governor's office. The rain had been so heavy over the past few days that the pungent smell of wet leaves from the tall trees filled the air, even inside the hall. Strangers gave us bananas to eat as we waited for dinner. In the evening, military vehicles dropped off cooked rice and beans. Although the aroma of the meal was new to me, the smell of freshly cooked food brought warmth as parents looked relieved to feed their children. I do not recall whether the food tasted good. I do not even recall if I ate. I simply remember asking Mom if my sister, who was still sick, could eat the strange-smelling military food. Télesphore looked like he was enjoying it as he ate together with my cousins.

We stayed there for a week before being moved to *École Primaire* (EP) Gasenyi, a nearby primary school that had been converted into a large refugee camp for displaced families. For several days, we slept on the hard, unforgiving cement floor of a cramped classroom, our hips and shoulders bruised from the surface. The room smelled of too many unwashed bodies and fear. Eventually, a distant relative who lived nearby gave us a thin mattress to share. It wasn't much, but after the cement floor, it felt like luxury.

As DAYS PASSED AND we adjusted to the fragile sense of safety, a collective grief filled the halls and playgrounds. Children cried, calling for missing parents and siblings, while adults wept uncontrollably as news of lost loved ones arrived.

In the days to come, we learned more about the family members we had lost and the stories of how they had been killed. The news came in fragments, each revelation striking like a fresh wound. On my father's side, we lost my grandpa, four uncles, two aunts, and four cousins. On my mother's side, both grandparents, her youngest sister, and many other extended family members, along with friends and neighbors, were gone.

It had been total carnage. There were no funerals, no known burial sites to visit, and no place to pay homage.

Each name added to the list brought back memories of faces, voices, shared meals, and celebrations, all now gone forever.

I felt guilty for crying at Domitila's house when Mom wanted to cross the river to Rusagara to see her family. Maybe she would have said goodbye to them, but we could also have lost her in the attempt.

In Gasenyi, I didn't fully grasp the enormity of the situation. I was too young to understand that I would never see these people again. I had no capacity to grieve or comprehend the profound sorrow that filled the air. As the days passed, I missed people and longed to go home. More than anyone, I missed *nyokuru* Sophia, my maternal grandmother.

As a child, I had crossed the river from Bihogo to Rusagara to visit her and Grandpa. The path itself was an adventure—the runs down the hilly trails, the sound of the river, the sight of white egrets flying across the water to catch little fish hiding beneath white lotus flowers, the warmth of the sun on our backs as we climbed toward her house. She was gentle and warm, greeting us with a wooden jug of warm milk and freshly harvested pineapples. The milk still had foam on top, and the pineapples were so sweet they made my tongue tingle. The smell of cow dung from the barn still pierces my senses whenever I close my eyes.

She played with us, disciplined us, and taught us how to do daily tasks, her hands guiding ours as we learned to clean, cook, harvest food, and even watch adults milk cows. Her patience seemed endless, and her voice was always gentle, even when correcting us. The neighborhood itself felt like heaven. Healthy cattle provided milk, and the house was beautifully decorated, with cowhide chairs and well-tended backyard farms overflowing with fresh food. Along the neatly cut tree fences, colorful flowers bloomed. The bamboo forest was home to singing doves (wood pigeons), whose songs I have heard nowhere else since. The townsfolk were warm and welcoming. Love and life filled that place, and I felt its absence deeply.

At the Gasenyi refugee camp, all we had now was the stinky smell of survival.

International aid organizations had arrived in the wake of the war. The UNHCR (United Nations High Commissioner for Refugees) provided food. The Red Cross and MSF (*Médecins Sans Frontières*—Doctors Without Borders) arrived soon after to offer urgent medical care, treating malaria, dysentery, and the wounded. They occupied the nearby clinic, the major hospital of the provincial center.

WITHIN A FEW WEEKS at the camp, Mom began coughing frequently and vomiting blood. When she went to the MSF clinic, it turned out she was three months pregnant. All the while, she had cared for my sister and me at the dysentery clinic in Bihogo, carrying a baby in her belly. The fear of losing her and our unborn sibling was matched only by the weight of grief. *Did she feel joy for a new life, or fear for the future under these conditions?* I often wondered. Not only was my father gone, but her entire immediate support system was no longer with us. That night, Mom gathered us for the usual prayer—the Lord's Prayer ("Our Father"), with a steady emphasis on "Give us today our daily bread."

In all her strength, I know Mom worried most about feeding us. Our daily meals were plain white rice with cooking oil. So much oil coated the rice that it left a greasy film on my tongue, making each bite harder to swallow than the last. One way to make it manageable was to add scallions, which were cheap and shared among families. After a few weeks, I developed a strong aversion, sometimes vomiting at mealtime. The mere smell of oily scallions would turn my stomach. Mom cooked separately for me so I could have scallion-free rice. Though the oil remained, we couldn't waste what little we had. I often reflect on those days with some regret, wondering whether I was too picky and troublesome for her and my siblings. She already had enough to worry about.

Much of our daily routine involved people trying to maintain dignity despite the harsh conditions. Mothers fetched water to keep their children and belongings clean. They cooked meals. Children made soccer balls out of plastic bags to play on the playground. Schoolchildren wrote letters and numbers on the walls, almost as if determined to revive the school days we had missed.

I was always excited when a UNHCR plane delivered food supplies. In my memory, it was a massive plane—an Antonov AN-225 Mriya, perhaps. In retrospect, the landing space behind the school was too small for such a cargo ship. It was most likely an AN-32 transport plane. The engine noise roared from a distance, and we would run down to the playground to watch it land, unload the cargo, and take off again. The sound made our whole bodies vibrate, and the wind from its engines whipped dust and debris around us, leaving us in awe.

Different NGOs regularly visited the camp, taking orphaned children to orphanages and asking families if they wanted to send their youngest ones. These visits created a stir—hope and fear mixing as parents faced impossible choices. When my paternal aunt sent my cousin Eric, the lady recruiting asked Mom if she wanted to send me, too. She refused. Mom was still pregnant and couldn't fathom that I would grow up as an orphan in a distant home. I remember the fierceness in her voice when she said no, though her hands trembled as she held me close, like a hen protecting her chicks from an eagle. Ever since then, she has shared this story in her speeches or reflections whenever I experience major life events or achievements. She worried she had made the wrong choice, feared criticism from family, and yet feels proud that I proved her decision right. I sometimes wonder about the alternate paths —where my cousin and others ended up, where I did, and what became of all our lives.

That fall, all schools were closed with no reopening timeline. Older children learned ways to make money instead. The school sat on a steep hill near the central market. Many local merchants carried their goods on bikes to sell at the market. Because of the hill's steepness, they usually needed help to push the heavily loaded bikes.

We waited at the bottom of the hill for incoming cargo, negotiated a price to help push it, and then moved it to the top. The bikes were heavy with produce and goods; the hill seemed to grow steeper with every step, my small body straining against the weight. All I earned were mere pennies. Télesphore, older and stronger, made more, and on some days we could buy onions to cook with the rice, and occasionally even amaranth greens. The smell of fresh vegetables was the only reminder of the farm life left in Bihogo. Our family stayed in the camp from October 1993 until May 1994. Despite Mom's successful fight against sending me to an orphanage, I would not remain with them the entire time.

IN APRIL 1994, I fell sick. The fever burned through me, making the world swim in and out of focus. I had malaria. We had no medications, and Uncle Papa Gede, the younger brother of Jean-Berchmans, insisted on taking me to ease Mom's burden. One afternoon, he arrived on a motorcycle. I was dizzy, the world spinning around me. After checking my fever, he took me to his home in another province, Ngozi.

On the way, we stopped at a small bar-restaurant to grab food. He bought beef skewers and plantains to share, and an orange soda for me. I took a sip of the soda but was too weak to eat. I rested my head on the wooden table and napped until my uncle finished the meal, and we continued on the motorcycle. The vibrations rattled my bones, each bump in the road sending waves of nausea through me.

When we arrived at his house, they gave me fever medication, and I collapsed into a deep sleep. I would spend the next few months there, playing with my cousins and slowly regaining strength. Even in the company of my uncle's family, I remember randomly crying at night, or suddenly while playing with my cousins. Homesickness struck without warning—in the middle of hide-and-seek, or whenever something reminded me of my siblings or life back in the village. Or perhaps my body was grieving.

In May 1994, I received news that my family had moved to a new refugee camp. A month later, Mom gave birth to a baby boy. The frequency of my tantrums increased. I would suddenly refuse to eat in the middle of dinner and run to the bedroom. When the twin cousins my age asked why I was crying, my older cousin, Amandine, ran after me and gave me a big, comforting hug. I had many crying tantrums, and while the younger cousins didn't know what to do, I am still grateful to Amandine for her patience. She always knew how to make me feel better.

One July night at dinner, my uncle announced he would take me home the next day. I ran to pack my things, my body shaking; I could barely stand still to fold my clothes. Amandine came to check on me and helped me pack.

"Will you miss us?" she asked, gently nudging my shoulder with her finger.

"Maybe!" I answered, giggling with excitement. I was ready to see my new baby brother, and I was even more excited that I would no longer need to take care of my sister.

I woke up bright and early, had breakfast with my cousins, and said my goodbyes. We mounted the motorcycle and headed back to Muyinga, this time to a new location, the Mukoni camp.

Chapter 7

SCHOOLCHILDREN IN WARFARE

Uncle Papa Gede and I arrived at the largest camp in central Muyinga, Mukoni camp, where the blue-and-white UNHCR tents, which would become my new makeshift home, stretched to the horizon. To prepare for the upcoming school year and reopen schools, the UNHCR had built a large new camp to bring together refugees who were occupying primary schools near the provincial capital. It was about five kilometers from the provincial center, seven kilometers from the EP Gasenyi camp, and seventeen kilometers from Bihogo.

Like a strange city, the plastic sheets flapping in the wind created a constant background rustle. The air smelled of cooking fires and too many people living too close together. As we made our way through the camp toward my family's tent, many children played, their laughter and shouts forming a stark contrast with the grim reality of our situation.

When we arrived, Mom was carrying Elysé on her back. He was only two months old. She hugged me and turned around to show me his sleeping face. He looked tiny and fragile, his small fists pressed against his cheeks. I was excited to have a new little brother to care for, though the responsibility felt heavier. I knew at that point how quickly life could change. I also knew it was my sister's turn to take over some of the household duties.

Although it was fun for the children to play together in a central location without having to run far from the safety of the protected camp, a dark shadow hung over the neighborhood. The camp's location next to a major military base, less than half a kilometer away, meant we lived with constant reminders of the ongoing conflict. There were already talks of a budding rebellion against the government, and the smell of warfare lingered in the neighboring hills and on the roads.

THE PROXIMITY TO THE military base, supposedly for our protection, meant enduring the relentless soundtrack of war. Every day, on the way to Sunday Mass or the market, we watched soldiers train, their bodies moving in formation, their weapons glinting in the sun. The sharp cracks of gunfire during military drills made us jump, each shot bringing back memories of that October week. The rhythmic thump of marching feet, the shouted commands, and the occasional roar of helicopter blades cutting through the air became our daily background noise.

Being children, we would run to the fence to peek inside whenever there was a commotion at the base. The metal links of the fence were warm from the sun as we held on to them to watch the camp, curiosity overriding fear. Sometimes we saw emergency helicopter landings, the wind from the rotors whipping up dust and debris, forcing us to shield our eyes. Other times, we heard screams from inside the base, sounds that should have sent us running but drew us closer, our young minds not yet fully comprehending the darkness we were witnessing.

What we didn't realize then was how this exposure was shaping us. Many young adolescents, watching the soldiers day after day, became fascinated by military life. The uniforms, the weapons, the sense of power—it was seductive to children who had felt powerless for so long. Some of these kids eventually became soldiers themselves, trading their childhoods for combat boots and rifles. As for me, even the sound of a helicopter still triggers fear in my body to this day. I am privileged not to have become a child soldier.

The camp's location near the intersection of Route Nationale 6

(RN6) and Route Nationale 12 (RN12) meant we were at a crossroads of commerce and conflict, between promise and peril. These major arteries of trade brought supplies to keep the country alive, but also made us vulnerable. At night, the darkness would come alive with different sounds—the screech of brakes, shouts, sometimes gunfire or explosions. Young men from the camp, the older ones ready to join military life, would target these merchant trucks, seeing them as a means of survival when aid ran short.

The middle of the night was their time, when the darkness could hide their desperation. I was too young to take part but old enough to understand their pattern. They would stop a truck, search it, and demand ransom. If the drivers resisted, we would see the results in the morning.

Early mornings, we went to fetch water at the nearest fountain. The air was sharp with cold; our bare feet numbed by the damp ground. Often, conversations started immediately.

"Did you hear another van was burned last night at the corner?" one kid would exclaim, his breath visible in the morning chill.

We would all ask for details, our water jugs forgotten for a moment. Though we probably only heard snippets of adult conversations, we pieced together our own versions of events. But curiosity demanded more than secondhand stories. We would agree to go see it ourselves after dropping off our water. Meeting at an agreed spot, we would plot our approach to the site, hearts racing with a mixture of fear and excitement that only children can feel when confronting the forbidden.

One boy would approach slowly, hiding behind the rocks to confirm it was safe, then signal the rest to follow. Once gathered, the bravest among us would poke at debris around the burned car while flies began to gather, and we covered our noses with our shirts. Most often, what remained was a blackened metal skeleton, the acrid smell of burnt rubber and fuel still hanging in the air. The ashes would still be warm, sometimes smoking in the morning dew. A few feet away, beyond the larger stones that marked the hill's base, we would sometimes find what we pretended not to be looking for—the bodies. Some were burned beyond recognition, others bore wounds from desperate attempts to escape. The morning sun would cast long shadows across these scenes, making them seem both more and less real somehow.

Other than curiosity, I don't know what else we were doing out there. We wanted stories to tell our classmates at school that day—the stories that would make us seem brave, worldly, as if witnessing death had made us more grown-up. By the time we had scoped out the incident, it was around 8 a.m., and we'd run home to get ready for school. At the end of the school day, we would come home, either fetch more water or run to the playground to play childhood games.

In this camp, the games I played most were hopscotch, hide-and-seek, football, and, on nights when we had shadow puppets, projecting animal shapes on the plastic tents. We played late into the night, running under the moonlight until we were exhausted—or until parents came looking for us around 9 p.m., at which point we went to sleep in complete, blissful ignorance. The contrast was stark: laughing and shouting in the same spaces where we had seen death that morning, playing while others had screamed their last breaths.

Some days, these memories surface on a random morning or evening, and I briefly think, *Well, dang, that was crazy!*—before moving on with my day. But the memories never truly leave; they sink deeper, becoming part of who I am, childhood wounds slowly transforming into scars over the years.

I RESTARTED FIRST GRADE in September 1995. I can still smell the fresh, brand-new khaki uniforms and the sharp scent of Bic pens and pencils I packed in a plastic bag on my first day of class. The uniform was stiff with newness, its creases sharp enough to cut. The plastic bag crinkled with each step, a sound that carried possibility and hope.

On school days, we had a simple routine that structured our chaotic lives: I would fetch water in the morning, my shoulders aching from the weight of the jug; go to school; return home for lunch, if we had food; go back to school for the afternoon; come home at 5 p.m.; fetch water again in the evening; play soccer or other games with the children on the playground; go home for dinner; then play some more with kids in the nearby tents until bedtime.

To sustain us, Mom sold vegetables and sorghum beer in the market. She also began commuting back to Bihogo to plant and harvest food, often gone for days or even weeks, leaving us to fend for ourselves.

So on weekends, life followed a different rhythm. We would sell gum, peanuts, and cigarettes on the streets and at bars. In the village, there was no drinking age, and there were no rules against children selling cigarettes. Bars were gathering places where parents of all backgrounds brought their children. Nursing mothers with little kids would come to the bars to drink. It was not uncommon to see a woman carrying a toddler on her back, giving alcoholic drinks to her child, only months old, to quiet them while the adults socialized. In the countryside, a seven- or eight-year-old conducting business in public spaces was not unusual. As children living in a refugee camp, our primary directive was survival.

Business knowledge was passed down from older children to younger ones, like an unwritten survival manual. I learned from kids in my neighborhood that they were making money selling items on the streets. I asked my older brothers if I could join. They agreed, with one condition: I had to control myself and not consume the products so that we could make a profit. I asked Mom for investment money and bought one pack of cigarettes and one pack of gum to sell.

After a few rounds, I learned two harsh lessons about the adult world. First, that adults could be deceitful. Some would take a cigarette, promise to pay the next day, then turn hostile when I came to collect.

"Hello, can you pay me for the cigarettes from yesterday?" I asked a man who had told me he knew my mom and needed a few cigarettes, promising he would pay the next day.

"What? What are you talking about? I wasn't even here yesterday," he replied, giving me an intimidating look, as if I accused him of wrongdoing.

I checked my packs. I was confident I had counted correctly, and the money matched, except for three cigarettes.

"Yesterday evening, you paid for the two gums but not the cigarettes. I gave you three."

"Get out of my face and don't disturb me again!" he yelled. Crying, I asked Samuel, our older, taller neighbor, if I was mistaken.

"No, we saw it yesterday too. That guy is a liar. Never sell him anything again. We all avoid him."

Reeling from the reality of immoral men, the knot in my stomach on the way home gripped my spirits.

The second lesson was about my own weaknesses: I couldn't resist eating the gum I was supposed to sell. For weeks, I barely broke even, watching my small investment disappear, one piece at a time, into my mouth. More experienced kids were succeeding and learned that peanuts were a better choice. Customers usually asked for them before getting too drunk, and there was a bigger market for peanuts compared to cigarettes and gum. Roasted peanuts were also less tempting to eat than sweet gum.

Samuel and the other older kids knew peanut suppliers. One reliable vendor was only 3.7 km away, about a one-hour walk. I started joining them on these trips. The two-hour round trip to get freshly roasted peanuts wasn't just about business—it was a fun activity that built camaraderie among the children. We played games along the way, daring each other to run across the streets as cars approached, almost to see who was the fastest. One of my favorite games was a test of bravery. The challenge was to stand on the white line in the middle of the two-way RN6 highway and count how many cars could pass before giving up. Most drivers would honk loudly to scare the player away. I was so competitive that my childhood friends still remind me that I won every time, holding the record throughout those years (sorry, Mom).

When we were not on the streets doing business, religious practices anchored our weeks. Sunday mornings meant Mass, a brief escape from camp life into something more dignified. We would wake up bright and early, clean up, and dress in our best shirts and shorts, the fabric often worn thin but carefully washed. The walk to church gave us glimpses of a different world: the bustle of Muyinga city, and the gigantic buildings that seemed full of wealth. I was particularly fascinated by the fancy Safari Lodge hotel across from the Catholic cathedral. I would stare up at the second-floor balcony where businessmen relaxed with a drink, imagining what luxury lay behind those windows and dreaming of a better life someday.

Besides Sunday Mass, I went to the cathedral on Saturdays to prepare for First Communion, which I received in third grade. The neighbor kids my age and I spent Saturday afternoons at the church learning catechism, memorizing prayers, and reciting the rosary.

Often, the normal rhythm of our days was interrupted by civil war. The threat of rebels coming to school or attacking the camp arrived unexpectedly. One Saturday morning in second grade (Saturday classes were later abolished), we were in school when gunshots rang out. Rebels had passed through the nearby bushes, coming into contact with patrolling military, and had to be chased away. We hid under the wooden desks until the shooting stopped, and the headmaster announced that we needed to run home.

The cries of younger children were only soothed by teachers reassuring them that the military patrolled the main road we needed to take. We ran home that morning to find the camp in a state of panic, parents waiting in tears for their children to arrive. By early afternoon, the news spread that the rebels had been pushed out, and life returned to normal. After church duties that night, we went to a nearby convent, right next to EP Mukoni, to watch TV as we usually did. That evening, a big soccer match was scheduled, but because of the earlier fighting, the broadcast had been interrupted, so we ended up watching the Formula 1 Grand Prix instead.

For much of my adulthood, I had forgotten about this event—until last year, while watching *Drive to Survive* on Netflix, I experienced a major déjà vu. Goosebumps covered my body when I realized that the first time I had ever seen the on-screen box showing the drivers' names and positions was during that Saturday evening in second grade, at the convent in Mukoni. *Those were crazy days*, I thought as I continued watching the show.

ON THE DAY OF my First Communion in third grade, I woke up early to shower and dress in the brand-new white shirt Mom had bought me.

I also had a brand-new white rosary and candle, all part of the ceremonial procession. Mom stayed with us that week to prepare food and sorghum beer for the guests on Sunday. My godfather had come all the way from Gasorwe to be there for the big day.

"Shower first; don't be late. Your godfather will wait at the entrance," Mom said, brimming with pride. I put on my fresh clothes and ran to the cathedral.

I had to arrive early, by 7 a.m., so I could stand in line with all the children receiving their First Communion and sit in the front rows. The dry summer air felt holier than usual against my face as I gripped my candle and rosary inside their sealed plastic bag. They had to remain untouched until after the benedictions. Around me, children in bright white clothes moved toward the church—some walking quickly with their families, others balanced on bicycles, carried by fathers or older siblings. The solemnity of the day was only outshone by the summer sun bouncing off the paved road.

As I approached the church, my godfather waved from a distance, signaling me to come to him. We hadn't seen each other in a while because of the war. He was Hutu, and the conflict had strained many relationships, including ours. Still, I had always known him as a good man and never feared he would harm me. When I reached him, he pulled me into a big hug.

"You have grown so much. Your father would be proud of you," he said.

"Thank you. We should go—it's time," I replied, cutting the conversation short when I noticed the children lining up at the church's right entrance.

I was ready for the ceremony. We formed a line and entered the church when Holy Mass began. Sitting in the front with all the other children felt like front-row access to heaven. Dressed in white, we looked like angels for the day. The special Mass felt like the spiritual purification we had been prepared for. When the priest began the benedictions, he instructed us to light our candles and put on our rosaries, symbols of our transformation.

We were now worthy of receiving the body of Christ.

When it was time for communion, we were the first to approach the altar. I stepped forward, placed my left hand over my right, and presented my palm just as I had practiced countless times.

"The body of Christ," the priest said, placing the Eucharist—the small, white, circular wafer I had watched adults receive for as long as I could remember. Taking it for the first time felt like crossing a threshold into spiritual maturity.

"Amen," I replied softly, lifting it with my right hand and placing it on my tongue. I bowed, then made the Sign of the Cross—In the name of the Father, and the Son, and the Holy Spirit—as my fingers moved from forehead to chest, from left shoulder to right. I returned to my seat, knelt, recited the *Our Father*, and sat down once I finished.

That wasn't so hard, I thought, absorbing the weight of this new chapter on my spiritual path.

At the end of Mass, the priest reminded us to remain pure and repent our sins, to stay worthy of the sacrament we had received. A quiet sense of growth washed over me. We left feeling responsible, as though goodness itself had been entrusted to us.

Outside the church, my mother, siblings, and family friends waited to congratulate me. We walked home and shared a meal, celebrating with home-cooked food and sorghum beer. My mother looked happy as she hosted the gathering, her laughter carrying over the voices of guests inside and outside our tent. As I chatted with the other children, Mom spoke with my godfather. She didn't seem afraid. They were simply catching up.

"Can I go play now?" I asked, eager to excuse myself as the adults settled in to celebrate.

"Sure. Don't go too far, and come back to say goodbye to people," Mom replied. I took off with my classmates toward the soccer playground for our usual late-afternoon games.

WHILE OTHER KIDS PLAYED, I often sat nearby, lost in thought about building things, soccer balls made from plastic bags, toy cars carved from dry sorghum and maize stalks. I could put together a working model in less than a day.

That afternoon, we had a soccer match. Butoyi, a self-appointed coach, organized games between the living quarters. I played as a right winger and was supposed to start that day. As the players gathered, I remained seated. I think the coach assumed I was having a rough day. In truth, I was watching a plane fly overhead, long white trails stretching behind it. I realized I had never asked myself what those trails were. My thoughts wandered to the plane's material composition, then to the white streaks it left behind. Why would a flying metal object produce fog in the sky? The coach snapped me out of my wonder when he called my name and waved me onto the field. We won. Soccer was fun, but my mind was often elsewhere, fixated on how things worked. In those early school years, I grew comfortable being lost in the beauty of learning, quietly contemplating the unknown.

In primary school, I ranked first or second in my class from grade one through grade four. The rewards for top performance were precious: new school supplies at the end of each semester. For the top five students, these items mattered more than the report card itself. Pride swelled in my chest as I displayed my bounty, the most notebooks, the most pens and pencils. I showed them to neighbors like treasures, each fresh notebook representing not only academic success, but hope for the future. I couldn't wait to present them to Mom and see her face light up with pride.

The rhythm of school fostered a competitiveness that became my motivation. Acing every test and homework assignment became my directive. In fourth grade, a new girl named Clarisse joined our class. She was brilliant, having transferred from a private school, and Mom mentioned that she came from a well-off branch of a distant family. On our first math test, Clarisse outscored me. I became so competitive that I asked to change seats so I could sit in the front row. Every morning, our teacher gave us multiplication challenges, and Clarisse and I raced to finish first. She beat me several times. Her French was also far better than mine, and my jealousy pushed me to practice speaking French with my friends whenever I could. We battled fiercely for the top spot, and she won, much to my dismay.

By mid-1998, at the end of fourth grade, Mom decided we would move to a new camp closer to Bihogo. The long commute on foot to work the farm, while leaving us alone for days, had become unbearable. Often, while she was gone, we would run out of food as we waited for her return. One day in third grade, we came home from school, and Télesphore, stoic as always, sat us down and said, "We ran out of beans, so today all we have is *ugali*. Mom is coming tomorrow; we need to get through today." We ate in silence. We had been taught never to beg. Elysé, the youngest, could barely swallow the plain *ugali*. When I returned to school that afternoon, I felt weak as I went to fetch my classmate. Perhaps he noticed my lack of energy, because as I waited outside his tent, his older sister quietly packed food for me. After we left the camp, we sat on the roadside beneath a large eucalyptus tree, and I ate. Even now, I can almost smell the sautéed beans and amaranth from that early afternoon. When I finished, we tossed the plastic bag away. Realizing that fewer and fewer students were still on the road, we ran to reach EP Mukoni before the afternoon session began.

I later realized that Mom was also exhausted from having to return to reports about our mischief, especially my middle-child antics. Nearly every time she came back from days in Bihogo, neighbors complained that I had been fighting other kids, or sometimes my own siblings. She grew so weary of trying to discipline me that once she handed me the stick commonly used to punish misbehaving children and told me to beat myself.

I still remember the look of exasperated disappointment on her face when she returned to hear that I had been fighting with Télesphore for two days, chasing him around the neighborhood. Someone reported it to her, and when she arrived, I was called forward to explain myself. I had no explanation. I stood there, on the verge of tears, her disappointment echoing through my childhood and adolescence. It was the last time she ever needed to beat me.

In July 1998, we packed our few belongings, said goodbye to our friends, and boarded a UNHCR repatriation truck to Gasorwe camp.

Chapter 8

THE ALTAR BOY RETURNS TO THE SHADOWS

Nine miles away from Mukoni, Gasorwe camp is located at another intersection of RN6 and a road connecting it to RN12. The road runs from the Gasorwe town center to Karuzi. It was the same road the military jeep took in October 1993 to rescue survivors from the hills of Bihogo and neighboring Karuzi villages. It was also the same road Mom, Violette, and I walked to meet Dad on our way home on that fateful night. The camp sat directly across the street from the Gasorwe town center, where we first met other refugees before being taken to the provincial capital. It was only three to four kilometers from where our childhood home once stood.

The short distance was convenient because Mom could now work on the farm all day and return home by dusk, no longer leaving us alone for several days at a time. However, it was also painfully close to where we had lost our loved ones and our belongings five years earlier. The same neighbors still lived there. The presumed burial site of our father and uncle remained nearby. The land where our house once stood was now the same place where we spent days working the fields and harvesting what we ate. Both those who killed our relatives and forced us from our land and those who saved us and helped us escape continued to live in the same village. We greeted one another, each exchange marked by varying degrees of fear and hesitation.

Returning for the first time to the Bihogo home from which we had been chased felt like striking an unhealed wound. Only the cement and stone foundation of our childhood home remained. Memories of Nkurikiye and my escape, and of Ndiroreye attacking us, felt sharper, more tender, and more vivid than memories of the woodpeckers that once perched on the avocado tree in the backyard or the singing doves that once roamed between the banana trees.

When we went to Rusagara, where I used to visit *nyokuru* Sophia, the former paradise had become a ghost forest. The transformation was brutal. There were no houses, no cows, no pineapples in the backyard, no cats, and no carefully preserved tree fences for playing hide-and-seek. The bamboo forest stood silent, with no doves singing their familiar songs. Standing there, I could almost see the ghosts of what had been and nearly hear the echoes of those long-ago afternoons.

Unlike the six-year-old who had simply tried to make sense of unfolding events seven years earlier, I was older now, and the fear was far more intense. The weight of those shadows pressed against my body like a heavy stone and pierced my psyche like tropical thunder at the height of the rainy season.

Some days, it felt as though killers could show up at our camp at any time and repeat what had happened. We also woke up at 5 a.m. and spent days down in Bihogo. Mom reassured us that the worst people had been imprisoned, but the truth was that many people died trying to return to their original villages. While the mass killings had stopped, the conflict had evolved into a sustained civil war. Despite ongoing UN peacekeeping and reconciliation efforts, rebel attacks on camps and clashes with the military guarding them could happen at any moment.

Every so often, fighting would break out. Rebels would come through, and it would feel like a state of war all over again. Each camp had a small military unit guarding it, which helped. However, gunfights between armed rebels and the military intensified the fear. Eventually, the gunshots would stop, and after a few hours, we would either return to sleep or stay awake until sunrise. Adults usually sent the children to sleep while they kept watch through the night. In the morning, the camp chief would announce that the rebels had been pushed out, and life continued as usual until another gunshot was heard. Another trigger for me was helicopters. They symbolized either the arrival of the military or the emergency transport of a high-profile individual, both of which reminded me of the events between 1993 and 1998.

The first task most mornings was to determine whether it was safe to go to school. Our school was in the neighborhood, about a 10-minute walk or run, and it was surrounded by large bushes. These bushes were potential hiding places for rebels. If there had been an attack the night before, we often had to wait for the military to thoroughly search the area before school could resume.

The school playground was also where we played. After school, we went home to complete our chores, then returned to the grounds to play football, known as soccer in the US. We often played until 9 or 10 p.m. During holidays or on days when there was no school, I went with Mom to work on the farm. Despite the fear and trauma, the land remained our source of survival.

Making new friends, I had learned, was easy in the close quarters of camp life. We lived near a mosque, and instead of relying on adults to tell the time, we used prayer calls to structure our days. The 5 a.m. call for *Fajr* prayer became especially important. I learned to fetch water before the early call, sometimes waking up at 3 a.m. to go before dawn. This routine began because two of my neighbors who fetched water with me were Muslim and preferred to go before prayers. I enjoyed the competitive aspect. In addition, since the spring supplied water to the entire camp and nearby villages, it often became crowded. Standing in line under the tropical sun was far worse than waking up in the cool darkness of early morning.

The morning water runs were mostly silent. We tiptoed out of the house to avoid waking those still asleep and met outside at the gathering spot. Apart from the distant sounds of cars on the roads, the night was quiet, punctuated only by the songs of crickets and night owls under the moonlight. A chilly breeze brushed against our skin now and then, but running kept our blood warm until we returned with gallons of water as the camp gradually awakened.

FIFTH GRADE BEGAN IN the early fall of 1998. I carried the same determination; no one would outshine me academically. Our teacher, Mr. Claver, was a young military man and a recent college graduate serving in the draft. From humble beginnings, he came from Ruyigi, a province I had heard much about—my father had worked there. He wore a military uniform every day and walked to class carrying only a pen and a notebook. The blackboard was his canvas. He had a restless energy, and his eyes were twin stars that sparkled with delight. He moved with purpose, and with every sentence, his lively spirit commanded attention.

In the cramped classroom, I sat with two other students, Daniel and Thomas, neighborhood friends from the camp. We were in the front row, the short kids, while taller students like Samuel, whose family had also moved from Mukoni to Gasorwe that summer, sat in the back. I was appointed class president. The role's primary responsibility was to maintain order, primarily by reminding students to remain silent when unsupervised and by reporting anyone who misbehaved. I was short and skinny, so although the appointment fed my competitive spirit, I was nervous that the older, bigger boys might bully me if I told them to stop talking.

One day, Mr. Claver was running late, and the classroom grew loud. I asked everyone to stop talking, but the big students ignored my repeated requests. I wrote the names of the offenders on the blackboard. The bullies erased my list, and Daniel and Thomas started teasing me. Frustrated, I added their names as well.

"But we are friends, and we weren't talking before the argument started," they protested.

"I don't care. Everyone is getting a punishment today," I said.

The commotion became so loud that the sixth-grade teacher intervened. When Mr. Claver arrived, he called up the names on the board and disciplined the students with a wooden stick. Almost a quarter of the class received the punishment. Watching the stick thud on palms and buttocks, seeing the terrified eyes and trembling pleas, I felt guilty for some of the students. To make matters worse, Mr. Claver had brought a bundle of algebra test results. After the punishment, he handed out the papers and read everyone's scores aloud, turning the moment into a lesson in accountability. It was not the kind of educational moment I had hoped for.

"Not surprising. Libère is the only one who got 100 percent on the test. He's set for life, this one. You all should be as focused as him," Mr. Claver said. I knew, from the moment I became class president, that he liked me, but I did not want attention at this level. I was small and did not want to be bullied.

The intimidating stares from the bigger boys made me want to run, as I knew they would confront me after class. As expected, they circled me later to air their grievances.

"We know you're the favorite and that you'd report us to the principal if we did anything. We'll just crash you on the court," said Claude.

I didn't respond to the threat.

As promised, every time I played volleyball or soccer, some of the big boys made it a point to direct the ball toward me at every spike or kick attempt. In soccer, I could outrun them, but in volleyball, it was harder. That year, I gave up athletic pursuits and focused entirely on academics. I told Superintendent Joseph that I did not want to be class president in sixth grade, and they appointed someone else.

Outside of school, I had church duties on Saturdays and Sundays. I was entering adolescence, and in retrospect, being part of the church helped maintain discipline.

I was still quite rebellious, but Mom had stopped physically disciplining me as I got older. She now knew I took faith seriously and would often simply quote the Bible or ask me to confess to the priest.

One time, I had a fight on the playground with a kid who kept tackling others. It started as an argument to make him stop, but I ended up beating him and leaving bruises. When Mom heard about it, she sat all of us down and recounted how several families had recently complained about our behavior. In a tired voice, she delivered words that still echo in my mind: "From this day forward, I'm done disciplining you all. You are free to go out and do whatever you want. But if you mess up your life and end up on the streets, it's on you. God as my witness, I've done my best."

My siblings and I looked at each other in silence. For once, we had no clever comebacks. We quietly ate our food and went to sleep. We went to confess the next morning.

In Burundi, fifth grade is when most children prepare to receive the Sacrament of Confirmation, the third sacrament of initiation into the Catholic Church. Preparations begin the year before. Participation in theological and pastoral activities is a prerequisite for this milestone. Typically, girls joined the choir or dance troupes, while boys became altar boys. Following this tradition, I joined the altar boy group, attending practice every Saturday afternoon to learn the processions for Sunday Mass.

On the first Saturday, I arrived at the church as the afternoon sun slanted through the tall windows, casting long golden rectangles across the cool stone floor. The air inside carried that familiar church smell, a mixture of incense that had seeped into the walls over decades, melting candle wax, and the faint mustiness of old hymn books. My bare feet made soft, padding sounds against the smooth floor as I joined the other boys already gathered on the front seats near the altar.

Father Bernard, a tall man whose cassock always smelled faintly of tobacco and wood smoke, walked in from the back and stood in front of us. Severin, the most senior altar boy, stood next to him. He was tall and muscular, in sixth grade at the same primary school where I had just recently started. Severin also played volleyball and ran track; he had beaten everyone at a recent school meet. His stature alone commanded obedience.

"In the name of the Father, the Son, and the Holy Spirit."

"Amen," we responded in unison.

Father Bernard gave a brief speech welcoming us into the sacred practice and left us with the senior altar boy. After learning the process in theory, it was time to put it into practice.

We took turns in groups of four, going through the process as if it were during Mass. When it was my turn, Severin handed me my first alb, the long white liturgical robe. The fabric was rough cotton, starched so stiff it nearly crackled as I pulled it over my head. It fell past my knees, making me feel both important and slightly ridiculous. Severin showed me how to tie the rope cincture around my waist, three loops, he emphasized, representing the Holy Trinity.

We spent hours learning the choreography of the Mass: where to stand, when to kneel, how to hold the thick brass cruets containing water and wine. The cruets were heavier than they looked, their cold metal surfaces slippery with condensation. I learned to walk with measured steps, not too fast, which would seem irreverent, and not too slow, which would disrupt the Mass's rhythm. On major events like Christmas and Easter, the front altar boy carried the processional cross. It stood taller than me, polished smooth from generations of hands. In my first year, the experienced boys carried it until I was ready for front duties in sixth grade.

I was terrified of ringing the altar bells during consecration. Three precise rings at each elevation, the timing had to be perfect. Too early and the priest's prayer would be interrupted; too late and the moment would pass unmarked. The bells themselves were beautiful: four brass spheres attached to a wooden handle, each producing a slightly different tone. When rung properly, they created a cascade of sound that seemed to make the very air shimmer. During practice, my nervous hands often made them jangle discordantly, earning disapproving looks from Severin. I repeated the movement again and again until I got it right.

The thurible, or incense burner, was reserved for senior altar boys only. We watched enviously as they practiced swinging it in perfect arcs, smoke billowing in grey and white clouds that caught the sunlight streaming through the windows. The chains clinked rhythmically, and the burning charcoal inside glowed orange through the perforated brass. The incense itself came in small amber chunks that looked like tree sap, releasing thick, sweet smoke that made my eyes water and clung to our clothes long after Mass ended.

By my third Saturday, muscle memory took over. I could light the tall altar candles with the long brass lighter without trembling, touching flame to wick in one smooth motion. I knew which genuflection was a full kneel, both knees, and which was a quick bob, right knee only. I had memorized the Latin responses, *"Et cum spiritu tuo,"* even though I didn't understand their meaning. The words felt ancient and powerful on my tongue, connecting me to centuries of boys who had stood in this same spot, wearing the same rough alb, performing the same sacred duties.

During Sunday Mass, the church transformed. What had been a practice space became a theater of divine mystery. The congregation's murmured prayers created a low hum that seemed to rise from the floor itself. The air grew thick with incense and expectation. Standing next to the priest at the altar, I could see his hands tremble slightly as he elevated the host, hear his whispered prayers that the congregation could not catch, and watch the candlelight reflect off the golden chalice.

My mother's pride was visible from where she sat, always in the same pew, third row on the right. Her eyes followed my every move-ment, and I felt her prayers for my vocation wrapping around me like an invisible cloak. This was more than serving at Mass; it was her hope made manifest, her dream that one day I might stand at the altar not as a boy in an alb, but as a priest in vestments.

AFTER OUR ESCAPE IN 1993, Mom decided not to buy us shoes until we went to boarding school, since our Bihogo house had been ransacked and everything else burned to the ground. Daily survival had been the priority. But after the summer of fifth grade, she was pleased that I had become a disciplined altar boy that she bought me flip-flops.

"You have been good this year. You can have shoes now," Mom said after Mass, where I was the lead altar boy.

The coffee harvest was good that year, and living closer to the farm allowed us to better care for it. With the money she earned, Mom bought us new clothes and flip-flops before the new academic year began. I chose a green shirt covered in white and pink flowers, paired with light teal shorts and those bright blue flip-flops with patches of white, my two favorite colors. When I got home, my neighborhood friends were waiting to fetch water as usual. I slipped on my brand-new flip-flops, eager to show them off.

"You can wear those on Sunday. Right now, we need to go before it gets dark," one friend said.

"Yeah, they're brand new; you're not supposed to wear them down the hill. The boulders would damage them," the other added.

"You're right. Let me put them back."

I ran inside to place the flip-flops in the transparent plastic bag, grabbed my water jug, and joined them. We ran down the usual hill, hurrying to beat the sunset.

In the summer of 1999, many of my friends, classmates, and I were anointed in the Sacrament of Confirmation. The processional celebrations were as grand as those I had experienced during my First Communion in the previous camp. Once again, my godfather joined us at church and at the celebrations with family and neighbors in the camp. This time, I had my new flip-flops and wasn't entering the Holy Mass barefoot. Both Confirmation and the flip-flops became symbolic markers of my transition into the final year of primary education.

Sixth grade, which started that fall, was significant because a national exam determined which school we would attend for middle and high school. I was determined to earn the highest score possible to secure a place at a boarding school. I would wake at 3 or 4 a.m. to complete my chores—mostly fetching water and firewood, then go to school early to study. We had no electricity to study at night, so waking early meant making the most of daylight hours for learning. Mom insisted that we only use candles or petrol lamps if necessary.

The exam took place in late May or June, at the end of the school year. In the days leading up to it, friends and family sent well-wishes and advice.

"Don't eat *intore*. It's bad luck," they would say.

Intore, or African eggplant *(Solanum aethiopicum)*, is one of my favorite vegetables. I never understood why it was considered bad luck, only for that specific test, but for a few days beforehand, I avoided it completely.

When the morning came, I woke early, showered, and gathered my pencils. The principal had advised taking at least three new pencils and two erasers, just in case anything went wrong. Gasorwe III hosted the examinations for the four primary schools in the area. The building had once served as a dysentery quarantine site where my sister and I had been patients a few years prior. The memory was unpleasant. In my clean khaki uniform, I silently prayed that I wouldn't be assigned to the same room. Forget the eggplant; that would have been really bad luck.

The morning was foggy, strange for early summer, almost like an omen. I tried not to dwell on the memories of October 21, 1993.

As we lined up according to our assigned numbers, I noticed that my test was in the building next to the quarantine block and felt relieved. *No bad omens today.* I entered and took my seat.

The proctor distributed the tests on bound papers, with a pink sheet on top and a white one at the bottom. I had seen this pink sheet on my brother's tests in previous years. The exam lasted several hours and covered mathematics, French, science, and Kirundi. The proctors handed out the test sheets one by one, in that order, with a bathroom break in the middle. In primary school, math and French were my favorite subjects, so having them first in each session helped my brain work efficiently. The headmasters of all four schools were present, along with a committee of selected supervisors. There were about 100 sixth-grade students at the school that morning.

The headmaster began with a speech emphasizing the importance of the test and reminding us that cheating on a national exam carried serious consequences. We also knew that the tests were meant to start at the same time nationwide. While there was no technology to enforce this precisely, 9 a.m. was the expected start time, not 9:02. The brief speech added the formality the occasion demanded. Some students were sweating nervously. Others asked to go to the bathroom. But the rules were the rules.

Once preparations were complete and 9 a.m. struck, the lead supervisor signaled us to begin. I opened my math test and quickly skimmed through it before starting. I completed it without much difficulty, though one problem left me uncertain. I was ready for French as soon as the new test sheets arrived, accompanied by the ringing timers and announcements.

At the end of the exam, we headed home and discussed the answers with each other. Some proudly shared their solutions, while others realized which questions they had missed. The fog had lifted, and the summer sun shone brightly, almost as if it were marking the start of a new adventure. As we walked home to remove our uniforms before regrouping for an evening soccer game, I thought about the changes ahead. *The next school year would begin at a new school, likely a boarding school in a different town. I will be moving again in the fall.*

The Education Ministry would announce the results later in July, usually posted on public government buildings. Each student's name, score, and assigned school would be listed.

ONE JULY MORNING, my friend Daniel came running to my house.

"The results have been posted! You're going to attend Lycée Kanyinya!" he shouted, nearly out of breath.

"Where are they posted?" I asked.

"The communal news board."

I dropped the clothes I was washing into the basket and started running. Daniel followed.

"Where are you going?" I called over my shoulder, outpacing him.

"Lycée Rugari."

"Congratulations!" I knew about that boarding school, thirty-three kilometers from Gasorwe, near the Tanzanian border. Télesphore had been placed there a few years earlier.

I knew little about Lycée Kanyinya. I had only heard of it, and as far as I could recall, it was an all-girls school run by nuns.

"Isn't Kanyinya an all-girls Catholic school?" I asked again, noticing my friend starting to tire.

"Wait for me! The announcement says it's going co-ed this year. You're in the first co-ed class."

At the communal board, I ran up the steps, squeezed through the crowd of students learning their fates, and pressed forward to the front. The announcements were encased in the usual bulletin board mounted on the light green wall. The rectangular case held multiple clippings, some old—perhaps wedding announcements from last month. In the middle, a fresh white sheet of paper with crisp black ink gleamed through the reflective glass. I slid my fingers over the glass, scanning the list until I found my name. There it was: my name, my score, and my future—Lycée Kanyinya, a boarding school in Kirundo province near the Rwandan border, forty-seven kilometers from Gasorwe. I looked for other familiar names; only two other students I knew would join me.

There is a common ritual in Burundian education in which older high schoolers haze new 7th graders, marking the transition from primary school to adolescence. I had prepared myself for bullying at boarding school—but I hadn't expected the first bullies to be my own blood. Télesphore and Marius, my second cousin, were already in high school, a few years ahead of me, and they took it as their duty to perform the initiation. Kanyinya was a girls' school, they argued, and I would need proper hazing to become a real man.

One summer day, we were working in the fields by the river as usual. Marius' family was tending their plot a few meters away. At lunchtime, the cousins gathered and announced it was time for my initiation. The challenge: I had to jump across the river. They turned into drill sergeants.

"We, the seniors, command you to jump this river. Right now!"

I was furious. I always thought the practice was antiquated, almost cult-like. But tradition demanded obedience. I stood, found the narrowest section of the river, and jumped. I nearly fell in. It wasn't a large river, though, and for an athletic kid, it was manageable.

"What next?" my reckless self asked, trying to rebel against the absurdity of the rituals. There was one problem: the river was quite deep, and I didn't know how to swim. The odds of drowning were not zero. Village tales spoke of people who had drowned, their bodies carried away into the abyss.

Fear quickly replaced anger. After the first jump, they pushed me toward a wider section of the river. Then another. Then another.

I was beginning to run out of strength, and the family watching started to worry.

"Hey, hey, boys! Let my son eat lunch. You can go haze at your own schools," my mother shouted, cutting through the commotion.

"You got lucky this time," they muttered as they backed off.

Fear. Anger. Anxiety. Excitement. These marked my final summer at Gasorwe camp. I was leaving the familiar, even though the familiar was sometimes harsh. Catholic boarding school awaited, and my mother was pleased. She had always hoped I would become a priest. *Perhaps the strict structure of boarding school would offer a refuge from the constant dangers of refugee camp life*, I thought.

> *"So live your life that the fear of death can never enter your heart. [...] Prepare a death song for the day when you go over the great divide."*
>
> — TECUMSEH

August 2000. Gasorwe, Burundi. Family photo in the Gasorwe camp. This is also the oldest known photo of Libere.

Part Three

NOT CALLED FOR PRIESTHOOD

"Sometimes it is the people no one imagines anything of who do the things that no one can imagine."

— ALAN TURING

Chapter 9

ADOLESCENCE AWAY FROM HOME

My cousin Bukuru, the uncle Julien's first born, had watched me grow up in Bihogo and throughout the refugee camps. As one of the first family members to finish high school and earn a teaching diploma, and was now a first-grade teacher and a father of two with parental opinions. Like most family conflicts, Mom and our paternal cousins did not see eye to eye. They had opinions on how she should raise us. Among other grievances, they often criticized her for not buying more farmland for us to inherit when we grew up and started our own families. My mother, unable to ride a bike, could not take me to Kanyinya. Since she had spent all the funds on my clothes and school materials, she could not pay for a taxi. Bukuru would have to bike me all the way to Kirundo, thirty two miles away.

I did not sleep the night before as I packed my belongings and prepared for the 4:30 a.m. departure. We strapped the duffel bag to the far edge of the bike's passenger seat, and I sat between my uncle and the bag as he pedaled. I wasn't strong enough to pedal both of us uphill, so I pushed the bike and bag whenever we climbed.

We rode along the paved roads of RN6 and RN14, the major high-ways connecting northern Burundi to Rwanda, sharing the road with cars and large commercial trucks. The early morning was forgiving; the fog and cool breeze made the ride manageable. Mist clung to our clothes, and the silence was broken only by the sound of bicycle wheels on pavement and the occasional passing vehicle. Later, we endured the scorching late summer heat, stopping once for lunch, then continuing through the hills of rural Kirundo, dodging trucks and cars along RN14. The relentless heat and the smell of hot asphalt mixed with diesel fumes reminded me constantly that I had left the comfort of home behind.

We arrived at Lycée Kanyinya in Kirundo around 5 p.m. I wore my khaki primary school shirt, dark blue pants, and brand-new black shoes. We entered through the small gate at the corner of the two main red brick

buildings and immediately faced the administrative offices on that quiet Sunday afternoon.

"Hello, I am Sister Claudine. What is your name?" the disciplinarian asked, pen poised over her list as she had seen us enter through the lancet window of the office.

"Libère Ndacayisaba," I said, brimming with pride at joining a new school and the prospect of boarding life.

I had expected a much older nun, but she was young and thin, dressed in a light gray tunic and white veil, as pure as the feathers of the egrets that flew over the river in Bihogo. Her welcoming smile reflected her friendly nature, and her voice was crisp and melodic. Her presence radiated a sense of calm holiness.

"Welcome to Lycée Kanyinya. Follow me to your dormitory," she said, signaling for us to follow.

We parked the bike in the entrance hall, and I grabbed my black-and-red Adidas Diablo duffel bag, which contained all my belongings, trailing behind her through the corridor.

THE ARRIVAL AT LYCÉE KANYINYA was a significant milestone: my first time away from family, my first time living in another province, and my first time sharing a living space with strangers. It felt like a reward for the hard work I had done in primary school and for my performance on the national exam. After a decade in multiple refugee camps, I was finally going to live in a safe and supportive environment. Here, they would feed me full meals; I would not worry about being hungry. I would no longer need to push heavy commercial bikes for a few pennies. I would no longer have to sell peanuts, gum, or cigarettes on the streets. I could focus entirely on learning and becoming an excellent student. I was entering adolescence, and it felt good.

"What's with the khaki shirt? You're not a schoolboy anymore," Sister Claudine said as we walked down the short steps, almost like a hazing ritual. She pointed out that khaki was a primary school uniform, and I would no longer wear it.

"You will now dress properly in black or dark blue pants and a white long-sleeved shirt."

"Yes, ma'am. I know the required uniform," I replied, almost to communicate that I understood the responsibilities that came with transitioning from boyhood to adolescence.

"And you're wearing your uniform pants on a Sunday? Save those for class days. We allow students to wear regular clothing on weekends," she added as we made our way across the campus courtyard.

"I understand. I have two additional pairs," I said, hoping to end the conversation.

At home, buying multipurpose pants for daily wear made financial sense; that was how we made choices in the refugee camps. I had three pairs to rotate and did not mind wearing the uniform any day. I was here to learn, not to dress up.

As more students arrived, I noticed that most were wearing casual clothing, keeping their middle school uniforms packed away. Nice jeans in various colors or fashionable shorts were common among older students and those whose families could afford multiple casual outfits.

I quickly realized how economic realities shaped even simple choices for my mom as we grew up. I also understood that the green flowery shirt and new flip-flops she had bought me were her way of making sure I felt presentable at school. By that afternoon, I could already feel adulthood beginning.

"Don't forget to fold your shirts properly. We don't like wrinkles here," Sister Claudine reminded me, concluding the day-one onboarding.

"I will do my best," I said.

Bukuru noticed I was under scrutiny and interjected.

"Don't worry, he is disciplined. Their father taught them how to iron and fold clothes properly since they were young."

"That's great. We're happy we got a good one," she replied.

On the way to the dormitory, we passed the library on the right and the chemistry lab on the left. On the second block of buildings, there was a large cafeteria on the right and an enormous hall on the left. Each space promised new experiences and new knowledge.

The third block of buildings was the dormitories. Girls occupied the right side, and boys had the left. The solid brick structures had blue doors and windows, their weathered walls silently telling stories of generations of students who had passed through these halls. At the back of each dorm block were showers and washrooms. Steam and loud noises would soon drift from these facilities in the early mornings, as hundreds of students prepared for their day.

After the brief tour, Sister Claudine took me inside the dorms and showed me my bed: the lower bunk of a two-story structure. The metal frame creaked slightly as I tested the mattress with my hand. The hall was massive, probably housing 200 to 300 bunk beds, sectioned according to class rank. The room stretched so far that the beds at the far end seemed to blur together, like railway tracks converging at the horizon. What struck me most were the lights. Unlike primary school in the refugee camps, where we relied on petrol lamps to illuminate the night, here there was electricity. Bright lights everywhere. *I could pray at the chapel anytime. I could study at any hour of the day.*

I would bunk with my future classmates on one end, while the far edge of the hall was reserved for the oldest boys, in twelfth and thirteenth grade. Their section seemed almost mythical to me, a place where giants dwelled. It reminded me of what former primary schoolmates who had joined the military used to describe: neat rows, precise spacing, and a subtle hierarchy embedded in every corner. Some beds were made, while others held only empty mattresses.

"More students are still coming in. Most of your classmates will arrive later tonight," she said, smiling reassuringly, though it did little to calm my nerves.

A few groups were already chatting in the dorms and outside, all appearing to know each other well and clearly having formed friendships. Their loud shouts carried a confidence that only comes with experience.

Sister Claudine left to receive more incoming students. Her footsteps echoed down the hall, gradually fading until they merged with the general murmur of activity outside.

Bukuru needed to return home. I walked him to the gate where his bike was parked and said goodbye. My throat tightened as I watched him mount the bicycle, knowing this was the moment I was truly alone, away from family for the first time.

"Be well. We will come to visit you frequently," he shouted as he disappeared into the evening light. His words, like a promise, lingered in the air, though we both knew the distance and cost would make visits infrequent.

Homesickness rose like a wave, threatening to overwhelm me as I stood there, staring at the spot where Bukuru had vanished. I knew nobody at this school. In fact, I knew no one in the entire province. The loneliness felt heavy, pressing down on my shoulders like a loaded backpack. As I walked back toward the dormitory, I wondered how I would make friends. This felt different from the refugee camps. In the camps, friendship came as naturally as breathing. Children played together in dusty streets, sharing whatever little we had. Here, I felt I was no longer a child and could not simply play my way into belonging.

To familiarize myself with the boarding school, I decided to retake the tour. This time, I moved slowly, trying to memorize every detail, as though mapping the geography of my new, contained world. I began at the library, peering through its windows. Inside, shelves of books stretched across the room, filled with volumes on countless subjects. The sight made my heart race. I had never seen such a collection before, not even in my dreams. These books were larger and more sophisticated than the primary school texts I knew, with their childlike illustrations. The subjects alone felt vast. Music, astronomy, French literature, English, biology, geography. Each book seemed to hold a fresh adventure waiting to be explored. I wondered what secrets they contained. Mathematical equations and celestial diagrams caught my eye, as did anatomy illustrations and detailed world maps. For a few minutes, the excitement of learning softened my home-sickness.

I moved on to the empty classrooms. They looked refined and orderly, with larger blackboards and neatly arranged wooden desks and chairs. *This was where learning would happen.* Each empty seat seemed to wait patiently for tomorrow's lessons.

Next, I hurried to the chemistry lab. Through the glass window, clean beakers and graduated cylinders appeared neatly arranged, almost inviting me inside. Bottles of different colors and sizes lined the shelves, capped carefully like a pharmacy cabinet. *Those must be chemicals. Would we mix them? That sounded thrilling and dangerous. How exciting.* My imagination ran wild with visions of bubbling solutions and colorful reactions. Unlike the classrooms, the lab tables were long, metallic, and fixed in place. They looked sturdy, as if built to withstand mistakes. Scratches across their surfaces told silent stories of experiments carried out by students who came before me. *How soon will I be allowed to use the laboratory?* I wondered

Next to the chemistry lab stood the chapel. I knew I would visit it daily for prayers. Though smaller than the churches in Muyinga and Gasorwe, it appeared more refined. Everything felt cleaner, newer, and carefully maintained. The familiar scent of incense and candle wax filled the air, a smell I associated with holiness. This was clearly a school run by nuns. Their orderliness and attention to cleanliness impressed me. I knew I could learn much here, even about how to keep myself and my space tidy.

In the courtyard, the Burundi flag stood tall at the center of the school, fluttering gently in the evening breeze. I knew that was where we would line up every morning to sing the national anthem before class. The plants and flowers in the courtyard were vibrant, reminiscent of church backyards where greenery is meticulously preserved.

Bougainvillea vines cascaded over the walls in deep purple waves, while carefully tended roses stood like sentries along the pathways.

I walked past the cafeteria, or rather the dining hall, and noticed that the tables were numbered and neatly arranged, grouped in a way that mirrored the order of beds in the dormitory. The large hall on the left caught my attention because it felt unfamiliar. I had never seen anything like it before. It was a theater hall that also doubled as a space for dances and special events, and at times was used by physical education teachers for indoor sports. Its high ceiling and cement floor would soon echo with performances, laughter, and the squeak of athletic shoes.

Life at Lycée Kanyinya became enjoyable. Each day brought discoveries, fresh challenges, and steady growth. Seventh grade passed quickly. I made friends, settled in, and found my group. Like most teenagers, I experienced crushes and heartbreaks, both at school and back in my home village. These fleeting affections of adolescence bloomed and faded like seasonal flowers, leaving behind sweet memories and the occasional ache.

As time went on, loneliness lingered, largely because I missed my family. The distance was too great for them to afford visits. I missed working on the farm, tending the coffee trees, and the familiar Sunday routine of serving as an altar boy. We had no phones to call one another, so we wrote letters. Each month, I wrote to my mother, telling her about life at boarding school, mostly to reassure her that I was doing well. Every letter was carefully composed, filled with small stories meant to bridge the distance between us. I wrote about my classes, the friends I had made, and how deeply I missed home. I also made specific requests for the meals I hoped she would cook when I returned for the next holiday break.

I sent letters to the church where I had served as an altar boy. Church leaders met monthly, and we handed the letters to the supervising nuns, who then passed them on to the priests at our local churches. During announcements, church officials would mention when letters arrived from Kirundo, and my mother would collect mine from the small office near the church entrance.

I often imagined my letter traveling the same route I had taken to reach Kanyinya. I pictured my family anxiously opening it, wondering whether it carried good or bad news. My younger sister would read it aloud to my mother, having taken over my former role of reading letters sent to our home.

I wrote to my brothers, who were attending boarding schools in different provinces. Isidore was in Gitega at the school for the deaf, and Télesphore was at Lycée Rugari. Our letters formed a web of connection across the country, each envelope carrying news, encouragement, love stories, and the comfort of family bonds. I also wrote to former classmates who were now scattered across boarding schools nationwide. I wrote to old crushes, to people I had left behind, and to neighbors from home. And they wrote back.

The letters arrived like small gifts, their pages filled with news from home, gossip from other schools, and shared dreams and fears. They became what connected me to the rest of the world. Those envelopes were my window beyond the school gates and a reminder that loved ones were still thinking of me.

EIGHTH GRADE WAS A particularly difficult year. In 2000, the country, along with much of the Horn of Africa, faced a severe drought that led to a deadly famine. The northeastern region was especially vulnerable and took the hardest hit. As a result, schools struggled to feed students, and imported food supplies were often of poor quality.

There were reports that some vendors mixed sand into the flour we ate to increase its weight and maximize profits. Conditions in boarding schools became so dire that students began organizing protests. Often, we would find handwritten instructions posted in bathrooms and showers, outlining plans for an organized march the following morning. Older students, usually class presidents from the upper grades, determined the meeting place and time. Everyone was expected to arrive in full uniform, remain silent, and follow a predetermined route through town.

The instructions emphasized that participation was mandatory and warned of harsh punishment for anyone who attempted to alert the administration. Some marches were stopped before they began, but on several occasions we marched through the town center to the governor's office. Similar protests and acts of resistance were taking place on school campuses across the country. The famine was so severe that we heard stories of families feeding grass to their children. People we knew were dying of hunger, children were succumbing to malnutrition, and much of the north experienced rising cases of diseases such as malaria.

During the winter months, malaria was rampant. That year, Don, my classmate and bunkmate, and I contracted the illness and spent two weeks hospitalized at a nearby clinic. We were placed in the same room, in beds side by side, and treated with chloroquine and quinine. Although my family could not travel to care for me, Don's family showed remarkable generosity, bringing double portions of food and drinks so we could share.

The first week was brutal, but by the second week, we began to recover. Our classmates visited on weekends, and like typical teenagers, we spent much of the time talking about our crushes and planning how we would catch up on missed schoolwork. Those days in the hospital strengthened our bond. Our friendship lasted until tenth grade, when we were separated by transfers to different schools.

The rain that winter eased the drought's grip, and over the next two years, as I moved through ninth and tenth grades, both the economy and our nutrition gradually improved.

During those four years, I learned far more in the classroom than I had expected when I arrived that Sunday afternoon in seventh grade. Sister Claudine taught religious studies, and Sister Bernadette, older, meaner, and far stricter, taught music. Her presence alone evoked fear, and music days quickly became my least favorite. She entered the classroom like a storm front, her heavy wooden rosary beads clicking together with each step, announcing her arrival before she appeared. Deep grooves around her eyes and mouth suggested a lifetime of frowning, and her gray hair seemed to absorb all the light in the room.

In her presence, the classroom itself felt like a punishment. Out-of-tune singing on middle C sounded like a dying cat's wail. She carried a thin wooden ruler, which she snapped sharply against desks whenever we sang off-key, the crack making everyone flinch. Her teaching method consisted mostly of forcing us to repeat scales until our throats were raw, her own voice a harsh croak that bore little resemblance to singing.

"Do-re-mi-fa-sol-la-ti-do," we droned, while she paced behind us, occasionally stopping to yank a student's ear if they went flat.

The room always smelled of her lavender talcum powder mixed with the musty odor of old music sheets, pages yellowed and brittle with age. The hour-long classes felt three times as long, and we emerged with ringing ears and dampened spirits, grateful to escape her domain. To this day, the thought of learning music theory dulls my excitement about playing musical instruments.

Physics, mathematics, and biology became my favorite subjects in middle school. Physics and math classes were held in the afternoon, when sunlight streamed through the school's arched windows, illuminating dust motes that drifted like tiny planets in their own orbits. Our teacher, Monsieur Pascal, had a habit of dramatically dropping objects, stones, feathers, wooden blocks, to demonstrate gravity, each striking the concrete floor with its own distinct sound. At other times, he hurled them across the classroom to explain projectile motion. The chalk squeaked against the blackboard as he derived equations, leaving white dust on his dark fingers, which he absentmindedly wiped onto his black trousers, creating ghostly handprints.

Mademoiselle Catherine taught physiology and cell biology with impeccable mastery. She recited the parts of the ten organ systems of the human body with intricate precision, like an orchestra conductor who had memorized every note, every cue, every pause. She could draw the respiratory system and label every part within the first fifteen minutes of class, all without glancing at her notes. In cell biology, she described the malleable nature of living cells as microscopic bags filled with fluid, explaining how that fluid itself contains even smaller bags. These organelles work together to sustain us as living organisms. She brought molecular and microscopic processes to life in her morning lectures, and to me, there was nothing grander, nothing more captivating.

⚓

IN NINTH GRADE, I performed chemistry experiments, memorized the periodic table, and learned about acids and bases and what happens when they mix. The chemistry lab felt like a world of controlled danger and thrilling transformations. Glass beakers clinked against ceramic surfaces as we set up experiments, their transparent walls revealing solutions that shifted from clear to vivid purple with a single drop of indicator. Sister Marie, with steady hands and thick rubber gloves, carefully poured concentrated sulfuric acid into a heavy brown bottle and demonstrated the proper pouring technique. Always pour acid into water, never water into acid.

When I carried out a neutralization reaction and watched the vigorous bubbling as acid and base met, I felt like a magician. The heat caught me by surprise as the test tube grew warm in my hand and thin wisps of vapor rose from the solution. One memory stands out clearly: the rancid smell of sulfuric acid made my nose wrinkle instantly. We wore stiff white lab coats that never quite fit, sleeves too long and shoulders too broad, making us look like children pretending to be scientists. The periodic table became my constant companion, its colorful squares holding secrets I was determined to master.

Almost as a continuation of my fourth-grade competition with Clarisse, Marcus and I challenged each other to memorize the entire periodic table. There was a famous mnemonic: *He-He, Li-B-Be-Cee-No-Fe-Ne, Napoleon-Mange-Six-Poulets-Sans-Chlore...*, continuing left to right, then downward, repeating the pattern to the end. And yes, the third line translates to "Napoleon eats six chickens without chloride." It sounded like a hymn verse, and it made perfect sense to us. We would recite it from memory, racing to see who could go faster and reach further down the table. It was an elegant system of memorization, and the knowledge stayed with me well beyond those years.

Even now, whenever I pass a periodic table in a museum or an academic hall, I silently recite the old mnemonic and smile at its absurdity, briefly reconnecting with memories of middle school life.

⚓

BEYOND ACADEMICS, I learned how to socialize and navigate my teenage years at the boarding school. Although the Catholic faith remained central to educational life, the administration was not overly strict and allowed students time to go out, socialize, and spend time beyond the school's gated brick walls.

In the same rhythm as other boarding schools, we had *sortie* (a "day-out") once a month. Students with families nearby could go home. On some of these *sortie* Sundays, friends invited me to spend the day with their families. On other Sundays, I went to see movies or stayed at school to study. Traveling home for a single day was too expensive for other out-of-town students, and for me, so we had to wait until the end of the semester. We returned home for two weeks during Christmas and Easter, while summer marked the real vacation.

The spring term ended in the first week of July, and we were not expected back at boarding school until September. During those breaks, I returned to my family in the Gasorwe camp and reunited with old classmates who were also home from their respective boarding schools. Traveling from Kirundo to Gasorwe was sometimes difficult. Most often, Mom mailed me cash or sent it with someone traveling to town so I could afford a bus ticket. When money was tight, I borrowed enough for part of the trip and walked the remaining distance.

One Easter holiday, the return home was especially hard. I walked half the distance home, carrying my bag and weighed down by exhaustion. Seventeen kilometers, ten miles, with my backpack pressing into my shoulders. As I climbed the hill behind the old primary school I had once attended, songs from the nearby Pentecostal church echoed across the landscape, rich and reverent as ever. The grass beneath the tall cedar trees was a vivid spring green, stirring memories of where we used to gather after long soccer games on the school's dusty grounds. The scent of eucalyptus, carried by eastern winds, mixed with the freshness of cedar leaves, filled my nostrils, welcoming me back.

Before I reached home, a friend saw me and ran toward me. When I asked why she looked so distressed, she told me that rebels in the capital had shot and killed my uncle Gilbert, my mother's youngest brother. To protect my studies, my family had chosen not to tell me. Grief, sorrow, and exhaustion settled heavily over us. We sat beneath the cedar trees where we once played and talked quietly for a while. After catching up on life in the camp, we continued walking toward my home, only to find it empty. Mom was still at the farm, my baby sister and younger brother were at school, and my older brothers had not yet returned from their boarding schools.

I went instead to my friend's house, where her parents welcomed me and fed me as I tried to eat, grief and loneliness pressed in, over-whelming and inescapable.

"Did you miss your friends here?" her mother asked, perhaps noticing how unusually quiet I was.

"Yes, I did."

"Eat up, and you two can go visit everyone," she said, her words carrying a quiet reassurance that things would be all right.

Finding comfort in community during loss was familiar to me by then. It is a shared experience among those living in refugee camps. Loss becomes familiar, and bonds form easily, almost instinctively. Soon after, we left to visit different houses, checking who was home and willing to spend time together.

That was the routine of every holiday return: looking forward to seeing everyone, asking what had changed, and slipping back into a familiar rhythm. Time at home meant helping Mom on the farm and attending church on Sundays.

School life continued with its steady pattern of departure and return. It took time to adjust to moving between two homes. Saying goodbye every few months, writing letters, and waiting for replies. Some farewells lingered longer than others. The September departures were the hardest, following an entire summer spent with family and old friends and, most importantly, free from schoolwork.

Tenth grade was the year of the national examination, and it demanded focus and discipline. Friends and family understood the pres-sure that came with it. I was content to remain at Lycée Kanyinya if that was where I was placed. I had settled in, built friendships, and grown accustomed to the rhythm of leaving and returning. But because I was performing well, I knew they would likely send me elsewhere.

I wanted to move to Bujumbura, the capital, to experience city life. My uncle strongly opposed the idea, insisting that city life would be a distraction and that I needed to attend an even better school. He recommended seminary schools instead.

During the summer break before eleventh grade, while working on our sorghum farm, Mom expressed how proud she was of my performance on the national exam. I felt a level of attention and affection that, as a middle child, I was not accustomed to receiving.

In a more deliberate tone than usual, or perhaps because I was older and listening more closely, she explained why seminary schools would be good for me. She spoke of how I could become a priest, then an archbishop, then a cardinal, and even a pope. She made it sound as though my path would secure heaven for everyone. I could become the Bishop of Rome.

Almost as if answering her prayers, Papa Chris managed to secure me a place at Petit Séminaire St. Pie X de Muyinga, where he and his brothers had studied. Despite my desire to live in the city, it was decided that I would attend the seminary for grades eleven through thirteen.

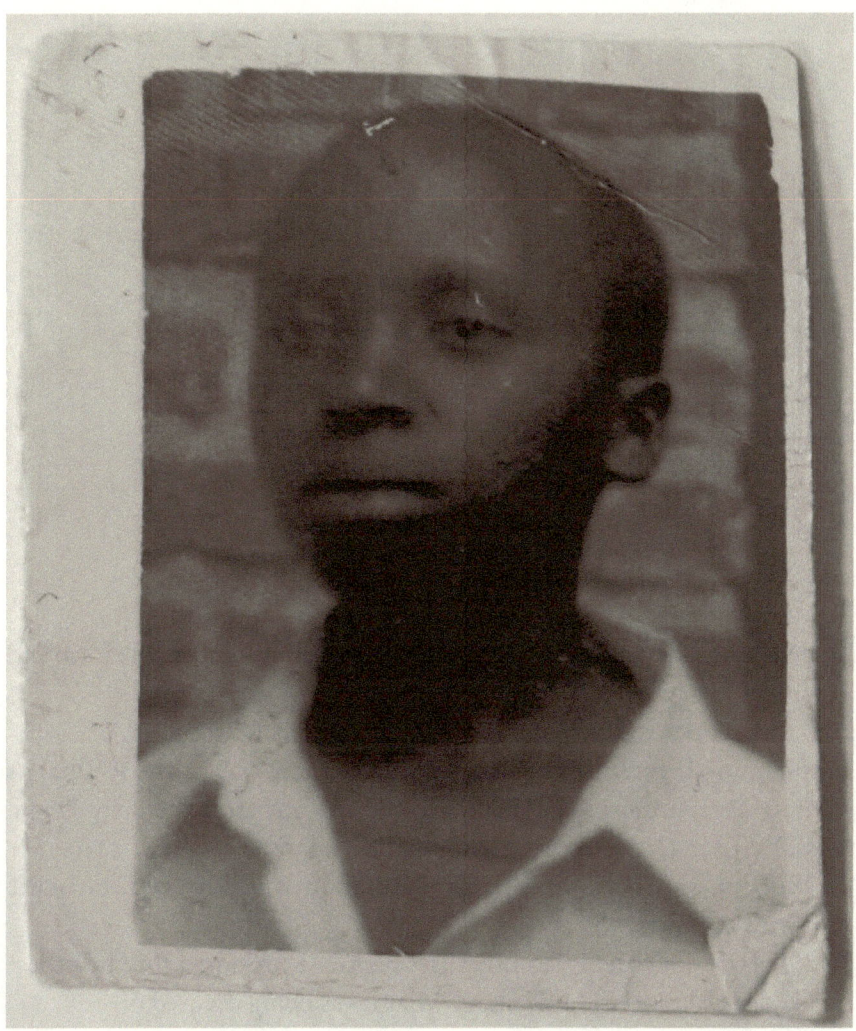

September 2000. Kanyinya, Kirundo. Portrait of Libère starting 7th grade at Lycé
Kanyinya

Chapter 10

SCIENCE WAS NOT THE SIN

I felt a hand land on my shoulder from behind and turned around instinctively.

"Please do not touch me."

Standing before me was the ordained deacon, one of the seminary's strictest disciplinarians. He had followed me out after the daily 7 a.m. Mass. His face carried the stern expression I knew all too well.

"Libère, you have broken the meditation rule," he said, his voice firm with authority.

"That is not true. I was quiet last night," I protested. My heartbeat quickened as I tried to understand what I was being accused of.

"I caught you whispering to another student. An appropriate punishment awaits you."

Uncertainty hung between us in the cool morning air.

PETIT SEMINAIRE SAINT PIE X de Muyinga, located nineteen kilometers from Gasorwe and about a kilometer from where the Mukoni camp once stood, is one of the country's most devout and strictly spiritual minor seminaries. It was the kind of institution designed to shape future priests and cardinals, a place that functioned more like a monastery than a school. We often hear that the first Burundian pope or saint could be among us. Nearly every morning at 7 a.m. Mass, we were reminded to watch for signs of being called to serve and spread the Gospel. The priest emphasized that we were already disciples of Jesus.

I lived with a constant fear that I was sinning whenever I imagined pursuing a different professional path. Science fascinated me, but what if I missed a sign that Jesus Christ had chosen me for something else? What if I ignored a calling?

At any given time, two or three disciplinarians patrolled the campus throughout the day. They were themselves graduates of Catholic seminaries, trained as guardians of doctrine and discipline. With their rigid posture and unblinking stares, they projected an intensity that kept everyone on edge.

One of the cardinal rules of the school was absolute silence between 10 p.m. and 7 a.m., designated as meditation hours. No one was allowed to speak, let alone whisper. There were no exceptions. The school sat between two mountains, and the silence at night was so complete that even the smallest sound felt amplified. Sharp objects were forbidden, so instead of imagining a pin dropping, it felt as though you could hear birds chewing.

In hindsight, I was still a growing teenager, fresh from Lycée Kanyinya, a progressive coeducational school. I had suddenly found myself in a small, all-boys boarding seminary governed by austere religious discipline.

That night, I had whispered with my bunkmate about a biology test we had taken earlier. We believed the disciplinarian had already left the dorm, but later we learned he sometimes stayed hidden, listening for students who broke the silence. A few of us were written up for minor disciplinary violations.

The confrontation that followed the next morning escalated everything. I was expected to listen without speaking back. When I pushed his hands off my shoulders, the act was interpreted as physical assault. In a matter of moments, I had committed multiple serious offenses, each compounding the last. Assaulting a disciplinarian, whether intentional or not, was grounds for expulsion.

A few weeks after the incident, Emelyne, a nun in training and one of the disciplinarians whose family had once lived near us in the Mukoni camp, stopped me to speak. She informed me that because of the serious offense I had committed, the administrative council had decided to expel me. She urged me to keep a low profile for the remaining weeks of the academic year. She emphasized that they had chosen to let me finish the year and that the offense would appear on my transcript. Still, she reassured me that I would be able to continue my education elsewhere, since most schools would not place much weight on seminary rules.

Within the seminary's rigid schedule, the only free time we had during the week was on Saturday afternoons. Saturday mornings were reserved for cleaning. We washed clothes and scrubbed dormitories, classrooms, the chapel, and every corner of the campus. Each grade was assigned a specific building to clean every Saturday morning. The afternoons, however, were ours. That was when we could relax, pursue hobbies, and take part in recreational activities.

Beyond playing soccer and volleyball on the school grounds, I tried to learn how to play musical instruments. I started with the guitar, but my fingers were too short to move quickly between the strings and maintain a melody. I also disliked the lingering pain that followed each practice session. After a few weeks, I gave up the guitar and switched to the piano, forcing myself to set aside the resentment I had developed toward reading musical notes.

One of my talented classmates agreed to teach me. He was one of the designated piano players during Mass. Nearly every time I practiced, I found myself playing *À la claire fontaine*, a song we had learned back in first grade during French class. I was drawn to it because it echoed the sadness I carried during that period. After long hours of cleaning the campus, sitting quietly in the chapel, and practicing piano, I often felt a deep sense of nostalgia that I could not yet put into words.

The song's origins date back to the seventeenth century in France, and over time, it became popular in many French-speaking countries, including Canada and Belgium. We likely inherited it during the Belgian colonial era. It has since appeared in numerous films and television productions, adapted by different creative teams. Its soft, pentatonic melody makes it an effective teaching tool for young students.

Nearly every morning in first grade, we would stand neatly in our khaki uniforms, like a small orchestra preparing to perform. The teacher would signal us to begin, and we would drum our little hands against wooden school chairs while singing from our tiny lungs. We sang the song long before we understood its words or meaning. It was not until eighth or ninth grade that I had developed enough comprehension to recognize the quiet melancholy embedded in its lyrics.

At the Saint Pie X small seminary, the campus felt like a photograph drained of color, reduced to shades of grief. It stood barely a mile from the Mukoni camp, a place tied to memories of loss and fear from my childhood. Nearby was a military camp, where I had seen former classmates become child soldiers and where the sound of helicopters came to signal danger. The surrounding hills were places where friends and I once searched for firewood, often wandering into forests rumored to shelter rebels. I traveled the same roads each day to and from campus. Mukoni camp no longer existed. It had been demolished. The children I had grown up with, from first through fourth grade, had all returned to distant parts of the province their families originally came from. The seminary was also only a few miles from the primary school I had attended, where I had first learned *À la claire fontaine*. Perhaps that was why the song carried such weight for me. In that state of quiet sadness, it was inevitable that it would be the first piece I played on the piano.

ON THE FINAL DAY of school, we gathered in the large hall for the annual reading of class rankings. In Burundi, this tradition marks the end of each academic year. School officials read each student's name aloud, starting with the top-ranked student, and announce the class position and overall academic percentage. This ritual begins in first grade and continues through secondary school and beyond. At smaller schools, where space allows, the entire student body attends. That was the case at the seminary. Everyone was present. I already knew what awaited me.

When my name was called, the Rector, the head of the seminary, announced my overall score. He paused briefly, then added, "Please see me after today's procession."

I stepped forward to collect my report card. Aside from a few classmates who had been quietly asking me for updates since the incident, the rest of the school turned to watch. Faces shifted. Some students looked stunned. Whispers followed me as I moved.

I walked to the front, where the professors and administrators sat on the raised stage, accepted my report card, and returned to my seat. Though I had prepared myself for this moment, the walk back down the aisle felt heavy, as if unspoken judgment pressed in from every side. The sadness settled in as I sat, listening while more names were called.

Being among the top students in my class was not enough. I felt as though I had failed my teachers, my uncle who had sent me to one of the country's best schools, and my mother, who dreamed of my becoming a priest. I believed I had failed the Church, the faith, and the calling I was supposed to recognize. My throat tightened as the weight of those thoughts settled in.

After the ceremonies, I walked to the Rector's office. I had never met him one-on-one before. He reminded me of my offenses: breaking the silence rule, talking back to the disciplinarian, and pushing him. Following the advice I had received, I kept my head down, nodded, and left once he finished speaking. I gathered my things and exited the school grounds, avoiding conversation until I was far away. Some classmates waited on the hill to ask what had happened. I told them I had been expelled and continued toward RN6, where we would catch a bus and part ways forever.

When the news reached my family, reactions were mixed. Papa Chris, who had encouraged me to attend the school, was deeply disappointed. My mother was furious at the school, convinced I had been expelled because I was Tutsi. She remembered past incidents of ethnic discrimination in seminaries, from the time she, Papa Chris, and Gilbert were young. Despite her anger and sense of betrayal, the fault this time was mine. I apologized to everyone for my behavior and the disappointment I had caused. Part of me began to accept that this chapter was over. But what if no one accepted my blemished transcript?

That summer, shame weighed heavily on me. Instead of taking part in the theater activities I had enjoyed since Kanyinya, I worked on construction sites to earn some money. A project was underway to build rainwater tanks in the refugee camp before winter. I asked the head engineer for a job. I felt too repentant to enjoy leisure, and some days I wondered if working construction was all my life would amount to. For the first time, grades on a report card felt irrelevant. I no longer thought I was better than anyone else. *Perhaps I could still become a good man, like my father, no matter how far I went in school.* On better days, I sent messages to family members, asking for forgiveness and seeking advice on where I could continue my education.

When Mama Gede learned about my expulsion, she asked about my grades, requested a copy of my transcript, and promised to find another school. She had experience in the education sector and knew school principals, especially in the Ngozi province. I spent the summer worrying about my future. Mom's words about taking responsibility for mistakes rang in my head like church bells.

Late in the summer, good news arrived. Lycée Don Bosco, a seminary run by a more progressive Catholic congregation, had accepted my transcript and offered a transfer for the following year. The stress and anxiety I had carried all summer lifted, like a backpack set down after a long, arduous trek. A fresh surge of excitement followed, brightening the prospect of the year ahead.

LYCEE DON BOSCO WAS another Catholic boys' school run by the Salesians, a more progressive and less strict order. Unlike my previous school, where Mass was mandatory every day at 7 a.m., Don Bosco only held Mass on Sundays, and attendance was optional. Some local students did not even live on campus, and not all students were Catholic.

One challenge was that Don Bosco was in Ngozi, a different province, fifty-two kilometers from Gasorwe. This meant I was moving again, this time to a third boarding school. I also faced the challenge of being admitted into the *Scientifique A* section, a notoriously difficult math and physics track in Burundian high schools. The *Scientifique B* track, which focused primarily on biology and chemistry and was more popular, was full.

I felt partially elated. I had found a new school, and it was better. I was also partially nervous. Only a few students were admitted to this track; there were sixteen of us, compared to more than forty in *Scientifique B*. Don Bosco was one of only four or five high schools in the country with teachers qualified to offer this level. The school always ranked among the top two nationwide, so the pressure to excel was high. These classmates represented the best of Burundian intellect. Yet, because of the small class size, we worked together more than we competed. In a class of eight students, the difference between second and sixth place was small. We understood that our ultimate challenge was the national college entry exam.

The school's progressive culture and proximity to city life made Lycée Don Bosco a launchpad for my future. Beyond the advanced lessons in mathematics, physics, economics, and philosophical theology, we had much more freedom to leave campus on weekends. This freedom allowed me to dream of a life outside the priesthood. I lived with less Catholic guilt; pursuing secular ambitions was acceptable, as long as one remained a morally good person. I realized that a love of scientific inquiry was not sinful—the expulsion from my previous seminary had not been about my intellect or curiosity.

Ngozi, the third-largest and most prominent city after Bujumbura and Gitega, had enough infrastructure by 2007 to support internet cafes and connectivity. I began spending many Sundays in internet cafes, researching schools abroad and planning how to continue my education outside Burundi, all while trying to maintain good grades.

The internet cafes were a window to the outside world. They were typically filled with people sending emails to loved ones abroad, reading about international news, or checking the state of affairs in other countries. Business-minded visitors worked on import-export projects, while some foreigners stopped by to share photos or messages with families across the globe. Young students explored the digital world, marveling at its possibilities. The rooms smelled fresh, with crisp tropical air, welcoming visitors almost as if inviting them to stay longer. Music played softly in the background, mostly gospel songs from Burundian and Rwandan artists, blending with the clicks of keyboards as messages traveled from that little room in Ngozi to every corner of the planet.

Unlike Petit Séminaire Saint Pie X, the student community at Don Bosco was vibrant, progressive, and entrepreneurial. They defied the stereotype of students being only nerds or geeks. Even the disciplinarians were different from those at my previous school. They played sports with us, joked and laughed alongside us, and inspired a sense of success that went beyond academics and religion. I felt at home on that hill of Burengo. The school challenged us in class and in life, and the support around me encouraged me to dream bigger.

In the last year of school, thirteenth grade, we prepared for the national college entrance exam. Like sixth and tenth grades, this year was intense, marking a pivotal moment in our educational journey. Studying abroad was a dream for many, and I searched for opportunities to secure such a chance. Only the top one to two percent of students nationwide earned national scholarships for overseas study. Historically, recipients were sent to countries such as Russia, Cuba, Algeria, and, more recently, China, to earn bachelor's degrees before returning to Burundi. These students were considered national treasures, often going on to become ministers, governors, and leaders of major institutions.

The challenge was that corruption sometimes interfered. Each year, reports surfaced of bribery, with children of government officials taking the places of high-achieving students. Villagers whose children were denied opportunities rarely discovered the manipulation, as these schemes were conducted at the highest levels of the Ministry of Education. The *abanyabururi* were a powerful syndicate, descendants of the southern Bururi province who, after toppling the monarchy in the 1960s, came to occupy the highest offices in the government. From the 1960s to the early 2000s, they effectively ruled the country. According to the stories I heard, they controlled the national scholarship system. If you were not an insider, your scores or even your name could be swapped or falsified. That was the conspiracy.

As a villager from the Northeast, I knew from a young age that gaining a national scholarship would be almost impossible. I had also met some of these intellectuals who had studied abroad under government programs. Many of them were drunkards, abusive to their wives, and willing to accept bribes. They were not the role models I wanted to emulate. Mostly, I did not expect to ever be selected for the national scholarship. From my internet research, I had already discovered alternative ways to study abroad. At Don Bosco, I had learned that English was becoming the international language and that mastering it would be crucial for future success. I began searching for colleges in English-speaking countries. The United Kingdom seemed promising, but the colonial connection made it feel out of reach. Burundi had been a Belgian colony, not part of the Commonwealth, and French was our main language. Other than Chris, who had studied mostly in English in Kenya and at private schools in Bujumbura, I had not heard of anyone from Burundi studying in England. I also considered schools in Africa. South Africa, Kenya, Uganda, and Tanzania all had prestigious universities and were relatively close to one another. The United States was another option if I could secure a student visa.

As I prepared for the national exam, I often sneaked out to internet cafés to do research and email Isidore in the US. He was my direct link to understanding the American education system. I asked him questions about college admissions and visa procedures. He was also coming home that July for summer break, so I prepared to meet him, gather as much information as possible, and begin assembling an application for study abroad.

Before all that, I had the college entrance exam and graduation to prepare for. Since my primary goal was admission to study abroad independently, this exam was not my top priority. International universities didn't care much about it; they focused on grades instead. I also knew that, broadly speaking, scores could sometimes be manipulated through bribery. So while other students worked to rank in the top 98th percentile, I focused on scoring high enough to qualify for either the College of Engineering or a math and physics program at the University of Burundi or an equivalent institution.

The exam day in June felt like just another summer day in Ngozi. The bigger event for me was Isidore's visit for the upcoming graduation in July. I took the test, then went shopping for a suit for the ceremony. That's what seniors do after exams. My family had pooled money for a tailored outfit, and the debate over the color had raged for days; my cousins were graduating too. I wanted a white suit with a blue shirt and a black tie. Nearly everyone thought it was a terrible idea. Who in the red dusty village in northeastern Burundi owns a white suit? It wouldn't even survive half the ceremony. Some cousins, though, argued that I should get whatever I wanted; it was my day, after all. I went to the tailor for sizing, then left everyone to argue and headed to the internet café to check emails from Isidore and the U.S. college admissions offices. I have no idea who made the final choice, but on graduation morning, I picked up a dark brown three-piece suit, a dark red shirt, and a black tie. I hated it. I felt like a style-less, terribly dressed mortician. At least my shoes were perfect, shiny black and white, and I loved them. They made up for the terrible suit. We got dressed and headed to the ceremony. Speeches were made, graduates were called, and in classic village fashion, my family arrived late. My classmates and I took photos and said our last goodbyes. *Would I see them again?*

BACK IN GASORWE, preparations were underway for a joint celebration: my high school graduation and welcoming Isidore back to Burundi. Friends, family, neighbors, and everyone important in our lives were invited to bring gifts. Such ceremonies are culturally significant; they mark life transitions, almost like a rite of passage. My uncles, cousin Bukuru, and other cousins attended. *nyokuru* Helena had also made the trek. Though she had lost her teeth and needed a cane to walk, her eyes were sharp, and her pride was clear as she watched all five of us thriving.

We rented a classroom at the local primary school. There was food, drinks, an MC, and a DJ. As is customary during celebrations, Burundians love to give speeches. Traditionally, it's men who stand up to speak. One by one, the MC called people to say a few words. Most were uncles and "wise men" of the town. Even if someone tried to control who spoke, a few tipsy individuals would inevitably rise to share something. Some speeches were full of pandering, attempts to be in my or my brother's good graces. I remember a photo of my younger siblings and me rolling our eyes at one of these moments. It's all part of the culture; this is common in the village.

Isidore and I spoke last, as custom dictates. This was our moment to thank everyone who had helped us reach this stage of life. When it was my turn, I thanked Nkurikiye and Domitila for caring for me and looking out for my family over the years. I thanked the teachers from Mukoni and Gasorwe. I thanked Bukuru for taking me to Kanyinya. I thanked Mama Gede for helping me recover from the seminary expulsion. I thanked all those who had looked forward to seeing me upon my return from boarding school.

Amid the celebrations, the uncertainty of where I would go to college sat in my throat like a heavy log. A visceral feeling of dissociation washed over me. I could sense the approaching homesickness and the melancholic weight of once again disconnecting from family and friends. Perhaps this is a universal feeling with change, the fear of the unknown, the crossroads filled with uncertainty. Even though I had not yet received results from the college entrance exam and my visa applications were still in early stages, anxiety was already bubbling up.

On a bright morning in early August, Isidore and I took the five-hour bus ride from Gasorwe to Bujumbura. He was heading to the capital to prepare for his flight back to San Francisco. Along the way, he filmed the landscapes of Burundi, capturing the hills, valleys, and the thousand winding roads that define the country. That trip marked the end of my life in the camps and my Catholic boarding school experience. After a few return trips to Ngozi and Muyinga to secure documents for my visa application, I left for Bujumbura one last time in October 2007. I had no idea that I would soon secure my F-1 visa to California, and that this would be the last time I'd see Gasorwe. Between the challenges of settling in California, pursuing higher education, and the geopolitical events that unfolded in Burundi, eighteen years have passed, and I still have not returned to my village.

July 2007. Gasorwe camp, Muyinga, Burundi. Libère, Isidore, Violette, Mom, Elysé, and Télesphore at the ceremony.

Part Four

THE COLD START PROBLEM

"You must attend to your business with the vendor in the market, and not to the noise of the market."

— BENINESE PROVERB

Chapter 11

FOOTINGS THROUGH THE FOG

"Wake up. We need to get ready for school," Isidore nudged me from my deep slumber in our small room at the San Francisco Church convent. It was Monday, January 28; the morning after my long flight across hemispheres.

My eyes barely opened. At first, it felt like a dream. He ran to shower first. I got up and peeked through the window. Thick fog hung between the multistory buildings, confirming this was not a dream. I was no longer in Burundi.

"It's your first day of school!" he announced, still wrapped in his towel as he returned from the shower. "We need to hurry. It's almost two hours from here to Ohlone College."

I showered, dressed, and we set off. New backpack, new pens, new notebooks. The rush of blood through my veins reminded me of my first day at Mukoni Primary School in September 1995.

We walked a few blocks to Montgomery Station and boarded the BART train toward Fremont, a one- to two-hour commute to Ohlone College. I memorized each station as we passed, in case I ever had to travel alone: Embarcadero, West Oakland—transfer station—Lake Merritt, Fruitvale, San Leandro, Bay Fair—another transfer station—Hayward, South Hayward, Union City, Fremont.

The late January morning was cold, foggy, and windy, making my body ache. Isidore had said Fremont was warmer, that we wouldn't need gloves. I had been foolish to trust him. When we stepped off the train at Fremont Station, the wind cut through me. Waiting for the bus felt like a cold hell. Fortunately, as the sun rose, temperatures slowly increased. The heated train and bus were a small comfort. *What a luxury*, I thought.

Adjusting to the weather took time. The Bay Area's Mediterranean climate was nothing like Burundi's tropical heat. The dry air made my nose run constantly, and I worried I might be sick. The cold was relentless. I had never kept my hands in my pockets for so long. I realized pockets were probably invented to warm hands, not carry things. Scarves, I discovered, were more than just fashion.

From Fremont BART, we took bus number 217 to Ohlone College, feeding coins into the small payment machine to board.

"You just get on without negotiating the price?" I asked Isidore, marveling at the efficiency and calculating how much one might save if the familiar bargaining was allowed.

The bus was packed with students, all faces full of excitement for the first day of class. New backpacks and the air of scholars surrounded me. Seeing so many white, Asian, and Black students, I began to understand that California had a high concentration of immigrants and international students. Culturally, this diversity felt both challenging and full of opportunity. *What are the cultures of everyone's countries of origin? How is their food different? Do they come from politically stable nations, or have they also experienced war? What are the traditions and customs of their homelands?* I didn't yet dare to start conversations.

THE FIRST TASK WAS to report to International Student Services and present my visa documents. When we arrived on campus, it was as majestic as I had imagined. Palm trees lined the walkways, giving the grounds a sense of openness and calm. Unlike the Catholic boarding schools I had attended in Burundi, there were no gates surrounding the campus. It felt as if the students were trusted independent adults, free to pursue their goals without supervision. This feeling thrilled my adventurous spirit.

Isidore led me to the International Student Services office, where I met Jeff and his team. They collected my documents, confirmed my information had been entered into the system, and officially enrolled me at Ohlone College. Afterward, we went to meet Elena in her office on the same floor.

"Oh my God, you are here! Welcome to Ohlone College. It's so nice to meet you!"

Even with my limited English, I sensed the genuine excitement in her voice and body language. Her spoken English was as clean and crisp as in her emails. *How many years will it take me to be this good?*

"Thank you very much." I replied. I wanted to say more, but I was stunned by her energy and not yet confident enough to hold a full conversation. She was also pregnant and I had never seen a pregnant foreigner before. I wondered if she was doing okay. My memory flashed back to Gasenyi camp when mom was expecting Elysé. *Perhaps pregnancy is easier in the U.S., healthcare and medicine is very advanced after all.*

From our email exchanges, I had expected a white woman. Instead, she was of Chinese-Hawaiian descent. Back then, I didn't notice such subtleties. Growing up, anyone who wasn't Black was simply "umuzungu," meaning white. Standing in the Ohlone administration building, I noticed the differences. Jeff was definitely white; his hair and eyes reminded me of the lady who helped me at Chicago O'Hare airport. Elena, on the other hand, had features similar to those of people I had seen in Kung Fu movies. It feels almost embarrassing now to admit, but that's how my twenty-year-old self, fresh off the plane in America, interpreted things.

Next, I went to the counseling office, where the advisor checked which placement tests I needed to take. She emphasized that the tests were meant to help me prepare better and told me not to worry.

"Some courses may start tomorrow morning, so please be ready. I will email you," she said gently, watching my face as if to make sure I understood. These small acts of consideration helped ease my transition.

"Thank you." I nodded and entered the test room.

At the front desk, the personnel asked for my student identification card and pointed me to a cubicle.

"You have two tests today: one in mathematics and another in English. Good luck," she said with a strict tone that reminded me of the instructions I had received for Burundi's national exams.

While the pressure of testing felt familiar, the language barrier made it harder. The math test covered algebra, trigonometry, calculus, and geometry. The English test included reading comprehension, writing, and listening. Jet lag was hitting me. My eyelids grew heavy, nodding forward and jerking back up. The computer screen blurred, while the footsteps of other test-takers briefly roused me as I struggled to focus. That afternoon, exhaustion battled my will to succeed. Almost dozing off, I shook my head hard to stay awake and make sure I finished everything before leaving the testing room.

Later, Isidore came to find me and introduced me to a few people. I don't remember their names; my brain was fried after the placement tests. The bus and train rides home that evening were a blur. I took a nap along the way.

The next day, we followed the same morning routine. On the bus, I scanned for familiar faces but found none. That week, I noticed that classes rotated on different days. It was nothing like high school, where I had a small group of classmates taking the same subjects at the same time, Monday through Friday, for the full academic year.

I was placed into Algebra II for mathematics and English as a Second Language (ESL). I felt proud not to be in the beginner ESL classes or the English Institute, which served students below the ESL level. For math, I was frustrated. Part of me blamed my English skills and the jet lag. Another part wondered if I was actually inadequate, not good enough for college in America. The counselor explained that I could retake the placement test the following year, which would allow me to advance. When I did retake it, I skipped trigonometry and was moved into the calculus series.

⚓

As THE FIRST WEEK progressed, the glossy vision of the proverbial American dream and the pursuit of happiness that I'd held would soon collide with the harsh realities of immigrant life and the difficulties in adapting to a starkly different culture in California.

When I landed in San Francisco in January 2008, I had $300 cash hidden in my pocket. This was money my brother had left in the bank in Burundi when he visited that summer, and he had asked me to bring it with me. The $1,300 flight ticket and the $200 SEVIS fee, a charge for registering international students in the DHS system, were money I had borrowed from my uncles.

On paper, my plan seemed simple: get a part-time job on campus, earn scholarships, pay back the money, and sustain myself. I knew how to work hard; those 3 a.m. wake-up calls to fetch water or work on the farm had prepared me for this. My motto was, "I'll rest when I'm dead." I wasn't so sure about the scholarships, but my brother assured me there were plenty. He was confident that I would excel and that the money would follow. Initially, his confidence helped mask my own doubts.

Reality, however, didn't match the plan. Books were expensive. International student tuition was staggering. Rent, utilities, and food added to the burden. And my family back home expected support. I was in the U.S., after all, and my brother had been sending money for the past two years. An R1 visa meant that the congregation housed Isidore. They fed him and paid for his education. He even received a weekly allowance, part of which he sometimes sent back to Burundi. My situation was different. Every necessity had to come from my own effort. The weight of family expectations, combined with the gap between their perception of the U.S. and the reality I faced, was overwhelming. Having mostly known boarding school life and eating what we grew on the farm, I had no concept of the cost of living, much less of life in California.

During my first week of school, I sat in the library, the reality pressing down on me. I thought about where I could get advice and remembered Mukasa. He had gone through this process and could offer pointers. I emailed him, but didn't hear back that day. Then I remembered; *Facebook*. He had mentioned it in Brussels. I had just created an account. Isidore had insisted I get one since it was where I could meet friends and send messages more easily, as I didn't yet have a phone. I looked up Mukasa and added him as a friend. We exchanged messages. Through him, I learned what it meant to be a junior in college; I would be a junior three years from now. Mukasa was in ROTC, preparing to serve in the army and eventually become a U.S. citizen. He gave me tips on finding scholarships and suggested renting books instead of buying them. I knew I didn't want to be a soldier, but I wondered what other paths to citizenship were available.

On that first Tuesday, I went to my Listening and Speaking ESL and Algebra classes without books. While the algebra professor noted that books were optional, the ESL professor strictly emphasized that books were required. Feeling inadequate for not having the required materials, the basic tools needed just to begin learning, I slid lower in my seat, keeping my empty desk space hidden behind the student in front of me while others flipped through their brand-new textbooks. *I need good grades to get scholarships, and I need books to get good grades, so school materials must be the priority*, I'd calculate.

That Wednesday, I looked up the cost of the first-semester books and realized there was no way I could afford them. Even renting was out of reach. I messaged Isidore about the costs and asked if he knew how I might secure the books, or at least rent them more cheaply. As I clicked between the tab showing the price of the books and the one with my homework, a student stopped by my desk carrying four brand-new textbooks, the exact ones I needed for the semester.

"Hi, I'm Nathan. These are yours," he said in a reassuring voice.

"Your brother said you need them."

The sight of the books tightened my throat with emotion. He did not leave a note or anything, but I knew Isidore did not have the money to buy them.

"Thank you," I said, though the words felt inadequate. This had been the most significant expense weighing on me that semester. I felt a deep sigh of relief.

"You're welcome. Good luck with your classes," he said as he walked away.

I messaged Isidore to ask who the man was and whether we owed him money or needed to return the books at some point. He told me it was a kind gesture and that we owed nothing. Nathan was the president of the Associated Students of Ohlone College that year and had heard about me from Isidore and Elena.

The worries I had felt in earlier classes dissipated. I could now show up like everyone else and focus on learning. The first semester's grades would allow me to apply for scholarships. Although other needs remained, this was one less burden.

I spent my first week living in the convent in San Francisco, where Isidore was staying, and we commuted daily to Fremont for school. Commuting for the two of us alone burned through $200 that first week. In an effort to live closer, we spent the next two weeks in the dorm room of one of Isidore's friends at California State University, East Bay, within walking distance of the Hayward station. This was, of course, against university rules, so we slipped in and out of campus like shadows, careful not to cause problems for them.

AFTER TWO WEEKS, the situation became too risky and burdensome, and we ended up at a Motel 6 in central Fremont. We borrowed money for a few nights, uncertain where we would go next. It felt as though we were living on borrowed time. Each night, we wondered if we would have enough for the next. Each day is balanced precariously between hope and homelessness.

After the nights at Motel 6, my brother's friend, who had rented a multi-room house on Mission Boulevard, offered us an available room. We could live there and pay when we were able. It was a significant relief, but it also carried the weight of owed debt. We slept on a thin mattress in the small shared room. Three other tenants occupied the remaining rooms. All were deaf.

The temporary living situations, much like the refugee camps, brought a constant anxiety of displacement. To some degree, I was accustomed to this kind of transient life. I had one suitcase and did not own much to hold onto. I had no childhood memorabilia to carry with me either.

By mid-February 2008, something far more significant was

unfolding and affecting nearly everyone: the 2008 global financial crisis, often referred to as the Great Recession, the worst economic downturn since the Great Depression of the 1920s and 1930s.

I had not yet adapted well enough to understand the full scope of the problem. Unbeknownst to me, everyone was struggling. Gas prices began to rise at an alarming rate. On my first day commuting to Fremont for school, I noticed that gas station prices were more concerned with converting dollar amounts into Burundian francs than with understanding inflation. At one Shell station on Mission Boulevard, gas was $1.20, give or take $0.30 depending on the type, during that first week. A few weeks later, I noticed the price creeping up, eventually reaching $2 at most East Bay gas stations.

It did not concern me just yet. I had heard news about the growing global crisis and how it was affecting the petroleum market. In my eleventh-grade economics class, I had learned basic macroeconomic concepts. OPEC countries controlled oil pricing and sometimes restricted exports in response to market conditions and geopolitical tensions. *Perhaps this was a temporary issue, a minor disruption not worth worrying about.*

Later that year, the stock market crashed. I would come to learn about Lehman Brothers, the housing crisis, subprime mortgages, Fannie Mae and Freddie Mac, the major banks deemed too big to fail, and the deeper complexities of the stock market, wealth distribution, and economic inequality in America.

There was much to learn in my new life, but that February, my primary focus was settling into the basics. I needed a job and a pathway toward permanent residency. I asked Elena if she knew of any job openings.

"Yes, the cafeteria, the bookstore, and other customer service roles around campus usually have openings."

"I believe human resources may have an opening too. Let me ask around."

"Thank you."

Later, she sent me a list of people to contact about the jobs. When I met with them, I could barely sustain a conversation, and it quickly became clear to all parties that my English was not yet fluent enough for those roles.

I realized that tutoring might be my next option. I knew foreign languages. After reviewing the course descriptions for the college's beginner French classes, I felt qualified to tutor French. I asked Elena about tutoring.

"Good idea! There is a language department, and you can most definitely tutor French," she replied, her face lighting up at the possibility that this might work out. "I will speak with one of the faculty members in the French department, and we'll see how it goes."

I waited for news about the tutoring position. Hope. Anxiety. In mid-February, Elena emailed to say that she had heard back from Dave, the French professor. He asked that I email him so we could meet and discuss the job opportunity.

I wondered whether I should write the email in French or in English. Elena had suggested that I copy her on the message, so I wrote another clumsy email,, still learning to use an English keyboard instead of the French layout I was accustomed to. To this day, I remain deeply grateful to the members of the Ohlone College community who showed such patience and gentleness as I adapted.

The following week, I heard from the French professor, who invited me in for an interview. I was unsure what he might ask, but at the very least, I knew I would meet someone who spoke a familiar language. His name was not French, nor did it sound West African, Caribbean, or even Canadian. I could tell it was either Spanish or Portuguese.

When I reached his office, a small room beneath the math and physics classrooms, I was beginning to understand the building names and numbers. I knocked on the door, my heart pounding with anticipation.

"Yes, come in."

I stepped inside, shook his hand, and we began with small talk in French. He asked where I was from and how I was finding life at the college. I asked how long he had been teaching there. He spoke with a clearly Iberian accent. He held a degree in literature and was multilingual, teaching French, Spanish, and Portuguese at local colleges. I wondered whether there were truly no native French speakers in the area to teach college-level French. My thoughts drifted to the Bay Area's socioeconomic makeup and higher education in the United States. There was still so much I had to learn.

"You've passed the listening and speaking component. Now let's do the writing part."

He handed me a half-page paragraph written in English and asked me to translate it into French. The text described a family event. I turned to the table behind me and began translating the passage onto another sheet of paper. The ticking clock on the wall felt like a reminder of the moment's urgency. I worked quickly and handed him the translation without rereading it. I wanted to impress him badly so he would allow me to tutor both Level 1 and Level 2 courses he was teaching.

"Qu'est-ce qui s'est passé ici?" he asked after reviewing the page and spotting a typo.

I looked again. I had skipped a word in one sentence.

"Ah, désolé, je n'ai pas vérifié," I replied, internally groaning at such a careless mistake during an important encounter. I had fumbled my first impression, and in that moment, self-doubt and the fear of losing this opportunity crept in.

I corrected the error and handed the paper back.

"Très bien. Félicitations!" He shook my hand. I got the job.

"I will send you the class schedules. Come to class on Thursday afternoon to meet the students. I will notify HR, and you will start tutoring next week."

"Thank you so much," I replied, overwhelmed with relief.

Tutoring turned out to be an enjoyable activity between classes. The classrooms were smaller than those for general education courses, such as algebra. About half of the students were adult professionals taking French for pleasure or as a hobby; their relaxed approach to learning sharply contrasted with my own urgent need to succeed. The other half appeared to be students fulfilling a degree requirement.

"Class, please welcome your French tutor for the year. Libère hails from Burundi and will be available in Hayman Hall for French tutoring. Please check with the front desk for hours," he announced.

I stood and waved to the class.

"Bon après-midi. C'est Libère, enchanté."

"Enchanté," a few enthusiastic students replied.

OVER THE NEXT FEW weeks, I showed up for tutoring hours, checked in, and waited in the designated room for students to arrive. Some days, no one came. On other days, especially the one or two days before an exam, a large group would arrive with questions and a desire to practice their French. The ebb and flow of attendance followed the academic calendar.

There was deep satisfaction in helping others succeed. After exams or assignments, some students stopped by to show me their scores and thank me for the help. I felt proud and fulfilled. In this vast land and unfamiliar culture, I had found something meaningful to contribute, even within just three months of arrival.

More importantly, the modest but steady income from tutoring was enough to cover my share of the rent and school materials, though food remained a daily uncertainty. Some days, I avoided passing the Ohlone cafeteria altogether so I would not smell the teriyaki chicken I loved but could not afford.

There was one couple who attended nearly every tutoring session: Linda and Jonathan. They were older, retired, and taking the course in preparation for a trip to France. They mainly wanted someone to practice conversation with. Unbeknownst to the college, I spent much of my tutoring time chatting with them. As we got to know one another, they learned that my pay depended on student attendance. At one point, they even offered to tip me. I told them it was not allowed, but I was deeply grateful for their generosity. They assured me they would continue showing up as often as possible so I could earn enough to settle into my new life in California. Another kindness that became a brief anchor.

February 2007. Hayward, California. Libère (right) and Isidore (left) in a friend's dorm. The same shirt and Burundi flag necklace Libère wore on his flight from Bujumbura are worn here. Photo © Isidore Niyongabo

Chapter 12
SANCTUARY AT LAST

"Congratulations. You have been granted asylum. Here is the relevant paperwork to present as evidence of your change of status," the officer said. "Your work authorization card is also included in this folder, and you are now legally permitted to seek employment."

"Thank you very much." I said as I took the envelope and walked out of the USCIS office in San Francisco. It was on January 7th of 2009, after a grueling year in search of permanence in America.

WHEN I LEARNED ABOUT Mukasa's path to citizenship during my first week in the Bay Area, I began asking around about alternative ways to convert my F-1 visa into a green card for permanent residency. The answers varied. Some people joked that the fastest option was to marry a U.S. citizen, a suggestion that felt both wrong and deeply insulting. Others mentioned that there were multiple legal pathways and advised me to consult an immigration lawyer. When I asked how to find one, the conversation inevitably shifted to how expensive legal services could be. While discussing the French tutoring job, Elena also reached out to an immigration caseworker named Josephine, a kind woman from Sierra

Leone, to ask about a process called asylum. She referred me to an immi-gration center in San Jose, California. The center, a large three-story building on Moorpark Avenue, soon became a familiar place as I attended multiple appointments.

The waiting rooms were usually crowded with immigrants from all walks of life, and the atmosphere carried a heavy mix of hope and anxi-ety. A Vietnamese couple sat quietly in a corner wearing traditional clothing. I could not tell whether it was an expression of cultural pride, similar to my Burundi necklace, or whether, like me, they had recently arrived and these were the only clothes they owned. A West African woman sat near the front, gripping her documents tightly in a trans-parent folder. Her serious expression conveyed determination, regardless of whatever persecution had brought her there. She sat upright, unfazed by the long wait, her focus intensified by her Afrocentric, colorful head-wrap woven with red, green, orange, and navy blue. Nearby, a thin and fragile woman whispered to her young son, trying to soothe him as he cried. Her red, tired eyes suggested she had not rested well in days. The language she spoke sounded Japanese, perhaps Korean. I wondered if she was a single mother. *What had happened to her? Where was the child's father? Was the baby safe?* I found myself imagining the kind of suffering or persecution she might have endured to end up in that room.

After multiple intake appointments between February and April 2008, including in-depth interviews about my childhood and a psycho-logical evaluation for post-traumatic stress disorder, the center concluded that I did not meet the criteria for the population they primarily served. My understanding was that their focus was on individ-uals who were survivors of torture, particularly cases involving domestic violence. However, the team agreed that my asylum case was strong and informed me of another organization that could assist. They transferred my case and introduced me to the East Bay Sanctuary Covenant, a nonprofit organization that provides pro bono legal immigration services. There, I met with the center director, two caseworkers, and the attorney assigned to my case. The only request they made was that I consider donating someday, once I was established in America.

Over several rounds of interviews, the team took meticulous notes and asked detailed questions about my life, from birth to the present.

They asked about life before the war, the onset of the conflict, time spent in refugee camps, and my educational path. They encouraged me to recall as much as possible and to verify details with family members when my memory was incomplete. They also asked about Burundi's ethnic groups, how the war unfolded along sociopolitical lines, and the current conditions facing survivors who still lived in camps.

Recounting the events of my first two decades meant revisiting deeply painful memories. These appointments continued from May through August. Some sessions felt therapeutic, though conducted through a legal lens. Others felt like reopening wounds that had never fully healed. I often had to remind myself that their goal was to document an accurate account of the political persecution and wartime experiences I had lived through.

"What date was your father killed, and who was responsible?" one of the law students asked, likely for the fifth time that summer.

I responded as I had before, recounting the events of 1993.

"Do you remember where you were on October 21, 1993, around 8 p.m.?" another legal clerk followed.

I answered again.

"In your best estimate, how many family members were lost during that week, and who were closest to you?"

I took a deep breath and named the loved ones who were taken during those tragic days.

"Did you ever feel that your life was in danger? Can you describe those moments?"

Once more, I retold the experiences. The man with the machete. The long nights hiding in the trees. The encounter with Ndiroreye. The announcement that all Tutsi males would be killed. The days in the camp when people were killed on the roads. The nights of uncertainty when rebels patrolled around camps and schools. The new reality of former armed rebels rising into positions of power, and the withdrawal of international peacekeeping forces shortly before I left the country.

"Should we take a short break and continue after fifteen minutes?" the law clerks would ask, checking to see if I wanted to pause.

"No, I'm okay. Let's continue," I would reply, swallowing hard as I tried to remain composed.

"We don't have to finish today. We can continue at the next appointment," one of them added, softening their voice, likely in an effort to ease the tension.

"No, let's finish as much as we can today. I need to return to class afterward," I insisted, my stubborn resolve showing through.

Eventually, they would insist on taking a break themselves, suggesting coffee and water. There was likely no urgent need for hydration. They understood that I needed a moment, and perhaps they did as well, after listening to the duplicate emotionally heavy accounts over and over. Some days were more challenging than others. The offices of EBSC became a rare safe space where I could confront the darker memories I had buried for years.

THE QUESTION ABOUT HOW many people I had lost was complicated. I had never tried to count them, nor had I allowed myself to fully revisit or honor their memory. Perhaps my subconscious resisted knowing. Yet now, I also felt compelled to understand who they were. I emailed Télesphore and asked if he could compile a list. A week later, he replied with a long list of names, those lost during the final week of October 1993. Some names felt distant, almost unfamiliar. Others belonged to relatives I had known only through stories, people who lived far from us but were still family. Some were so close that the realization that they were all killed within a few days made my skin crawl. The year 2008, which was meant to mark the beginning of my college education, became a second period of mourning. Revisiting these memories pulled me back into the shadows of the past. That list became what I called the "Wall of the Fallen"

Wall of the Fallen

Father's Side

1. Manariyo Vénant (Father)
2. Gahutu Mathias (Grandfather)

3. Nduwimana Julien (Uncle)
4. Mpunjireko Euphrasie (Aunt)
5. Euphrasie's husband and their four children (Cousins)
6. Tiyota (Cousin)
7. Rivuzimana Athanase (Cousin)
8. Nahimana Fidèle
9. Eduard Masengo
10. Thadée
11. Mvunamaboko Emille
12. Gahutu
13. Ruhaya François
14. Kinyogoto Pierre

Mother's Side

1. Ntahondereye Louis (Grandfather)
2. Nankware Sophie (Grandmother)
3. Niyonshimira Beatrice (Aunt)
4. Mutuku Anthoine (Grandfather's brother)
5. Butunguka Anthoinette
6. Gaswi Charles
7. Kadamari Chantal
8. Barinabiri Dominique
9. Habimana Prudence
10. Ciza
11. Ntakamurenga Andrée
12. Niyonzima Melchior
13. Mugisha Aimé
14. Rugurane Arcade
15. Kamwenubusa Julien
16. Nzorubara Nicodème
17. Civuze Emmanuel
18. Riyazimana Jean
19. Nankware Constance
20. Bukuru Désiré
21. Mphayokurera Evariste

22. Gahungu Berchmans
23. Kavakure Lazare
24. Nahimana Thomas
25. Ntezabanyanka Mathilde
26. Budangwa Judith
27. Kabageni Calinie
28. Hakizimana Donatient
29. Nahagera Renée
30. Kampayano Venantie
31. Ngiririnyatsi Rosalie
32. Riragonya Joseph
33. Mukeshimana Génerose
34. Ntahorija Venant
35. Ndorere Dismas
36. Sebahungu Pascal
37. Kanyoma Elisabeth
38. Nubusa Claudine
39. Kanyunzuguru Didace
40. Muhakwanke Pie
41. Nkonko Anatole
42. Ndihokubwayo Tharcisse
43. Gahungu Joseph
44. Gahungu Bernard
45. Kazogizogi Nabuyondi
46. Génerose
47. Nizigiyimana Pascaline
48. Boduin
49. Mvanda
50. Niyonzima
51. Muzige
52. Adélaide
53. Mavukiro Mathias
54. Nibigira Adelin
55. Bashirakandi Claver
56. Romuald
57. Kayumba Anatole

58. Masurubare

They were the souls who transitioned from this mortal coil. The lost ones whose graves we never found and whose tombs we will never get to decorate. I spent months poring over the list, saying my farewells. Mourning. Vowing to honor them. Slowly healing.

IN JULY, the legal team notified me that they had concluded I had a strong asylum case. They would apply on my behalf and represent me as legal counsel throughout the process. Between the racing thoughts during the waiting period, I still had classes to focus on. I buried myself in my studies in the hope of earning scholarships.

In October, as a result of my strong grades in the first semester, I was finally offered my first scholarship, the Ohlone International Student Scholarship, which waived my out-of-state tuition fees. It was my first real win. In my jubilation, I forwarded the notification email to Elena, Isidore, and even Télesphore, who barely understood English.

During the first week of December 2008, I received notice of an asylum interview appointment scheduled for December 22 at 9 a.m. in San Francisco. The timing was both fortunate and daunting. The financial crisis was in full swing, and the September 15 market crash was still sending shockwaves through the economy.

Five days before the interview, my attorney scheduled a preparation session. Acting as a DHS officer, she asked multiple rounds of questions to ensure I was fully prepared. Most of the questions focused on details of my life and felt straightforward. At the end of the session, she instructed me to arrive at 8 a.m. on the day of the appointment.

I did not sleep the night before December 22. I kept emailing my attorney with questions, and she remained reassuring, reminding me to focus on telling my story clearly and answering only what was asked.

The morning finally arrived, and I dressed carefully to honor the day's solemnity. I took the BART train early into San Francisco, arriving at the immigration office a few minutes before 8 a.m. I waited for my attorney at the coffee shop next door. When she arrived, we ate breakfast together, though I had little appetite. I asked if there was anything else I should prepare for.

"No, everything is ready," she assured me, confidence steady in her voice.

I knew we would not receive the results that day. She had already managed my expectations, explaining that it would take about two weeks to learn whether the case was denied or granted. Still, in her voice, I felt hope. I felt that, eventually, everything would be okay.

At 8:30 a.m., we proceeded to the lobby and entered the building, passing through the usual security scanners and checking in at multiple desks as we made our way to an upper floor. My attorney did most of the talking, holding a large folder filled with documents and standing firm, her voice commanding in the way lawyers' voices often are.

When we reached the interview floor, we entered and sat among the other applicants. The resemblance between that office and the U.S. consulate in Burundi, where I had obtained my visa, was uncanny. The waiting room was lined with desks, with people sitting in silence. There were secured doors where applicants were called in, one by one, as though heading into interrogations. Large American flags and multiple USA seals adorned the walls and walkways, as if reminding you whose authority governed these halls. A formal photograph of the current president hung alongside that of the highest-ranking official in the jurisdiction, the governor of California, displayed here in San Francisco just as the ambassador's photograph had been shown in Burundi.

Two minutes before 9 a.m., my name was called, and I walked in with my attorney. The officer was a young woman of Asian descent, her expression so stern that one might have mistaken her for a Navy SEAL or a high-ranking military officer.

"Good morning," she said in a tone so judicially authoritative that it sent a jolt of fear down my spine.

"Good morning," I replied almost in unison with my attorney, who had previously explained that she would respond to the initial procedural questions and signal when it was my turn to speak.

"This is a petition for asylum for Libère Ndacayisaba. Is that correct?" the officer asked.

"Yes," my attorney replied as she handed over the prepared paperwork.

They went back and forth, exchanging documents and addressing procedural and logistical questions. The calm on my attorney's face throughout the interaction gradually eased my nerves. I had been instructed to listen carefully to each question and to ask for clarification if I did not understand what was being asked.

As the exchange continued, I felt increasingly calm and secure. They both sounded as though they had my best interests at heart. I could not fathom returning to the shadows of Gasorwe. Despite the legal formality of the moment, I knew I was not on trial. This was an immigration case for the officer to evaluate. When my attorney gave me the signal, I prepared to answer the officer's questions.

"How old were you on October 21, 1993?"

"Do you remember the incident at your childhood home on Friday, October 22, 1993?"

Like a repetition of the summer sessions at EBSC, I answered in the same way I had responded to the legal team, maintaining my composure and simply sharing my life story. We went back and forth, and before long, the officer said those were all the questions she had.

"Is there any additional documentation we can provide to support the decision on this case?" my attorney asked.

"No, we have all the necessary documentation," the USCIS officer replied. "Please return in exactly two weeks." She checked off a few boxes and closed the folder of paperwork in her hands.

That would be 9 a.m. on January 7, I noted mentally.

"The decision on your asylum case will be communicated to you then. You do not need an attorney for this appointment," she continued, instructing me to report to the second floor.

The two weeks of waiting felt like an eternity. As usual, I tried to bury myself in schoolwork.

On January 7, I returned to the same office. I proceeded to the second floor and waited for my name to be called at 9 a.m. When I was finally summoned to the window, I was handed an envelope containing a set of documents.

"Congratulations. You have been granted asylum. Here is the relevant paperwork to present as evidence of your change of status," the officer said. "Your work authorization card is also included in this folder, and you are now legally permitted to seek employment."

I don't recall what the officer looked like. I barely noticed her in that stressful moment.

"Thank you very much." I took the envelope and rushed out to the train station, almost as if I were fleeing from invisible asylum thieves lurking near the USCIS building. Once on the train, I opened it and carefully read through the documents, checking repeatedly to confirm that the Department of Homeland Security had officially granted me both asylum and work authorization. I ran my fingers across the pages as I read through the documents. The papers were authentic, legitimate. I had, in fact, been granted asylum and work authorization. Like that Thursday when I walked along *Avenue des États-Unis* with my F-1 visa stamped in my passport, I clutched the envelope as though my life depended on them.

My life *did* depend on these documents. I could now work and study as a California resident. Twelve months from that day, I would qualify for a green card and permanent residency. I was no longer an international student and would no longer pay exorbitant international tuition. I was not required to remain enrolled in college either. More than anything, I had found sanctuary in America. The fear of war washed away. A stable life could finally begin. *Sanctuary at last.*

The first order of business was to repay my debts to my uncles and to Ohlone College. Before that, I needed to find a job, not multiple jobs. Before all of that, I had to go to Jeff's office to formally register my change of status from international student to California resident. Once that was cleared, I could stop school and focus on finding work.

The trip back from San Francisco to Ohlone College felt like the blink of an eye. With the same urgency I once used to push open the door of the internet café in Bujumbura to notify Jeff's team of my visa approval, I knocked on the door of the international students' office, handed over my documents, and requested a change of status.

"Congratulations on being granted asylum. This is great news," the office staff member said as she pulled up my information.

"Thank you."

"Unfortunately, it looks like it is too late to change your status for this semester since you are already registered. We can only apply the change starting in the fall."

"Do I still have to pay international student tuition?" I asked.

"Yes, unfortunately, there is nothing we can do about that."

Under F-1 rules, I could not even change to part-time status. *Bureaucracy at its finest.* I remained registered for thirteen credits. I ended up failing one of the three classes, the only F I would ever receive in my academic career. At that point, however, I needed to work full-time to survive. Grades could wait.

THAT JANUARY IN 2009, the United States was preparing to swear in Barack Obama as the 44th president. Against that backdrop of hope, the financial crisis that had begun with the market crash of September 2008 was in full force. Companies were going bankrupt, and others were laying off workers by the thousands. Housing foreclosures were rampant, and even the small room we had occupied on Mission Boulevard was no longer available after the owner lost the property. Isidore and I found another room to share in Hayward.

In February, Kendrick, a friend of Isidore who worked at Safeway, mentioned that his store in Pleasanton might have openings for bagging groceries and stocking shelves at night. He suggested I come in and speak with the manager.

One afternoon, I arrived with my résumé, knocked on the manager's office door, and introduced myself. Steve, the tall and imposing store manager, was dressed formally in a white long-sleeved shirt, black trousers, and a black tie, polished black shoes completing the look. It was clear he was in charge.

"It's great to meet you. Kendrick told me you were coming," he said in a welcoming voice, extending his hand for my résumé.

"Nice to meet you too," I replied, handing it over.

He scanned the page, looking for relevant experience. Aside from French tutoring, there was very little to see.

"Have you worked in a grocery store before?" he asked.

"No, I haven't. But I am willing to do any job and eager to learn from your team," I replied.

"Okay, good. We need people to help at the front, bagging groceries, or possibly assisting with stocking the shelves. Welcome to the team. I will send your information to HR. Donna will be your direct manager and will show you what to do."

I was quietly relieved to have secured a stable job.

"Thank you so much. I will do my best," I replied.

He briefly explained the onboarding process and introduced me to Donna, an experienced cashier who managed the front end. Donna asked for my shirt size so they could get me an apron and told me to return in two days to start work.

Landing this job while so many others were losing theirs during the economic downturn felt like winning the lottery. It was a stable position with benefits, including health care. I was also part of a workers' union. These aspects of the American workforce helped me feel grounded. The $7.10 per hour wage, on a full-time schedule, was the most money I had ever earned. *If I worked hard, I could eventually be promoted and move up. Maybe even become the next Steve.* I worked at the Pleasanton Safeway for the next two years, moving from bagger to night-shift stocker, and eventually earning a promotion to cashier, which came with a $1.50 hourly raise. I bragged about that promotion more than I did about my scholarship. I enjoyed the physical, repetitive nature of the work, and the long drives gave me quiet time to think. They were meditative. I processed my homesickness and reflected on plans for the future.

Between French tutoring and my Safeway job, I also took on several other menial jobs, living the life of a true immigrant. With daily necessities and debts to repay, every paycheck required careful planning. One portion went to rent, a small amount to food, one envelope to Ohlone College, and another to repay my uncles. After the spring term ended, I left college for the fall semester to take on additional work. I worked as a private tutor for high school math and physics. Payment sometimes came in the form of hot meals, which made my days easier. I also worked as a newspaper delivery carrier, a job Isidore and I secured together. Through it, I learned that working in America often required owning a vehicle.

Before I interviewed at Safeway, one of our roommates, who worked at a newspaper delivery warehouse contracted by the San Francisco Chronicle in the East Bay, mentioned that his supervisor needed extra hands. He offered to ask about potential openings during one of his night shifts. Night work, we reasoned, would be ideal since it allowed us to attend classes during the day. Angelo, the boss, an immigrant from Southeast Asia himself, greeted us warmly, with the understanding of someone who had walked this path before. He offered us water and asked if we could start that same night. We said yes, and he showed us how to fold the newspapers correctly and as quickly as possible. His instructions were clear and urgent. In this job, time was everything. The large truck arrived around 11 p.m. to drop off the San Francisco Chronicle deliveries and unload the bundles. The packages were distributed among the drivers. Each person unpacked and folded their own portion, and the driving shift began around midnight. You had until 5 a.m. to complete the deliveries. Sundays were the busiest, so finishing by 6 a.m. was acceptable. Failure to deliver everything on time affected the entire operation.

In the quiet hours of the night, the smell of fresh newsprint and the sound of paper being folded echoed through the large garage hall. I listened intently, trying to absorb every detail. A glance to the side showed our housemate already folding his portion for the night. That explained why we had stopped to grab coffee on the way. It was going to be a long night.

I asked how we could do the job without cars. He explained that he knew we did not have vehicles. He would help pay for them and then deduct a small amount from our paychecks each month to cover the cost. The next day, we would look for a car for my brother, since he already had a driver's license. For that night, Angelo drove his van, and we sat in the back, helping fold newspapers while observing and learning how the deliveries worked.

"Have you ever driven before?" he asked as we continued folding and securing each newspaper with a rubber band.

"No, but I can learn quickly," I replied, projecting as much confidence as I could manage.

"You should start practicing and take the test as soon as possible. You need a car to live in America. It is essential," he said with urgency, speaking both as a boss and like a concerned uncle.

"Yes, sir. I will start tomorrow."

The following day, our roommate, who had recently retaken the driver's test, gave me the California Driver's Handbook. I read it from cover to cover that morning, the words swimming before my eyes as I tried to absorb every rule and regulation. For a moment, it replaced my schoolbooks.

That afternoon, after classes ended, we went to the empty playground of a local high school. Sitting behind the wheel for the first time, the adrenaline of driving mixed with the promise of independence a car could bring. I practiced what I had learned from the handbook while Isidore watched and nodded along. We repeated this several times, and with each attempt, I grew more comfortable. I started paying close attention to the roads and how cars moved, checking whether drivers were following the rules I was learning. Silently, I flagged every mistake: drivers making illegal turns, not stopping long enough at stop signs, honking unnecessarily, crossing into restricted lanes, and parking without turning the front tires according to curb rules. It became a private game in my head, turning every drive into a learning opportunity. The intensity of studying for the driving test reminded me of preparing for national exams back in Burundi. After failing the driving test the first time for speeding in a school zone, I finally passed by being extra careful and driving more slowly the second time around. That night, I brought the news to Angelo, and the next day we bought a white 1985 Toyota Camry for $1,000. Although the car was older than I was, I felt rich and free. The smell of old upholstery and the ownership paperwork made me feel wealthy. The sound of the engine and the weight of the keys in my hand screamed freedom.

I now had a car that worked. I no longer had to wait for buses to get to class. I could sleep longer after night shifts and leave only fifteen to twenty minutes before class started. I could give friends rides, play soccer at the park, buy groceries, and try new foods. I could even take on another job and commute. The Camry sustained me for the next three years until it finally died one evening in the middle of Mission Boulevard in Hayward at 9 p.m., on my way home from class. But for those three years, it was my piece of the American dream.

Sometime that summer, Isidore's girlfriend at the time came over, and I asked if there were any openings at her job. She worked at an assisted living community for adults with developmental disabilities, Friends of Children with Special Needs (FCSN). These positions often paid better and sometimes included housing for staff members. They were, in fact, looking for a new hire. After being introduced to the head manager and completing an interview, I was offered the job. It paid $11 per hour, a significant step up from the $8.50 I earned at Safeway. Living in the community meant I no longer had to pay rent, which allowed me to save the money I earned. I started the job sometime in August.

As I paid off my debts to Ohlone College and my uncles, I gradually phased out some of the smaller jobs and returned to school part-time in the spring of 2010. I began with general education courses such as music, English, and history, easing slowly back into the more demanding core courses. I had chosen to major in Natural Sciences with an emphasis in Mathematics and Technology. Returning to school was emotionally challenging. Friends I had met during my first year steadily completed their two-year programs and transferred to four-year universities, while I continued juggling multiple jobs and only a few classes at a time. Most days, I felt as though I was falling behind. Each academic year required learning how to make new friends all over again. This cycle became part of my adaptation to life as a Burundian American immigrant, slowly settling into a country that was beginning to feel like a home, yet never thoroughly familiar.

Chapter 13

THE PARABLE OF
THE SECULAR SON

"Is Sunday Mass in this building for deaf people only?" I asked Isidore on my first Saturday night in San Francisco in January 2008. I had never intentionally missed a week of Mass in the last twenty years.

"There are hearing people too, but the Mass itself is in American Sign Language," he replied. That meant I would not be able to follow the prayers or hear the hymns that had anchored my Sundays since childhood. Isidore looked away, guilty but helpless.

That night, I felt something shift inside me. The certainty that God had carried me from First Communion in Muyinga, to my altar boy duties in Gasorwe, and through the convent and seminary halls of Kanyinya, Rusengo, and Don Bosco began to waver. Tomorrow would be my first Sunday in America, and already it felt foreign.

Sitting in the small church the next morning, I watched hands move in fluid prayers I could not understand, lips forming English words I barely knew.

The absence of Kirundi. The absence of French. The absence of song. It all settled in my chest like a stone. While everyone else signed their devotion, I silently recited the prayers in the languages I could recall.

"*Dawe wa twese uri mw'ijuru...*"

No, that did not feel right.

"*Notre Père qui es aux cieux...*"

That did not work either.

Each language felt like grasping at air. None of them seemed to reach heaven from this strange new place.

Let me try in English, I thought.

"*Our Father who art in heaven...*"

No. That was not how the prayer usually felt.

The disconnect washed over my spirit like the cold fog that rolled through San Francisco each morning. *Perhaps it's because the Mass was in sign language.* I reasoned. I told myself I would find another church, one where I could sing hymns the way I always had.

The next time I went to church, it was at the invitation of Elena and her husband, Carlos.

"Do you and Isidore want to join us on Sunday for church in San Jose?" Elena asked.

"Is it a Catholic Mass?" I asked.

"No. A Christian church. A friendly community of faith where everyone is welcome."

I paused.

"You also need food," she continued. "They have a food pantry where you can take supplies home for free." She knew we were short on cash.

"Okay, we'll join," I replied, already wondering if Elena, devout in her own way, was unknowingly guiding me toward a transactional relationship with the church. Come for bread, not the Bread of Life.

The church was evangelical, and I had prepared myself not to encounter the familiar structure of a Catholic parish liturgy.

What I was not prepared for was my first lesson in the economics of salvation.

As we turned off Mowry Avenue onto the I-880 on a bright spring morning in Fremont, I saw the first white homeless person of my life.

"Any $$ helps!" a sign on brown cardboard read through the window of the Honda SUV. I paused for a moment, and no one in the car said anything. I turned for a second look.

"Is that a homeless person?" I asked Isidore in the backseat. He chuckled, realizing I had just encountered a white beggar for the first time. He repeated my question to Elena and Carlos. They exchanged glances, part uncomfortable, part considering how to explain.

"Yes, Libère, even in the richest country on Earth, there are still homeless people. It's a complex problem, and some cities handle it better than others," Carlos calmly explained.

Later, during the church service, when it was time for tithing, I watched offering baskets pass along long, polished benches, filled with $20, $50, and even $100 bills. I thought about how much I could have used a hundred-dollar bill at that moment. Like a church bell, the Ninth Commandment rang in my head: *You shall not covet your neighbor's property.* My mind went back to the man on Mowry Avenue, who seemed to need the money far more than I did—perhaps for a shower or a proper meal. The contrast between the homeless man on the street and the spotless church, the expensive bags, Sunday clothes, and luxury cars in the parking lot struck me. It created a dichotomy that made me reflect on the role of faith and religion in American life.

Soon after, I learned about the prosperity gospel taught by many American evangelists. Browsing YouTube, I stumbled upon Joel Osteen, the famed televangelist whose Hollywood-like sermons were streamed live across the U.S. I watched as familiar Bible passages were selectively interpreted with a striking emphasis on the idea that God rewards believers with wealth and material blessings. If you prayed correctly and donated to the church, you would be rewarded with financial prosperity and even physical health. *Does this mean that poverty signals a lack of faith?* I wondered. I also learned that many of these preachers lived in extravagant mansions, owned private jets, and held assets valued in the millions. Such faith felt backward to me—not only because of the homeless veterans with signs reading *"God Bless"* who sat ignored on streets from San Francisco to Fremont, but because it contradicted what I had been taught. *Hadn't Jesus said it was easier for a camel to pass through the eye of a needle than for a rich man to enter heaven? Hadn't he blessed the poor, the meek, the suffering? Where was the Jesus who overturned the tables of the money changers in the temple?* It seemed the prosperity gospel had replaced the Sermon on the Mount.

The Intersection of faith, wealth, and human suffering became my unexpected theological education. Here, in the wealthiest nation on Earth, the land of opportunity, people slept on concrete between skyscrapers. Patients near death were denied healthcare because of pre-existing conditions. Mental illness wandered the streets unaided while church doors remained locked except for scheduled services. *If God blessed America, why did His children sleep on its streets?* I quickly understood that pain requires no visa and grief requires no passport. Suffering had followed me across hemispheres, only changing its costume.

There was, of course, another kind of ministry: kindness that transcended religious boundaries.

Though Elena's family always invited us to church services, there was no expectation to convert to American Christianity. They offered unconditional help when we needed it most. Whether it was access to the food pantry, introductions to the community and professional opportunities, or enthusiastic letters of recommendation for scholarships and transfer applications, Elena and Carlos always asked, "How are you really doing?" and provided practical solutions that did not suggest praying problems away. There was also Paul and Sarah, a local family in Fremont who hosted international students from Ohlone College for Bible study at their home, providing a warm meal each week. Prayers and Bible readings were shared without prejudice or expectation, and the community built at these gatherings felt more valuable than communion itself. Although I often began to see church as a resource center rather than a spiritual home—attending like a Pharisee of necessity, performing rituals for earthly bread—I began to appreciate what faithful ministry looked like: love without dogma.

THE FALL FROM THE Catholic faith paralleled a fallout with Isidore.

Except for school holidays, Isidore and I had not lived together since he moved to boarding school in Gitega, when I was starting first grade in Bihogo before the war. Now in California, reconnecting with him and meeting his friends proved challenging. His friends were a mix of college students and older professionals—some from wealthy families, others with stable jobs. They were also deaf, and since I didn't know sign language, I couldn't understand their conversations. From my vantage point, they seemed reckless and extravagant. They partied and drank hard—not the ceremonial sips of communion wine, but beer and stronger things. They stayed out late, went salsa dancing, and clubbing. They spoke of women in ways that would have earned us expulsion from seminary. The vow of temperance I had been taught seemed to dissolve in American freedom. One particular Saturday, we went to eat at a buffet restaurant. It was my first time experiencing a self-serve dining experience.

"Do we just eat it all?" I asked.

"If you can," one of the guys replied when my brother told them what I had just asked.

"Isn't that very expensive?" I pressed.

"No, it's one price for all you can eat. That's what makes it special," they explained. My mind tried to figure out whether this was sheer abundance or a recipe for a health disaster. We stuffed ourselves, and afterward, they planned to go out clubbing that night.

"Join us. They'll show you how to live the city life," Isidore urged.

"No, you go ahead. I have homework," I replied, noticing he was still the same old "life of the party" brother.

As they coordinated the time to meet up, they discussed what each had to do first.

"I just need to stop by Walmart to buy a new set of shirts to replace these," one guy said. I glanced around, wondering if anyone else heard that. No one reacted.

As we walked to the car, I asked Isidore if that's what he had said.

"Yes," he replied. "He doesn't like to do laundry, so he just replaces the pack of shirts like that."

They dropped me off, and Isidore changed into his weekend outfit while I sat down to work on my algebra homework, reflecting on the privilege of not doing laundry and simply buying new clothes instead.

"Indulging like your friend seems irresponsible, doesn't it? We don't have money to spend," I lamented the next morning.

"You need to chill and have fun. You're no longer in seminary; the rules are different here," Isidore said. *But were they? Or were we just different? Had we both been destined to live the biblical fable of the prodigal son? We have no father to return to.* My mother's words about taking responsibility for how our lives turn out rang in my mind like a distant horn.

The tension between us grew with each passing week. He had started spending money carelessly, going out on nights we couldn't afford. The money that should have gone home or toward rent disappeared into what felt like an expensive illusion of American success. I was so furious that I began airing my grievances with my family and his friends, hoping they would help me change his behavior. Our relationship progressively turned sour, and by early 2009, he had moved to Santa Rosa, partly for a new job. Partly, I suspected, to escape the mirror I had become, reflecting the promises we had both made and were now breaking, each in our own ways. He later moved to San Diego, then Austin, Texas, and we never lived together again. In San Diego and Austin, he found good friends who helped turn his life around, but the brother who was supposed to be my anchor in this new world had become transient.

COMMITTING WHAT I BELIEVED to be the original sin marked the ultimate fall from grace, though not in the same way Adam sinned.

Somewhere in my Catholic education growing up, the disobedience of Adam and Eve described in the Old Testament became equated with adultery. Priests often proclaimed from the altar that the original sin was sexual relations or eating from the tree of knowledge, a sin so severe that it made humans fallen creatures and justified human suffering. This interpretation of scripture had shaped my childhood with unwavering certainty. I had come to the U.S. with a steel-spined intention to remain pure, never to sin, to commit no sexual transgression until marriage sanctified it. Seminary education had carved these convictions deep into my bones. Chastity was not just a vow; it was supposed to be my identity.

It was not long after arriving in California that I learned one does not burn in hell or die upon the loss of chastity, at least not immediately, not visibly. I will not describe the details, but it did not feel like God was watching, despite His supposed omnipresence. The ceiling did not crack open. Lightning did not strike. The earth continued its rotation, indifferent to my fall from grace. Perhaps this was the real loss of innocence, not the act itself, but the discovery that immediate divine punishment was a myth.

A voice in my head reminded me that I had broken the seventh commandment. Worse still, having also disregarded the fourth commandment, I could not simply repent and be purified again. I knew I would not be able to overlook my survival duties and maintain regular Sunday Mass attendance. It felt as though I had excommunicated myself.

I wondered whether I had lost my salvation, but not with the indelible certainty I had been trained to feel. The Catholic guilt was there, but muted, like a radio station just out of range. What disturbed me more was how little it scared me. *Was this what damnation felt like, not fire and brimstone, but simple indifference?* I wondered.

I had been taught that some sins were more forgivable than others, though I never understood the hierarchy. Murder, apparently, could be absolved with proper contrition. Divorce, however, was considered a permanent spiritual stain. Stealing food when hungry was venial, but skipping Mass was mortal. Now that I had stepped back to think about it, the mathematics of religious morality never quite balanced. The seminary's careful categorization of sins seemed arbitrary, human rules masquerading as divine law.

My name itself, once a source of pride rooted in my Catholic faith and ancestral origin, became a reminder of failed holiness. Years into this transformation, while teaching hereditary traits at a Berkeley elementary school in the fall of 2012 as part of my year of concurrent enrollment at UC Berkeley, I noticed a little girl in the middle of the classroom staring at me almost blankly. Her gaze carried a deep curiosity, as if she were examining my very soul. I met her hazel eyes and smiled with a slight nod, giving her permission to speak. She quickly raised her right hand.

"Yes, Jane?" I acknowledged, curious to know what had captured her attention so completely.

The whole class turned, eager to hear what she could ask within the first two minutes of the lesson.

"Can I call you 'friendly bear'?" she replied, a wide grin spreading across her face.

The class erupted in laughter, and I joined in. I took a few seconds to think through how she had arrived at that idea.

"Aw. Yes, Jane, you may call me 'friendly bear,'" I replied, touched by the innocence of her request. As I reflected on her question, I realized how the child's simple, secular term of endearment felt more genuine than any religious meaning once attached to my name.

It soon became clear how she had arrived there. Before the lesson began, my colleague, who was co-teaching with me that day, had introduced me. After outlining the day's plan, she ended by saying, "Now, for the lesson on inheritance, let's welcome our friend Libère."

Jane, and perhaps some of her second-grade classmates, heard or interpreted my name as, "Let's welcome our friendly bear."

The irony of my first name was not lost on me. I was named after a pope who later became controversial for straying from orthodoxy. Perhaps it was prophetic. Pope Liberius is not a saint and remains the earliest pope not to be canonized. His legacy is tied to the rise of Arianism, and the Council of Nicaea ultimately sent him into exile. My namesake was a heretic pope. As for Ndacayisaba, I was slowly but steadily no longer praying to God. Each time I introduce myself by my full name, I carry both a papal blessing and a prayer I no longer say, a walking contradiction of faith lost and heritage maintained.

PRAYERS FROM HOME DID not bring me closer to God. If faith was abandoning me, or I was abandoning it, staying connected to my ancestry would provide the spiritual respite I needed. Between classes at Ohlone, I would escape to YouTube, searching for Burundian church songs that could transport me home, if only for three minutes. The familiar harmonies filled my headphones as I sat in the library doing homework or at Hyman Hall, waiting for French students who rarely came for tutoring. Gospel songs from the internet cafés of Ngozi mixed with hymns from childhood Sundays, each melody a thread connecting me to a life that felt increasingly distant. But even these songs began to feel hollow, performed rather than lived, a distant memory of a sacred life I once had.

The computer lab became my new sanctuary. There, surrounded by the hum of machines and the click of keyboards, I could access my homeland through pixels and sound waves. Burundian traditional songs played softly, the same ones that once drifted from the national radio at dawn, setting the rhythm of village days. French ballads that had echoed through the streets of Muyinga, Kirundo, Ngozi, and Bujumbura now provided the soundtrack to my homework sessions. Slowly, secular songs replaced sacred hymns.

On my newly acquired Verizon flip phone, a luxury that had cost me two weeks of tutoring wages, I learned how to buy international calling cards. Ten dollars for twenty minutes to Burundi, if I were lucky. Fifteen if the connection was bad. The arithmetic of love, measured in minutes.

When I called home, Mom's voice would crack with joy, then immediately shift to concern.

"Are you eating well?"

"Yes, Mom."

"Are you going to Mass to pray?"

"Yes, Mom." The lie came easier each time, like Peter denying Christ three times before the rooster crowed. *How could I dare tell Mom that I had broken the fourth commandment and no longer honored the holy Sabbath?*

"Good. I know you're focused on your studies, but don't forget to pray. We are praying for you every day."

"And we pray that God fills the basket from where your help to your siblings comes from."

Beneath this prayer, the implied need for financial help was understood. I knew the time of year. Violette and Elyse needed school supplies. Télesphore needed college tuition. This was the hardest cultural chasm to bridge. In the US, I was learning, most children grow up to become independent, with their financial obligations to parents minimal or nonexistent. I had listened to classmates speak casually of their parents' retirement funds, of boundaries, of "not being responsible for" their families' problems. Meanwhile, every dollar I earned carried the weight of five lives back home. The biblical commandment to honor thy father and mother took on economic dimensions that the apostles had never preached.

"I'll send something next month," I would promise, often calculating how many meals I could skip and how many extra shifts I could take. This was my tithe now, not to the church, but directly to those in need.

As months turned into years, the phone calls home became a litany of changes I could not witness, milestones I could not celebrate, and losses I could not mourn properly.

"Your cousin Francois got married last week," Mom would report. "It was a beautiful ceremony. Everyone asked about you."

"That's great," I would respond, calculating that Francois was three years younger than me. *When had he become old enough to marry? Was he financially ready to raise a family? Did they sing the usual nuptial hymns at the church wedding ceremony?*

"Remember Claudette from primary school? She has two children now." *The girl who used to share her lunch with me was now a mother twice over. Had she baptized them? Would they grow up with the faith I was losing?*

"Uncle Pascal's daughter is starting secondary school. She's very bright, like you were."

I started counting my years with these markers. The child who was born when I left was now walking, now talking, now starting school. My absence was measured in the lives of others. Each milestone was a sacrament I could not witness.

"Nkurikiye got married," came another update, months later. Nkurikiye, who had sheltered me that terrible night, had her hand pressed over my mouth to keep me silent as my father was killed. She had been like an older sister, protector, and friend. Now she was building her own family, while I could not even attend her wedding.

"She asked me to tell you she prays for your success," Mom added.

Success. *What did that mean anymore? I was surviving, yes. Learning, yes. But at what cost? Had I gained the world but lost my soul?*

But not all news was of growth and celebration.

"Domitila died," Mom said one October evening, her voice hollow across the miles.

Domitila. The woman who had hidden us during those terrible days in 1993. Who had risked her life for ours. Who had sent her children as lookouts, who had shared her meager food, who had lied to killers to protect us. A true Christian. I wondered if she had ever questioned God's plan that night.

"How?" I managed to ask.

"Sickness. She had been ill for months, but couldn't get medicine."

Medicine. From where I was sitting in Fremont, California, I briefly counted the medical facilities that surrounded me. *Perhaps if she had been here, she would still be with us.* I had sent money home the previous month, but it had gone to school fees. *If I had known, if I had sent more, could she have been saved?*

"*Imana imwakire mubwami bwayo*" (may God welcome her in His kingdom), I recited, maintaining the religious tone, as though to project that I had not completely lost all that the church had taught me. I clung to her kindness. Her toothless smile flashed in my mind as I recalled the days she fed us freshly cooked meals when our parents worked on the farm. I recounted the nights she protected us from killers and lamented with us as we counted and remembered those we lost during those nights. As I tried to focus on my classes, I imagined her reaching heaven and reuniting with those she could not save in 1993.

AS YEARS WENT BY, I created my chapel of resilience and new secular sacraments. They had taught me in seminary that when external circumstances spiral beyond control, creating internal order becomes essential. I have carried this lesson into my secular adulthood, though its application has evolved. Where once I had morning prayers, I now had morning coffee. Where once I had the repetitive comfort of Mass, I now had the rhythm of playing soccer, my feet on grass becoming a kind of Sunday service. Regular check-ins with family across continents replaced confession. The discipline of study replaced the discipline of devotion.

Small, consistent practices reminded me that even when everything else changed, certain rhythms could remain within my control.

The rhythm of survival quickly overtook the rhythm of worship. I often found spiritual meaning not in grand moments of divine intervention, but in the humble architecture of daily habits.

"You've become American," my old friends would say when I called on Sundays and mentioned that I no longer went to Sunday Mass. It was not a compliment. It meant I had become secular, a pagan.

I could explain why I worked on Sundays in a way they could understand. I could not explain why I no longer prefaced meals with prayer. I felt like Lucifer's son, cast out not from heaven but from the certainty of belief.

Yet even as formal faith faded, something else emerged. I found holiness in unexpected places: in the dedication of researchers working to cure diseases, in the kindness of strangers offering directions when I was lost, and in the diligence of community college teachers during office hours. The verses carved into my memory during those seminary years still surfaced, unbidden, in moments of stress or fear. Luke 16:10 would whisper to me as I counted out exact change for bus fare, or as I pushed myself to focus on smaller tasks:

"Whoever is trustworthy in very little is also trustworthy in great matters."

When anxiety about money, family, or the future threatened to overwhelm me, Matthew 6:26-30 would rise like a familiar song:

"Look at the birds of the air; they do not sow or reap or store away in barns, and yet your heavenly Father feeds them. Are you not much more valuable than they? Can any one of you, by worrying, add a single hour to your life?"

The words still brought comfort, even if I no longer believed in their literal truth. They had become philosophy rather than theology, wisdom rather than dogma.

The parable of the prodigal son promises that return is always possible, that the father waits with open arms. *But what if you can't return? What if the journey has changed you so fundamentally that the person who left no longer exists?* I was both prodigal and faithful, secular and spiritual. I honored my family, but couldn't honor their God in the way they expected.

When Mom asked if I was still going to church, I'd say yes, not mentioning that my church had become the library, my prayers were written in scientific questions and statistical analyses, and my communion was the shared struggle of other immigrants trying to build something from nothing.

I still have not returned to Sunday Mass. I may be able to reconcile this dichotomy some day. Reconnect the altar boy who once served with such devotion to the scientist who seeks truth through empirical evidence. For now, survival was the priority, a requirement for which neither God nor the secular world would punish me. It's the prime directive, older than any commandment: continue living, continue growing, continue becoming whoever you're meant to be.

And perhaps that, too, is a kind of faith—the belief that tomorrow might be better, that education might be salvation, that somewhere between the banana leaves of Burundi and the skyscrapers of America, there exists a space where all my secular and spiritual selves can coexist. This became my parable: not of a son who squandered his inheritance and returned home chastened, but of one who invested it in a different future entirely. Whether that makes me prodigal or prudent, faithful or fallen, I still don't know.

"Trust in Allah, but tie your camel."

— PROPHET MUHAMMAD

August 08, 2014. San Diego, California. Libère (left) and Isidore (right) after brunch on a Sunday morning. Photo © Sonia Holtzman

Part Five

ECHOES OF THE OPEN ROAD

"In the midst of winter, I found there was, within me, an invincible summer."

— ALBERT CAMUS

Chapter 14

THE SCIENTIST IN THE MIRROR

On the computer monitor, I stared at DNA strands sequenced from the material I had extracted from the legs of Tahitian mirids a few days prior. I realized I was looking at millions of years of insect evolution. A discovery. I emailed my mentor, Andrew, about what I was seeing. The next day, we reviewed the data again.

"How did you arrive at the five groups?" he asked, to ensure I had organized the data correctly for the analysis. I walked him through the analysis steps, and he checked the different modules in the software program to make sure I had used the correct parameters.

"The data looks good; this is great," Andrew said, with an excitement only matched by his love of a home run during a baseball game.

"What should we do next?" It was a question I would soon learn was the language of excitement and curiosity in research.

"We should sequence more specimens to make sure there is no bias." I pointed out that we were only looking at a few insects. I had learned about outliers and statistical significance in the research course that spring.

"Excellent. Let's do it. Check the vials in the other freezer; we have more specimens."

I spent the next two weeks performing microscopy imaging,

extracting and amplifying DNA, sending samples for sequencing, and, more importantly, making sure we had a balanced mix of morphology among the specimens. I processed nearly ninety insects. As the data came back, I immediately updated the inputs in the software and reran the analysis.

This was in mid-June 2012, inside Hilgard Hall at the University of California, Berkeley (UC Berkeley), where I was spending the summer conducting scientific research. We were studying the speciation of Tahitian plant bugs.

DURING THE PREVIOUS SUMMER, four years after arriving at Ohlone College, I had settled in and started looking for opportunities to do scientific research. The familiar palm trees and Mediterranean climate had become home, but my intellectual mind yearned for something more engaging, more challenging, more adventurous. Ohlone, a junior college, did not have research laboratories or opportunities for such endeavors. Each science class I took only intensified this hunger for deeper understanding, for hands-on experience with real scientific pursuits.

I searched and applied to universities in the Bay Area, looking for research internships. When I was not in class, I spent hours scrolling through university websites in search of a suitable opportunity. It needed to be an experience where I could work in a lab while maintaining my full-time studies and my job. I could not afford to be jobless; survival still had to come first. The delicate balance between pursuing dreams and paying bills was familiar by now.

I found a program at UC Berkeley that allowed students to enroll concurrently with community colleges. In this one-year program, the Environmental Science Leadership Pathway (ELP), we took a research methods course in the spring term, completed a summer research internship, and enrolled in a science teaching course in the fall semester. The program paid a stipend of around $2,000 for the spring and fall terms and about $5,000 for the full-time summer internship.

I spent weeks putting together my application, crafting the best statement of purpose I could. With an improved grasp of the English language, I was able to convey my short- and long-term aspirations with confidence. I also asked for proofreading help at the writing center. Mena, the head of English writing, read through the statement and added comments and suggestions for revision. When I went to pick up the printed copy I had given her, she offered a compliment that echoed throughout the rest of my career.

"You have a very good writing voice," she said, noting that she had fixed a few grammatical errors. Her words carried the weight of something I had been unconsciously seeking.

That single compliment erased the insecurities I had harbored since the first time I attempted to speak or write in English. Before college, I had always excelled at languages. French had been easy to learn; its rhythm and flow always felt natural and intuitive. Before the recent years of learning English and feeling inadequate, I had felt so confident in languages and literature that I used to write poems. Molière (Jean-Baptiste Poquelin) and Léopold Sédar Senghor were my favorite writers, admired for their poetic and, at times, romantic prose. As for English, I still felt like a newcomer.

Mena's seemingly small compliment washed away my doubts. Empowered, I felt that I had arrived. I transitioned from thinking of English as a second language to seeing myself as fluent. Like a lighthouse guiding a ship to safe harbor, her words showed me the way forward. If it were not for that single compliment, it is unlikely I would be writing this book today.

I applied and was accepted into the ELP program, a feat that ignited my fierce pursuit of scientific research.

When spring 2012 arrived, I stepped onto the Berkeley campus. With a brand-new Cal student ID in hand, the pull of academic excellence was immediate. The air itself seemed charged with intellectual energy, alive with possibility. From the names of Nobel Prize-winning scientists stamped across buildings and parking spaces to the storied discoveries lining the alleyways, the blue and gold colors themselves signaled prestige in knowledge. Each building seemed to hold centuries of discovery, each pathway once walked by giants of science. At the center of campus, Sather Tower stood like a temple of wisdom and enduring knowledge. My research course that semester met in a class-room on the first floor of Mulford Hall. Every Wednesday evening, I commuted on the BART train from Fremont to Berkeley to learn how to conduct scientific research. I felt that I had found my people and my place in the scientific research world. The classroom itself smelled of chalk dust and possibility.

I had met my classmates a few weeks earlier at a retreat organized for team building. They came from all walks of life, a group of future scientists and engineers selected from community colleges across the Bay Area. Robert, the program director, was a professor of environmental sciences. A former Navy officer, stoic as a ship captain, he mostly wore shorts and flip-flops. I learned that not all academics wear collared button-down shirts with bow ties, spectacles perched wisely, and mustaches that scream niche expertise. Scientists, it seemed, could look like anyone.

The research course, taught by senior PhD candidates working as teaching assistants, covered both the theoretical and practical processes of conducting sound scientific research. Their enthusiasm was contagious, and their recent experiences in the trenches of research made the lessons feel immediate and real. We learned how to formulate a scientific question, gather data, analyze it, and communicate findings to the world through either a poster presentation or a scientific manuscript. We collected and analyzed real datasets to demonstrate what we had learned. At the end of the semester, we presented a poster, inviting an audience to view our work and ask questions.

It was a carefully orchestrated course designed to map out the intricate steps involved in carrying out a rigorous scientific project and applying the scientific method. Even more exciting, it served as preparation for the summer, when we would have full-time positions in laboratories researching real, unanswered scientific questions. The prospect of contributing to human knowledge, even in a small way, filled me with a sense of purpose I had never known before.

LATER THAT SEMESTER, we were presented with a list of labs seeking summer research interns. I sought and selected labs whose projects included the use of computational tools to study biological questions. The fusion of biology and computational science was enthralling. At the time, Bioinformatics was becoming a critical skill for the modern biologist.

I was matched with the UC Berkeley Evolab (Evolutionary Laboratory), jointly led by Drs. George Roderick and Rosemary Gillespie are two of the most highly decorated scientists in the Department of Environmental Science, Policy & Management within the College of Natural Resources. My direct mentor was Andrew, a senior doctoral student studying the evolution and speciation of Tahitian plant bugs known as mirids.

My project involved using molecular biology techniques to extract DNA data that could be fed into an algorithm mapping genetic changes across evolutionary time. Studying evolution as an immigrant felt poetic; the premise of the research mirrored my own path of change and adaptation. By examining these insects and correlating variations in their DNA sequences with differences in size and color patterns, we hoped to determine how many distinct species existed across the Tahitian Islands and throughout French Polynesia.

Early that summer, Andrew was collecting specimens in Tahiti, which we would eventually analyze in Berkeley. I began my summer internship without him for the first two weeks. We scheduled several Skype calls to discuss the project and the scientific literature relevant to the research I would soon conduct. The other PhD students in the lab onboarded me, providing everything I needed and training me in the necessary skills.

June 4th was my first day, and Natasha, another senior PhD student in the group, discussed ongoing projects with me. I spent the next two weeks training at the bench while also helping her with her work on the characterization of California bees and reading literature for the mirids project. As part of my acclimation to the Evolab, we visited the university's Essig Museum of Entomology, a historic collection housing some of the most valuable terrestrial arthropod specimens. I could identify species of butterflies, bees, and other insects I had seen growing up in tropical Burundi. The colorful monarch butterflies resembled those that once roamed the Bihogo backyards of my childhood. The many species of bees looked like those that pollinated coffee farms across the hills of the Burundian plateau.

When I officially began my lab work, I was issued a well-fitted white lab coat. This was not the school lab coat I had used in chemistry and biology labs at Ohlone College and taken home. This was a sterile, research-grade coat made from a different fabric. Like a real scientist, my name was printed on it. *So formal. So cool.* I had a dedicated lab bench space, along with gloves and safety goggles. I was assigned designated micropipettes and fresh boxes of pipette tips in different sizes. I had my own section of the minus 80 degree freezer for storing mirid specimens and a dedicated box of biochemical reagents in the minus 40 degree refrigerator. I was given a detailed protocol outlining how to extract DNA from the thin legs of these fragile insects. When no one was looking, I would sneak past the window and glance at my reflection a few times. Just like in the movies, the scientist in the mirror looked real.

I had access to the microscopy room to capture images of the insects so we could analyze the details of their morphology. After shadowing my mentor as he performed imaging, followed by DNA extraction and PCR amplification several times, my turn came. I followed the standard operating procedure step by step, from microscopy imaging to DNA extraction, PCR amplification, proper waste disposal, returning reagents at the end of the workday, and cleaning my bench space accordingly.

I loved the routine. I repeated this process many times each day over the following weeks. The goal was to generate data for as many insect specimens as possible so that I would have sufficient time to perform analyses and prepare my poster presentation, which would showcase my research at the end of the ten-week program. Research presentations take the form of posters summarizing a project, essentially a polished version of a third-grade science fair. But before the science showcase could happen, there was a humbling lesson to learn.

⚓

WITHIN THE SACRED WALLS of the second floor of Hilgard Hall, I experienced my first experimental failures. One particular Friday, after I had been successful in generating data and working independently at the bench, my mentor was out of town. He is a devoted baseball fan, and that weekend he was in Los Angeles for a Dodgers game. While the team trusted me to work independently, I had no prior experience handling situations when things broke down.

That morning, I completed microscopy imaging, extracted DNA from three specimens, and began DNA amplification for each using PCR, Polymerase Chain Reaction. PCR is a common technique used by molecular biologists to produce millions of copies of a specific DNA region. It is similar to using a copy machine to reproduce millions of copies of a single page from a large book. To confirm DNA amplification, I ran a gel electrophoresis assay. This method allows researchers to visually assess DNA quantity on a transparent gel, using a specialized imaging instrument to capture images that display DNA band size relative to a reference control of known quantity.

A successful amplification experiment produces a thicker band compared to the reference control. That day, however, every gel image showed no amplification, and I could not identify the issue. As always, I had meticulously followed every step of the standard operating procedure, yet the results remained negative. Frustration set in. Nervousness followed. *What exactly had I done wrong?*

The molecular biology lab technician, the expert responsible for troubleshooting such issues, was also out of town. I reviewed the entire process from start to finish and still could not locate the problem. Andrew was available by phone and email, so we communicated back and forth to examine every aspect of the protocol, but we could not determine the cause.

I needed to confirm successful amplification before sending the DNA for sequencing to generate data for my poster. We attempted multiple solutions, but nothing worked. Eventually, I paused the experiment for the day. Already feeling guilty for interrupting my mentor during his trip, I placed the DNA vials in the freezer and went home, defeated.

On the train ride back to Fremont, I felt like a failure. My mentor had trusted me with precious specimens and a protocol I knew how to perform, yet I had failed. *How could I ever become a good scientist in the long run?*

Andrew had explained many times that such setbacks happen regularly in research. He suggested that the issue was likely something minor and unrelated to the experiment itself, and that we would resolve it on Monday. But in that moment, on that train, every click of the tracks echoed my doubts.

When we all returned on Monday, the two of us checked everything again and still could not identify the issue. We asked the molecular biology technician to help us troubleshoot. Within a few minutes, she noticed that the imaging instrument was the culprit. Someone had changed the parameters for gel imaging, and I had been using the wrong settings the entire time. An immense relief ran down my spine. *The data would be fine after all, but we still had to test it.* I quickly prepared another gel, loaded it, and, lo and behold, the thick band appeared. After confirming that we had enough DNA material remaining, we promptly prepared the samples and sent them out for sequencing.

This was followed by stories from lab members about the many experimental mistakes they had encountered over the years, some far more embarrassing and serious than mine. They joked that I had officially joined the club. Subsequent mistakes and failures in the years that followed taught me that failure in science often functions like a beacon atop a house, guiding a sailor toward shore and helping them anchor their vessel. New ideas, new questions, and new research directions emerge from failure and lead to discovery.

After a few weeks of data generation, we received our first set of sequenced results from the genomic sequencing core. The compressed software files felt like an envelope filled with payment and reward for all the experiments I had completed in the lab. I had never seen such files before. Andrew sent me instructions on which software to install and how to analyze the data. That night, at home, I downloaded the bioinformatics software and followed the steps to load the dataset.

After reading the documentation to understand the algorithms and mathematics behind DNA analysis, I ran the program on our data. The specimens clustered into distinct groups. To correlate morphology with these groupings, I examined the microscopy images. I found that the green specimens clustered together, the amber specimens formed a separate group, and the mixed-color specimens comprised a third distinct group. It was mesmerizing. I marveled at the colorful nucleotide sequences and their correlation with the insects from which they came. I was generating knowledge. I was more than just a cashier at a grocery store. The realization was deeply inspiring and profoundly humbling.

During the final two weeks of the summer internship, we focused on crafting the best possible poster presentation. We condensed the summer's research into a clear and visually engaging display designed to excite an audience of fellow researchers. After many drafts, the final version was printed, and I invited friends to hear about my work.

On presentation day, the years I spent feeling uncomfortable speaking English dissipated in the excitement of telling people about my research. Science felt like a distinct language in itself, and I was a native speaker. The research also felt like it belonged to me. My name appeared first at the top of the authorship. I led the research work and produced its results. I felt like a preacher delivering a sermon on that late July Saturday afternoon. With the Pacific winds and California sun streaming through the windows of the presentation auditorium, I stood before my first formal scientific poster presentation.

With my voice steady and my heart full of excitement, I told the story of my first scientific findings. I had mapped how mirids evolved and speciated over millennia. I had identified five groups of these insects that we were proposing to the entomology community as likely separate subspecies deserving further study. It was not just the act of sharing truly new knowledge, information the rest of humanity had not yet encountered, but also witnessing the audience's reactions. Their faces reflected awe at the complexity of the natural world and curiosity about what it all meant and what else might still be out there. This was my new identity. I was a scientist for life.

IN THE FALL, we took a course on how to teach science. More importantly, the core idea of the curriculum was that teaching deepens learning. We learned how to prepare lessons, develop teaching materials, and teach elementary school students. The target age range was second through fifth grade. I taught second grade at two local schools, one in Oakland and one in North Berkeley. My lesson plan was titled "Hereditary Traits: What Makes Us Special."

I chose this subject because of my continued search for identity in this country. I wanted the next generation to understand the complexity of diversity. It may have stemmed from my long-standing love for biology and my newly developed fascination with genetics. Whatever the reason, the lessons went well. Teachers were pleased. Students loved them. Jane even called me "friendly bear."

When the year at UC Berkeley concluded, the program hosted a holiday farewell party in mid-December. The cohort selected me to deliver the farewell speech. I was given three minutes to represent the student experience. Families and loved ones were once again invited to gather for the evening cocktail event. I prepared my speech and practiced it carefully. Aside from my mixed Kirundi-French accent, I was confident I could deliver a proper farewell message.

After the dean and program directors spoke, I was called to the podium. It stood several steps above the floor and was decorated with Christmas ornaments. *How formal, and what an honor.* Dressed in a black suit, white shirt, and black tie, I walked onto the stage, hoping to inspire my cohort. As underrepresented minorities in these revered academic halls and research towers, I knew we had much to prove, not only to others, but to ourselves and to the communities we represented. It felt like a preview of what lay ahead. For us to leave a mark would require Herculean effort. The promise of meritocracy does not favor lone adventurers who fall outside a narrow cultural mold.

I stood up there, unafraid, unshaken. It wasn't a science talk, so it was my first speech in English in front of native English speakers. I thanked the university for creating the ELP program. I remarked on my humble beginnings and noted what a privilege it was to be there. I thanked the program directors, the teaching assistants, and the labs that hosted us. In the eyes of the mentors, I could sense the pride everyone felt for all the students who had come with little to no prior exposure to scientific research. I concluded by encouraging fellow cohort members to continue dreaming bigger and pursuing science and technology for the betterment of human health. Or perhaps I was just reminding myself of the ultimate goal.

I was hooked on scientific research. I applied to other research opportunities, and I wanted to try one that would allow me to spend a summer away from California. I'd eventually land a great opportunity to be in New York for the summer in 2013. After multiple rejections and offers, I spent the summer at the Wadsworth Center in Albany. Unlike the environmental research at Berkeley, this was biomedical science. I would work on a drug discovery project, finding medicines for dengue, a major tropical infectious disease. *Perhaps one of these molecules will end up in a pill and be shipped to many villages across the globe.* I'd often hope.

I arrived in June, stepping out of the airport to a wall of humidity that clung to my skin. The air in Albany was thick with summer. It wasn't the dry heat of California or the brisk coolness of San Francisco's fog. No, this was different, reminiscent of the Burundian tropical air; dense, heavy, and almost alive, as if the air itself had joined me on this adventure.

I was a National Science Foundation scholar through its program Research Experiences for Undergraduates. The opportunity to spend the summer conducting scientific research on therapeutic drugs targeting the NS2/NS3 complex of the dengue virus was exhilarating.

Albany was nothing like I had imagined. The city was a mix of old and new, its skyline punctuated by the stark, modernist architecture of the Empire State Plaza, juxtaposed against historic brownstones that seemed to whisper stories of another era. My daily walk to the lab took me past tree-lined streets and brick buildings, their facades softened by decades of history and summer blooms spilling out of window boxes.

The lab was a world of its own, a place where curiosity and rigor intertwined. Days were long, filled with pipettes, assays, and the steady hum of machines analyzing microscopic interactions. My research on the NS2/NS3 complex, the component essential to viral replication, felt like solving a puzzle with no picture to guide me, each discovery a small but significant step toward understanding how to outsmart a virus that plagued so many.

Dr. Jason, a postdoctoral scientist in the virology group, walked me through the scope of the project. Young and knowledgeable, he came across as rather jaded. He spoke more about failures than successes. I would later learn that this outlook is common after the arduous years of PhD training.

"Cells are finicky," he repeated each time the bacterial cultures we grew for experiments failed to yield the expected amount of protein during purification. When the protein purification experiments finally began to work, we started screening for new molecules that could inhibit protein function and potentially prevent viral infections. I became obsessed with seeing results. Internally, I was convinced I could discover the next antiviral medicine that summer. I buried myself in the lab, at times even staying in the cold room, a specialized laboratory space kept at 40°F (4°C) for sensitive experiments, until midnight.

The other scholars were a diverse group from across the country. We bonded over our shared love of science, trading stories about our schools and our lives. During breaks, we gathered in the cafeteria, our conversations drifting between discussions of experimental results and plans to explore the East Coast on weekends.

THAT SUMMER I ALSO visited New York City and Boston for the first time. A group of us took the train down for the weekend, eager to experience the city that seemed to exist in everyone's imagination. When I stepped out of Penn Station, the city felt alive in a way I had never experienced before. Its streets were a chaotic symphony of honking taxis, rushing pedestrians, and flashing advertisements.

Times Square was almost too much to take in. Bright lights bathed everything in a surreal glow. Screens towered above us, displaying everything from fashion advertisements to Broadway showtimes. I stood in the middle of it all, turning in slow circles, as if I could somehow absorb the energy. It was nothing like Burundi's quiet nights or San Francisco's laid-back rhythm. This was urgency and spectacle compressed into a single block of chaos.

We walked along Broadway, taking in the sheer sensory overload. I thought about how far I had come, from the green hills of Burundi to the glowing chaos of Times Square. It felt surreal, as though I were living inside someone else's dream.

That summer was also a geography lesson. Growing up in Burundi, I had always known my country as small, so small that you could cross it in a day. California was vast, its endless highways and sprawling cities a reminder of just how large a place could be. But the East Coast felt different. In a single day, you could pass through multiple states, each with its own distinct character. On weekends, we toured the Northeast. We drove through Massachusetts, Connecticut, and Rhode Island, their borders marked by little more than signs on the highway. Things changed quickly: accents, architecture, even the way people seemed to move. It reminded me of Burundi, where every village had its own unique rhythm, yet was part of the same larger whole.

One weekend, I traveled to Boston. Walking the Freedom Trail felt like stepping into a history book. I stood in front of Paul Revere's house, its wooden exterior a relic from a time when the idea of freedom was still a fragile dream. The cobblestone streets led me past churches, graveyards, and the Old State House, where the Boston Massacre had ignited the flames of revolution. Boston Harbor stretched out before me, its waters glittering in the sunlight. I imagined tea floating in its depths centuries ago, an act of defiance that rippled through history. The city seemed to breathe with its past, each corner whispering stories of revolutionaries, scholars, and immigrants who had shaped it into what it is today. The food in Boston was unforgettable. We ate clam chowder at a small restaurant near the harbor, the rich, creamy soup warming us pleasantly despite the summer heat. It reminded me how food can connect you to a place, much like the bean stews and grilled bananas of Burundi connected me to home.

By the end of the summer, Albany had become a strange, humid kind of home. The research, the friendships, and the weekend adventures left their mark on me. I could navigate the labyrinthine corridors of the lab, decipher the complex language of proteins and enzymes, and, more than that, I had found my place in scientific research.

That summer became a bridge between the past and the future, between the familiar and the unknown. The East Coast had shown me the breadth of a country I was still learning to understand. It had given me Times Square and Boston Harbor, lab coats and laughter, history and horizons. I wanted to explore more of this country. I wanted to know what the East Coast feels like during the autumn and winter seasons.

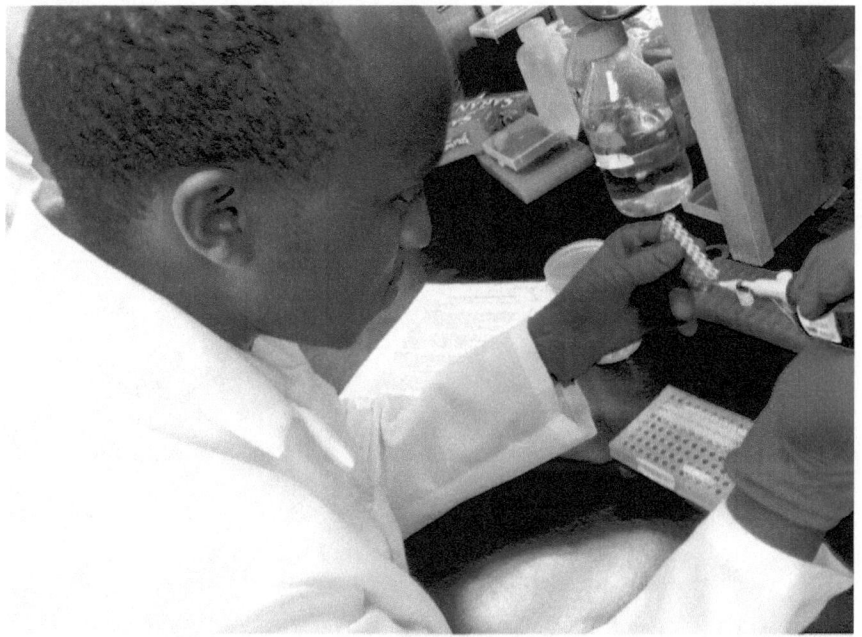

June 2012. Berkeley, California. Preparing an PCR experiment in Hilgard Hall Photo © Nerissa Ignacio

December 2012. Berkeley, California. At the pulpit, speaking to the ELP cohort and their loved ones in attendance.

Chapter 15

SEASONS OF THE COLD SNOW

I hailed a taxi outside the terminal, and as we started driving toward my new apartment, I asked the driver to stop. He glanced at me, confused, but obliged. I stepped out onto the snow-covered sidewalk, the icy wind biting at my cheeks. I bent down and scooped up a handful of snow. It was lighter than I expected, softer, and so impossibly cold that it instantly numbed my fingers. I held it in my hands for a moment, watching it begin to melt. The taxi driver leaned out of his window, smirking.

"Where are you coming from?" he asked, his tone both amused and skeptical.

"California," I replied, still marveling at the snow.

"Figured," he said with a chuckle. "Did you grow up there?"

"No, I grew up in Burundi. It's even warmer and more tropical over there," I responded with my usual brief note about my homeland, also noting the contrast to what I was experiencing.

"You're not ready for this," he replied, this time with a mildly concerned look.

He was right. I wasn't.

It was January 10, 2014, a crisp, cold early evening at Syracuse

Hancock International Airport. I had just landed as a transfer student to start my junior year at Syracuse University.

When I returned to Ohlone College in the fall of 2013 after my summer in Albany, I immediately applied to transfer to four-year universities. Perhaps it was the growing confidence in my scientific abilities or the excitement of a potential adventure outside the Bay Area that lit a fire to finish my tenure at Ohlone. I had decided I would transfer that spring. Most universities don't typically accept junior transfers mid-year, so I knew only a limited number of spots would be available. I didn't want to wait another full year. I had completed my requirements, and after all my time at Ohlone, I was ready to move on.

Back at coffee shops, I worked on applications as the summer sun gave way to fall clouds over the East Bay. As the fall term progressed, I applied to and received offers from schools in California, New York, Massachusetts, Pennsylvania, and Oregon for spring 2014 transfer admission. In the midst of deciding which university to attend, I also received two scholarships totaling $1,500: the Ohlone Foundation Award and the Osher Initiative for California Community Colleges. *Perhaps Isidore was right all along*, I thought at the annual scholarship ceremony where the awards were handed out. Elena and Carlos were in attendance. Their daughter was now five years old. It was perhaps the most fitting conclusion to my time at a college that had seen me through all my highs and lows.

Like most of my life decisions during those years, the decision to transfer to Syracuse University was mostly driven by finances and intellectual curiosity. Syracuse offered the best scholarship package and, aside from the California universities where I was a resident, it would be relatively cheaper to attend. The biotechnology major I was admitted into was also intellectually and professionally attractive. The combination of courses in gene and cell engineering, biomaterials, business entrepreneurship, and of course scientific research tugged at my scientific interests like a magnet.

Perhaps I also wanted to move away from California to experience more of the East Coast adventures I had briefly seen during the summer in Albany. The tales of changing seasons ignited a sense of wonder for what life was like living in these parts of America. Photos of a campus covered in white snow mixed with fall foliage looked like a catalog from a fictional planet.

Syracuse University, a private school, was still going to be expensive, but I had now learned about taking low-interest federal student loans and finishing my education faster. This was the American way of life. In fact, at this point I was regretting quitting school at Ohlone College during the recession. Federal grants and loans were an option that had been available but unknown to me. The objective was to finish as soon as possible and move on.

January 10, 2014, arrived with the same electric charge I had felt six years earlier when I left Burundi for the United States. Adventure coursed through my veins. Hope and uncertainty tugged at me equally as I loaded my two suitcases and carry-on into my friend's Prius on the way to San Francisco International Airport. The early morning in San Francisco was brisk, the city still wrapped in its foggy cocoon. *Farewell, Carl the Fog, until next time.* I said goodbye to the Bay Area, to its colored bridges and rolling hills, knowing the warm hues of California would soon be replaced by the stark white winters of upstate New York. Full of anticipation, the flight to Syracuse felt brief.

As we approached the town, I looked out the window to get a glimpse of the reality on the ground. Thick snow blanketed everything in white, stretching as far as I could see, much denser than my old memories of Brussels or Chicago. I had not traveled to snowy states across America. There were parts of California with snow, such as Lake Tahoe. Many of my friends used to go, but for financial reasons or perhaps because snow activities did not excite me, I had never touched snow. When I landed at Syracuse Hancock International Airport, the cold cut through my California jacket as if it were not there. I had packed for it, or so I thought, but nothing could prepare me for how cold it would be.

I soon learned that Syracuse carried the infamous title of snowiest city in America, and 2014 would become one of the harshest winters on record. Snow lingered on some mountains until early summer. I had wanted an adventure in the snow, and here I was.

As the taxi wound through Syracuse's neighborhoods toward campus, the city revealed itself as a place shaped by seasons far harsher than anything I had known. Through downtown, rows of red brick buildings lined the streets, their rooftops weighed down by snow clinging to them like a stubborn memory. Smoke curled lazily from chimneys, and the windows of small houses glowed warmly against the cold. We passed the main campus and drove to the South Campus apartments, where most students lived. The trees around Oakwood Cemetery were bare, their branches etched against a gray sky, and tombstones peeked out like frozen ghosts. My apartment was a modest three-bedroom with a drafty living room and a heater that hummed like an old man's sigh. Even the air conditioning system was strikingly different from California. That night, I unpacked my suitcases, the silence outside broken only by the occasional crunch of snow beneath passing footsteps.

I met my roommates. One was a reclusive, skinny South Korean senior whose major I never learned during the year we lived together. The other was an outgoing Nigerian and proud Yoruba, majoring in Accounting in the Whitman School of Management. We shared African food and attended the occasional parties when we were not busy studying. We also played soccer with other students, indoors in the winter and outdoors when there was no snow, which made my first year at Syracuse feel more familiar. What was unfamiliar was indoor soccer. For the first time, I bought indoor soccer boots, and my roommate and I joined a group that played on the second floor of the athletic building. The ball ricocheted off gymnasium walls instead of rolling across grass, our cleats replaced by squeaking rubber soles on varnished wood. The squeaks and sweaty indoor air made the beautiful game feel like an entirely different sport.

On my first day of classes, snowflakes landed on my eyelashes, blurring my vision until I learned to blink them away without breaking stride. Sometimes I paused, watching my breath curl into the air as the flakes accumulated on my coat before melting. The campus itself felt like a small, self-contained world. Red brick buildings dotted the grounds, their spires and archways dusted with snow.

I first reported to the Hall of Languages, where the College of Arts and Sciences, my home college, was housed. The tall clock tower at the entrance was only outshone by the Crouse College tower on the hill a few feet away. Crouse College, which I would later learn houses the school's Visual and Performing Arts, was covered in white snow, its brownstones and bell tower still visible just like in the photos I had studied before accepting my offer. It really does look like Hogwarts, I thought. On the second floor of the Hall of Languages, I met with my advisor to get my registration sorted, then headed to class in the new Life Sciences Complex, where biotechnology courses and research were primarily based.

On the way, I passed Hendricks Chapel. Its octagonal dome crowned the red brick walls, and the iconic Greek pillars framed the entrance like a cathedral. Though it was not St. Peter's Basilica, its grandeur made me pause and reflect on how far I had come from the smaller, simpler churches I had frequented growing up. I thought about the little chapels at Lycée Kanyinya, Petit Séminaire Saint Pie X, and Lycée Don Bosco. *Classic America, even campus chapels are massive marvels of architecture*, I thought, walking through the white snow in the quad where the Syracuse Orange flag fluttered, the seal reading *"Suos Cultores Scientia Coronat,"* knowledge crowns those who seek her.

Behind the chapel, the Carrier Dome rose, covered in white snow. I imagined myself soon watching basketball games there and eventually attending graduation in this grand stadium, just as I had seen in photos and videos of campus life.

That first week, my Californian shoes were soaked through by 10 a.m. each morning, my toes cycling from cold to burning to numb. After a few days, I realized I needed real winter boots. In my philosophy class, I noticed a girl wearing water-resistant boots with thick soles that looked like old soldiers' boots. I noted the Palladium brand and looked it up later. At $150, they were the most expensive shoes I had owned, and worth every penny. The Palladium Pampa Sport Baggy WP boots were tall, foldable, and incredibly comfortable. They rose above my ankles, lined with wool to keep my feet warm and layered with a water-resistant exterior to protect against thawing snow. That pair would last me through two winters in Syracuse and two more in Boston.

I also learned by observing how others dressed. In the dining hall, I would notice someone peeling off layers: a North Face jacket, a fleece underneath, thermals visible at the wrists. That night, I would search for each item online. Learning about thermal clothes became a lifesaver.

AS SEMESTERS ROLLED ON, March's gray slush gave way to May's tentative green, then September's maples bled red and gold before November stripped them bare again. I learned how to engineer genes to create novel medicines in my morning Applied Biotechnology class. I learned how to design implantable medical technologies, such as joint replacement devices, in the midday Biomaterials and Medical Devices class. I learned about computing and databases during the evening Introduction to Computer Science course. Each class fulfilled promises I had made at the embassy window in 2008.

Some classes were so small that, with about fifteen students in the classroom, the professor knew when someone had not done the reading; there was no back row to disappear into. Conversations in the dining hall were all in English, punctuated by lacrosse sticks leaning against tables instead of the mix of languages I had grown used to. At Ohlone College, I could see a student in a hijab comparing notes with someone in a Warriors jersey on their way to an American Sign Language class. In my biology classes of sixty, I counted three to five other Black students. We nodded at each other in the hallways like a silent alliance.

In my first year, the letter confirming I was on the Dean's List felt like a stamp of approval for my decision to choose the university. I had regained the academic zeal that had driven me through primary school and seminary education. As always, I looked for opportunities to do research, and even better, to be paid for it. Like clockwork, I applied to be a scholar in nationally funded TRiO programs. I was accepted into both the Ronald E. McNair Scholars and the Louis Stokes Alliances for Minority Participation (LSAMP) Scholars program. These programs provided a research stipend and professional support to prepare students for graduate school.

I joined a lab in the Department of Chemistry, doing computational chemistry research. I analyzed new molecules synthesized in the lab to determine which ones were most effective at preventing a bacterial pathogen called *Pseudomonas aeruginosa* from attaching and forming colonies in the lungs of patients with cystic fibrosis. *Each molecule I modeled could someday mean one less child struggling to breathe.* I often ran simulations late into the night.

As senior year approached, the inevitable decisions about post-graduation plans loomed. The TRiO programs strongly encouraged us to pursue graduate degrees, and I expressed my desire to go for a PhD. Deep down, the idea of committing the next five years to more schooling felt exhausting. Perhaps it was because I had lived through multiple hardships and sometimes felt drained by the nonstop hustle of life. Or maybe it was because I had recently taken the GRE, and the scores were disappointing. The TRiO program directors, an incredible team, reassured me that GRE scores, a standardized test built for American education, should not deter my ambition, as they do not necessarily reflect intellectual ability or potential for success in doctoral programs. In the background, I prepared multiple post-graduation plans. My notebook was filled with pages organized in variable orders: A) PhD programs, B) Master's degrees, C) industry jobs, D) post-baccalaureate options. Each plan included deadlines, timelines, application fees, and cost versus benefit calculations in the margins.

By early 2015, having gained experience in academic and government labs, I decided to pursue a summer internship in the pharmaceutical or biotechnology industry. I wanted to work with and learn from the people who produced chloroquine and quinine, drugs I had taken for malaria back in Burundi. That would be the ultimate next step. I applied and secured a summer research internship at Novartis.

Even though my degree would not be officially granted until all courses were completed in December, the graduation ceremony for the class of 2015 was in May, and I decided to walk with my peers. My California dreams of winter adventures had been fulfilled. As I crossed the stage in the Carrier Dome, I reflected on having survived the snowiest city in America in all its seasons.

February, 2014. Syracuse, New York. Libère in the snow, first week of classes, in front of Hendricks Chapel.

Chapter 16

KNOWLEDGE CROWNS THOSE WHO SEEK HER

S *uos Cultores Scientia Coronat;* "knowledge crowns those who seek her." That is the motto of Syracuse University. I liked this guiding principle. Perhaps that is why I attended two graduations in two consecutive summers. I wanted to be crowned. Attending two graduation ceremonies during a college career is uncommon. Doing it two years in a row is even more unconventional. But that has always been my thing: the unconventional.

IN EARLY 2014, during my first semester at Syracuse, I secured a summer research internship at the prestigious University of California, San Francisco (UCSF), which meant I would spend the summer back in the Bay Area. Around the same time, Ohlone College sent me a reminder to submit paperwork to graduate with the 2014 class, and I realized I could also attend the commencement ceremony. Graduation would make the trip back to my old stomping grounds feel complete, as I knew from my Burundian roots, celebration matters. It marks transitions and formally closes a chapter. In early May, I flew back to the Bay Area.

From 2008 to 2014, it had taken me six years to complete what others finished in the expected two. Part of me did not see that as an achievement. If anything, it felt like failure. Aside from Isidore, I did not have a large family who could cheer when my name was called or displayed on the screen. Most of the friends I had made at Ohlone College had already left to attend four-year universities and were now graduating with their bachelor's degrees. It felt humiliating to attend my community college graduation while peers I had started with were celebrating university diplomas. My transcript from Ohlone was also marked with W grades from the semesters I withdrew from classes to avoid failing when I could not balance multiple jobs with a full course load.

"We have to go to the ceremony and celebrate. It is still a huge achievement," Isidore insisted.

"You're right. It's a good way to close a chapter and honor all the hard work," I agreed, and we made plans to attend the commencement.

I landed at SFO just as I had in 2008, retracing the steps of another life. Isidore flew in from Austin, and we took the same BART ride, not to the church on Octave Street, but to the East Bay. The familiar BART announcements, the smell of coffee mixed with sea salt in the air, the fog rolling over the hills, everything felt like a homecoming and a farewell at the same time.

We rented a car and drove along the routes we used to frequent. We passed the Motel 6 where we once stayed and the small house on Mission Boulevard. The Motel 6 sign still flickered with the same irregular rhythm, casting its orange glow onto the cracked asphalt of the parking lot. We drove to Pleasanton to see the Safeway where I used to work. The automatic doors still released that familiar pneumatic hiss, and the fluorescent lights hummed the same tune that had accompanied my night shifts.

I stopped by UC Berkeley to see Hilgard Hall and reminisce about my first research experience. The building's brick façade had weathered slightly, the mortar between the bricks now hosting tiny colonies of moss that hadn't been there in 2012. Emotions ran high in the days leading up to the commencement ceremony as I reflected on how far I had come.

On graduation day, I put on dress shoes, pumpkin-colored chino pants, and a plaid dress shirt. The shoes squeaked slightly with each step, still stiff from the box. I aimed for a business-casual look, comfortable and unpretentious. I topped it off with my Ohlone dark green graduation gown and a cap with a dangling golden tassel. The tassel swayed with each step, marking the rhythm of transition. The polyester gown rustled softly, its synthetic sheen catching the morning light.

Isidore and I drove to the ceremony, once again recounting old memories. I had invited friends and was excited to see everyone. As I walked to stand in line, I recognized familiar faces, classmates from upper-level biology, organic chemistry, and physics courses. Along the way, strangers called out congratulations from all corners of campus. The support felt unreal, yet grounding. We took photos and reminisced about long days in labs and intense nights studying for exams in Hyman Hall.

The procession began, and the marching band played Sir Edward Elgar's *Pomp and Circumstance March No. 1*, commonly known as the graduation march. The brass instruments resonated through the warm May air, their vibrations echoing in my chest. The rhythm rose and fell. Goosebumps. Ceremonial joy. I marched with my head held high as the crowd cheered for the long line of graduates. The sun beat down on our black caps, creating a shimmer of heat above the procession. It felt like soldiers returning victorious after years of battle.

I took it all in. This was for me. For us. For all the hard days that had come before.

We entered the basketball stadium, converted for the day into a commencement hall, and joined families already seated in the rafters. The perfume of hundreds of flower leis briefly masked the gymnasium scent of varnished wood and old rubber. Row by row, we settled into our seats near the center of the stadium. The air was thick with anticipation. The wooden bleachers creaked under the weight of proud families, creating a symphony of groans and squeaks that followed every movement.

After the speeches concluded, it was time for graduates to be called and walk the stage. One by one, names echoed through the arena, each followed by cheers that rose and fell depending on the size and enthusiasm of the crowd.

When my name was called, loud cheers erupted from my friends, with Isidore being the most audible. His voice cut through the ambient noise like a foghorn, raw and unrestrained. Cameras were everywhere, capturing every ceremonial moment. The click and whir of shutters created a steady, mechanical rainfall of sound. It felt surreal and profoundly comforting to know I was not alone, that despite my nomadic life, the friendships I had built remained constant.

I walked off the stage proudly as an Ohlone College graduate. Outside, Isidore, Elena, and other friends waited with congratulatory leis, flowers, and cards. The weight of the leis around my neck felt like the collective embrace of everyone who had supported me through the years. Plumeria and tuberose petals released their fragrance with each movement, surrounding me in a soft cloud of sweetness. We took countless photos and celebrated the achievement. That Sunday, we shared a celebratory dinner, and I went to sleep filled with the immense happiness of closing a chapter that had once felt cold and lonely. There would be more blessings ahead.

THE FOLLOWING WEEK, I moved to San Francisco for the summer and began my research internship at UCSF's Cardiovascular Research Institute. I worked on computational algorithms to understand how certain proteins transport sugar in and out of the kidneys. I also searched for molecules that could help repair this transport mechanism in patients with type 2 diabetes. The summer became a blend of city life, biomedical research, new friendships from across the country, and steady growth as a scientist.

My mentor, Dr. David, slender with curly hair falling to his shoulders, looked like a Renaissance physicist. An Isaac Newton or a Niels Bohr. He seemed like someone who could recite the periodic table using a method far more sophisticated than the one Marcus and I had learned. And yes, he was a physicist by training. *Do they teach how to style when one wants to become a physicist?* I wondered, noting the familiar resemblance shared by physicists of both past and present.

Of the many lessons from this summer, one that stood out was how Dr. David showed me how to tackle unfamiliar areas of science with simplicity.

One afternoon, the team held a journal club, a meeting to discuss a scientific paper relevant to our ongoing work in the lab. The topic was theoretical physical chemistry, an area I had no prior exposure to. We were supposed to read the paper a week in advance. I had not. For one, the content looked dense and intimidating. On the other hand, the interns had partied all weekend, and I procrastinated until the evening before the journal club. During the discussion, we were asked to take turns explaining what we had taken away from a randomly selected figure. When it was my turn, I was assigned a figure I had not even glanced at. Like a deer caught in headlights, I stared at the page and said nothing for several long seconds. I was too embarrassed to admit I had not read it, and I froze.

Sensing my struggle, Dr. David stepped in.

"Here's a tip when reading a figure," he said. "Just read the legend. It tells you what's in the graphs."

I read the legend aloud, and as the words left my mouth, I felt the complexity dissolve, and my nerves settle. From there, the rest of the journal club unfolded as a true scientific discussion, the way it was meant to be. I carried that advice with me from that day forward, and every journal club after that became easier. As for procrastination, well, that remains a time management challenge I continue to work on.

After the usual end-of-summer scientific presentations, my experience at UCSF concluded in early August. I flew back to Syracuse to begin my senior year of college, carrying with me not only new scientific knowledge but also the reassurance that I belonged in these prestigious research towers.

IN MAY 2015, preparations for graduation from Syracuse University were in full swing. This time, I knew what to expect. I was ready to embrace the ceremony and enjoy every moment. I had not quit. I was finishing on time, had learned an immense amount, found my scientific focus, and secured another internship for the upcoming summer. There was much to celebrate.

I also learned that university graduation spans an entire week, with separate ceremonies for different colleges and departments.

Ahead of graduation week, I made plans and invited my brother and local friends. I decorated my graduation cap and went to the store to buy all the glam and embellishments we needed. The craft store smelled of hot glue and possibility, its aisles lined with rhinestones and ribbons ready to transform plain mortarboards into personal statements. The glue gun released wisps of chemical smoke as we worked, its molten adhesive stretching into fine threads between surfaces. When we finished, the top of my cap read, "I'm the first. Thanks, Mom!" The glitter caught the light from every angle, scattering tiny rainbows across the dark blue fabric.

I was still not financially able to cover the entire process required for her to obtain a visa and travel to the United States for a graduation ceremony. Just as it had been in 2007, the village remained her home base, and she did not even own a passport. The full process would likely take more than a year.

When people asked whether my family was flying in for my graduation, I would brush it off quickly. "It's too much hassle; it's just a graduation ceremony," I'd say, sparing them the explanation that my mother was likely on the farm, growing just enough food to support my younger siblings. Over time, I grew deeply grateful for the friends who showed up on my big days.

They had become my family, and their presence and congratulatory messages helped fill the void created by distance and separation. Anchors, transient as they may be.

Trying on the decorated cap heightened the excitement. The fabric of the gown was richer, falling in more elegant folds than the one I had worn at Ohlone College. In addition to the academic sash from Syracuse University, both the McNair and LSAMP programs had created custom sashes to honor their graduating scholars. With all three sashes draped over my gown, the ensemble felt noticeably heavier, almost as if it symbolized the weight of the achievements being celebrated. The silk rested cool against my neck, each sash offering a distinct texture: the McNair sash rough with embroidered lettering, the LSAMP sash smooth as river mud.

From Thursday through Sunday, the ceremonies and celebrations unfolded. There were events for McNair and LSAMP scholars, the Black students' graduation, the College of Arts and Sciences Convocation, and finally the university-wide commencement on Sunday, when thousands of graduates gathered in the famed Carrier Dome. Each ceremony had its own rhythm. Intimate gatherings highlighted individual stories, mid-sized convocations showcased departmental pride, and the final ceremony brought us together as part of something far larger than ourselves.

At the McNair ceremony, held in a wood-paneled room scented with furniture polish and accomplishment, we were called "scholars" with such reverence that, for the first time, I truly felt like one. The wooden walls absorbed and reflected every word, lending the room an acoustic warmth that enriched each voice. The Black students' ceremony pulsed with energy. Drums beat, voices rose in celebration, and joy radiated from collective triumph over systemic barriers. The vibrations of the bass drum traveled through the floor and into our feet, syncing our heartbeats with the rhythm.

The College of Arts and Sciences Convocation felt more formal, with Latin honors pronounced carefully and academic tradition hanging in the air like incense.

In the Carrier Dome, the sheer scale swallowed individual voices, creating a collective hum of anticipation. The air conditioning strained against the heat of thousands of bodies, forming pockets of cool drafts and warm air. May sunlight streamed through the upper windows, casting cathedral-like beams across the space. Dust motes floated through the light like tiny celebrants. Arranged by college and degree, thousands of graduates formed a vast sea of orange and blue.

The speaker's voice echoed through the dome, speaking of futures and possibilities, but my thoughts were anchored in the past. When we were asked to move our tassels from right to left, the gesture felt heavier than it should have, as if we were physically crossing from one phase of life into another. The tassel's threads brushed my cheek as it swung across my face, leaving a trail of goosebumps in their wake.

As I walked out of the Carrier Dome for the last time as a student, diploma in hand, I thought about my mother's hands, worn from farm labor yet always gentle when she blessed me. This degree was hers as much as it was mine. Each graduation had carried me further from the refugee camps, and yet, in another way, closer to fulfilling her prayers for my success.

At every ceremony, there were photo sessions, speeches, and countless words of congratulations. By the time it all ended on Sunday evening, I was exhausted but energized, ready to step into whatever came next. Between these two graduations, I had transformed from a community college student unsure of his place in American academia into a biotechnology graduate prepared to enter the pharmaceutical industry. Each ceremony was not only a recognition of what I had achieved, but also a promise of what still lay ahead. The tassels had turned, but the adventure continued.

May 8, 2015. Syracuse, New York. The graduation cap decorated ahead of the week's ceremonies (left) and in full commencement outfit (right)

Chapter 17

CALLED FOR BIOMEDICINE

The late March afternoon sun melted the last patches of snow outside Syracuse University's Bird Library when an email notification appeared on my phone screen. It was from the Novartis Institutes for BioMedical Research (NIBR). I had interviewed with NIBR's Informatics team for a summer internship a week earlier, two months before all the graduation commotion. It was the only company I had pursued for an internship.

"Congratulations!" the first line read. The email was from Dr. Lee, the person I had interviewed with and who would become my mentor at NIBR.

"We really enjoyed meeting you last week and are excited to offer you a position within our Informatics team. An official offer will follow tomorrow, and we hope you will accept and join us," the email continued.

I stopped studying and took a few minutes to take it all in.

"I got the Novartis internship!" I texted Isidore. The message arrived as I was already planning a summer in Boston, looking up places to explore around Cambridge, where my office would be located. On the team, I would work on a project developing machine learning algorithms to help scientists identify proteins responsible for disease, which could then be targeted with new medicines. I was ready to learn the craft of making medicines.

THE FIRST WEEKEND OF June, after Syracuse graduation, I reported to the Northeastern campus, where the NIBR program had arranged dedicated dormitories for the twenty-plus summer interns from around the world.

I spent my summer living in the Back Bay neighborhood in Boston and commuting into Cambridge for work. The group included students from many U.S. universities, as well as a few from France and Japan. We crossed the Charles River daily to reach the NIBR headquarters on Massachusetts Avenue, or Mass Ave, as Bostonians call it.

Cambridge was the epitome of intellectual pursuit, home to Harvard University, the Massachusetts Institute of Technology, and other prestigious institutions. It gave the same sense of immersion into an academic environment that I had felt at UC Berkeley in 2012 and UCSF in 2014, except this time it extended beyond a single campus. The city itself hummed with intellect. Beyond the two massive universities, Cambridge also hosted the largest concentration of multinational pharmaceutical and biotechnology companies, including Novartis, Pfizer, Biogen, Amgen, and Takeda. Even the streets seemed alive with biomedical and technological innovation. The air felt charged with possibilities, carrying the faint sense of discoveries discussed, break-throughs celebrated, and deals made to bring medicines to patients.

Bars with names like "The Miracle of Science" and "Thirsty Scholar" were a signature of Cambridge. Unlike San Francisco or Bujumbura, even the street graffiti seemed to resemble chemical struc-tures and mathematical equations.

The halls of NIBR were nothing like the academic labs in Hilgard Hall or Wadsworth Center. Almost as if to reflect the proportional value of what was being created in these buildings, security was nearly as strict as the one I experienced at the U.S. Embassy in Bujumbura and the Federal immigration office in San Francisco. Badge readers beeped at every door, their red lights turning green with a satisfying click that meant you belonged. My office was on the fourth floor of NIBR's northwest research tower on Massachusetts Avenue. The elevator, circular in shape, was designed to resemble a DNA helix when viewed from the outside, giving the immediate feeling that you were entering a sacred biomedical research space. Every inch of the building and laboratory space was spotless, projecting the importance of quality, safety, and efficacy, all hallmarks of effective medicines.

Unlike academic halls, everything felt intentionally immaculate and precisely managed, reflecting the urgency to get drugs to patients. I felt a deep connection to this mission and was ready to learn and contribute to the innovation at the heart of the medicines of the future.

From the first meeting to discuss the summer plans, Dr. Lee was as sharp as a tack and precise as an atomic clock. She had a German accent. I would soon learn that, although she was born in Asia, she had studied and worked in Europe for many years. The big boss, Dr. Harrison, was as calm as a placid lake in winter. Research results, I noticed, were what captured his attention. He could look at a figure for one minute and conjure ten new ideas to pursue next. My impression was that the only thing he liked more than data and algorithms for drug discovery was his husky, whom he often mentioned. *What a natural scientist.*

"The score on the second plot is interesting. I think you're onto something," he said during a one-on-one research update meeting when Dr. Lee was out of town.

"Have we tried the algorithm from that publication on the other two datasets? What happens if we split the data into two sets? What other approaches could we take?" He went on with new directions as I scribbled notes.

"How did you come up with all these ideas from that one plot?" I asked. *I want to be like him when I grow up.* I internally thought.

"Experience. You will get there. I've looked at thousands of these analyses."

I had watched him ask such revealing questions during team meetings, but only now did I realize what it took. PhD training would give both the skills and experience to deconstruct what looked like complex puzzles.

Dr. Lee, like my mentors before, taught me many lessons. During a late summer check-in, I wanted her opinion on my preparations for pursuing a PhD.

"I'm still deciding when to start grad school. Do you think I'm ready? And if I did the post-baccalaureate program, would you be my mentor?"

"You are more than ready." Her validation carried the weight and motivation I needed. At that moment, I made the definitive decision to pursue a PhD.

"And if you choose to do the post-baccalaureate program, I'd be happy to have you back. The whole team is impressed with your performance over the summer."

We discussed the logistics and planning. While I had walked at graduation in May, I still had three courses left for my degree to be conferred. Since I had the fall semester to finish at Syracuse, I planned to join the new post-baccalaureate cohort in January and then apply for a PhD in the next cycle.

"I'll work on formalizing your offer with the program's office, and I'm positive we will make it happen," she assured me.

As the internship came to an end, I received and accepted the post-baccalaureate offer, securing a paid full-time position and solidifying my plans through summer 2017.

IN THE FIRST WEEK of January 2016, I reported to 181 Massachusetts Avenue. The team had moved into the newly built NIBR headquarters. The institute had also changed leadership. Jay Bradner, a decorated biochemist, oncologist, and charismatic leader, started the same week I returned. He took the reins from Mark Fishman, who had been at NIBR's helm for more than a decade.

While the team I was rejoining was essentially the same, the names of departments and groups had changed. The old Developmental and Molecular Pathways department was now called Chemical Biology and Therapeutics (CBT) to reflect the new emphasis on chemical biology. Our group's name changed from Informatics to Data Science. Presentation slides and posters across the halls also displayed the updated branding, reflecting this new era. I had read the news and closely followed why the company was making these changes, and I was excited for all of it. Here, I would learn the intricacies of corporate restructuring and strategy. Jay Bradner's vision was that chemical biology was the future of pharmaceutical research, while data and machine learning would usher in a new era of therapeutic discovery. The prior molecular pathway–centric paradigm would give way to a chemical biology framework for therapeutic discovery.

In our group of over 30 computational scientists, I was the only one with just a bachelor's degree. I absorbed all the knowledge I could while imagining myself someday in Dr. Lee's, Dr. Harrison's, or Jay Bradner's shoes. *What was it like to run such a complex organization with so much at stake? Did graduate school prepare one for that?* I couldn't wait to find out.

In the back of my mind, some doubts lingered. I had the best mentors so far, but most people in these new research towers did not look like me, much less understand where I came from. I knew that being the first in my family to pursue a PhD was like building a complex engineering system without a foundation or a map. And that made me want it even more. I had two main objectives: excel at my work and learn everything I needed to be admitted to a top PhD program.

Besides leading a project to advance the group's larger research goals, the NIBR post-baccalaureate program provided access to Harvard courses and conference attendance. Every Tuesday evening, we attended a research seminar through the Harvard College of Arts and Sciences. To further enhance my knowledge, I also enrolled in a graduate-level cell biology course at Harvard Medical School in the spring of 2016. Being among first-year PhD students gave me a real sense of graduate education. As an affiliate, I wasn't officially a matriculated Harvard student, and since this course wasn't a requirement for my PhD application, I focused solely on the learning.

The lectures were a mixture of professors taking turns to teach in their areas of expertise. Their voices were measured, their lectures clear and simplified, and they made the formidable Harvard Medical School feel more welcoming than I had imagined. Some lectures, such as those on the nuclear pore complex and microtubule dynamics by Professor

Mitchison, were so invigorating that whenever I read new science on these topics, his voice from that winter lecture still rings in my mind, a vivid reminder of a winter full of learning.

Scientific research conferences were also invaluable learning opportunities. Whether it was the Intelligent Systems for Molecular Biology in Orlando, Florida, Quantitative Biology in Kauai, Hawaii, or other symposia I attended and presented at, meeting fellow scientists and future colleagues enriched my preparation for doctoral training. Of course, these gatherings included both well-mannered academics and ego-filled individuals. I quickly learned to navigate this balance of personalities in higher education.

At one conference, I was presenting my research when an older gentleman approached my poster.

"Hello there, I read your abstract. Tell me about your project."

"Of course, thank you for coming by," I replied, excited to discuss my work, just like other academics.

"My work focuses on developing proteochemometric machine learning models..." I paused, remembering the presentation lessons I had learned. It's essential to gauge the audience's scientific background so that the discussion can be tailored. This allows you to adjust your language and remove jargon if necessary.

"May I ask about your research area?" I inquired.

"Don't worry, I can follow along," he said. It sounded dismissive, but I continued, and a small audience began to form around my station. I described the methodological approach, and before I could even discuss my findings, he interrupted.

"Saying machine learning, or whatever everyone is calling it, will discover new drugs is nonsense."

"Why is that?" I asked, curious about his dismissive tone.

"Mathematicians like myself have been working on these methods for years. None of it is new, and none of it is truly an intelligent system."

"I agree that mathematics and physics form the historical foundation for new predictive algorithms..." I began.

"You don't know what you're talking about," he interrupted, walking away before I could finish.

I composed myself and continued describing our work to the rest of the audience. I noticed some attendees had bristled at his comments, but no one seemed overly concerned. We proceeded as usual. In fact, my poster was among the three presentations that received an award at that symposium. The experience was a mixture of challenges and achievements, a preview of the academic research world I would come to know well. Opposing schools of thought are common in research communities, and friendly competition often drives science forward. As much as his comments stung for a few days, I was learning. I was getting a glimpse of what lay ahead.

IN SUMMER 2016, preparations for PhD applications for the 2017 admissions cycle were in full swing. The intensity of the process reminded me of summer and fall 2007, when I had applied to study in the U.S. Except this time, I knew what I was doing. I didn't need to visit a crowded internet café. I had a MacBook Pro and worked on my applications in hip coffee shops like Darwin's, just next to NIBR, sipping creamy cortados like a proper Cambridge biotech professional.

I made my list of programs and prepared my application package, consulting team members who had PhDs for advice.

"It's easy to get into a PhD; it's harder to get out," advised Dr. William, a senior scientist in the group. He reminded me repeatedly to stay focused on graduating and landing a job in the industry after my first year. He was only half-joking, but the advice anchored me through the PhD years.

"Remember, the devil is in the details," Dr. Lee remarked when she noticed a typo on my CV. This advice became a guiding principle, whether I was writing code or analyzing results. Her insistence on precision and sharpness in research left a lasting impression.

When applications opened in September, I submitted my documents to the PhD programs before the November deadlines and waited. Interview invitations and rejections arrived between November and late January or February, depending on the program. I mentally prepared myself not to stress over the wait; I only needed one offer, after all.

By December and January, I had received four offers: three for classic PhD interview visits and one for a master's program that would directly lead to a PhD. The master 's-to-PhD option wasn't appealing, given that I had applied for direct PhD admission. I thanked them and moved on. The other three offers were from the University of Southern California (USC) Programs in Biomedical and Biological Sciences, Vanderbilt University School of Medicine Interdisciplinary Graduate Program, and the University of Pittsburgh Integrative Systems Biology Program.

Multiple flat-out rejections also came in between these offers. The rejection from UCSF arrived early and was heartbreakingly demoralizing. It was my top choice. I had spent a summer on the campus and loved it. I had even sent my application package to someone in the admissions department, who had given positive feedback. I strongly recommend that I apply to a specific program that they thought was the best fit.

A rejection from the University of California, Berkeley Computational Biology program followed, carrying the same heartbreak. A few weeks later, the Stanford University rejection came while I was in Los Angeles interviewing at USC. The email ping arrived with a shock that felt like a slap, the blue light from my phone harsh against the rays of the conference room where we were learning about the program. A few candidates sighed, and we exchanged glances, noticing that the email ping had come at the same time.

"Stanford?" I asked the closest fellow candidate.

"Yeah, it was my top choice," he replied. Both of us nodded and shrugged at the realization that we would not be spending the next half-decade in Palo Alto.

I was gutted. Three Bay Area programs I had applied to had rejected me, and the romanticized homecoming I had imagined was not going to happen. *Perhaps Los Angeles would be my new home*, I thought, turning my attention back to the program director, who continued discussing what made graduate education at USC unique.

I had visited the city once before, flying in from Boston during a January winter snow. It was a typical sunny weekend in Pasadena and East LA. The warmth felt like a physical embrace after months of Boston cold, the sun on my skin almost medicinal. That alone was an enticing reason to consider the program. After two days of interviews, lab tours, and interactions with faculty, staff, and current students, I was sold. The academic pursuits were innovative, the culture supportive, and the fun palpable. I waited for the offer with anticipation. When I returned to my research duties in Boston, I reported back to my teammates about the weekend in LA.

"You're going back to California, aren't you?" Dr. Lee joked.

"Well, I liked it very much. Let's see how the other visits go," I replied, trying to stay calm amid the interview process. I had flights booked to Pittsburgh and Nashville. I had never been to either city, so I expected the visits would be interesting and enjoyable.

The Pittsburgh interview was delayed because I had a conference in Kauai, Hawaii, during the weekend of the main visit. The program accommodated a separate weekend after my Hawaii trip. Another candidate joined me for this secondary visit. Like the other visits, the focus was on meeting faculty, touring labs and facilities, and attending presentations about the program and why it was an excellent place to pursue a PhD.

One aspect that stood out was how stressed the senior PhD students were. In conversations, they explained that the program guarantees every student will finish their PhD in four years flat. At first, this promise seemed appealing after all, everyone wants to complete a doctorate quickly, but the seniors made it clear that this guarantee came with significant stress. That was a dealbreaker for me. I realized this program wasn't the best fit for my training. I received the admissions offer soon after the visit.

The visit to Nashville for Vanderbilt University was a more pleasant experience. The routine was familiar: meeting potential advisors, attending sessions about the program, touring the campus and labs, and learning about life in the university town. The senior students seemed happy, and the faculty were welcoming. However, as we toured the local neighborhoods, it felt like a cowboy town, a country music city, and I didn't feel like enough of a cowboy to fit in as a local in Tennessee. Or perhaps I had already subconsciously decided on attending USC as I had received an offer the week after the Los Angeles trip, which had the most excitement than all others.

IN THE MIDDLE OF a research seminar at Harvard Medical School, my phone vibrated against the wooden desk, partially drowning out the professor's explanation of how kinesin dysfunction correlates with neurodegenerative disorders. It was two weeks after my on-site USC interview. I peeked at the screen and noticed a voicemail had been left. Time slowed during the evening session as I anticipated listening to it. When class ended, I rushed out of the Tosteson Medical Education Center and stood in a corner to check the message, snow falling in the usual Northeast winter. A few snowflakes landed on my phone, instantly melting into tiny droplets that blurred the numbers. I slipped on my gloves and listened. It was the chair of the Medical Biophysics track calling to share good news and asking me to call back. I knew what that meant. I dialed immediately.

"Hello, I'm sorry I missed your call. I was in class," I said, nearly interrupting his greeting. Then I paused to hear the news.

"Hi, thank you for calling back. I wanted to relay the good news from the admissions committee: they have accepted you into the 2017 incoming class. We were very impressed with your candidacy, and we hope you will select our program. I wanted to call personally and share the news. A formal offer letter will follow shortly."

I held my breath.

"Thank you so much for calling with such great news. I will keep an eye out for the offer letter and stay in touch as I go through my other interviews."

"Great. Besides the program, I am available for questions you may have about the PhD program and life in Los Angeles. Please reach out anytime."

As the call ended, I froze for a few seconds to collect myself, but I couldn't. I jumped up and down, shouting "Yes! Yes!" with my fist in the air. My breath formed white clouds in the cold air with each exclamation, like visual punctuation marks. Students walked through the hall, but I barely noticed anyone.

Soon after, I received and declined the Pittsburgh and Vanderbilt offers. I accepted and signed the USC admission offer ahead of the April

15th deadline. My plans for the next five or more years were set. I had a city to move to. Financially, the PhD stipend, while not a large salary, was sufficient for a modest living in Los Angeles. Unlike 2008, I was fully proficient in English, accent aside. While confident in my preparation for PhD studies, the nerves of acclimating to a new city and university, and doing something no one in my family had ever attempted, remained. I was ready for it all.

The plane lifted off from Logan Airport, and I watched Boston shrink below, its skyline giving way to clouds. Somewhere ahead, Los Angeles waited, with its palm trees and promises, its laboratories and hypotheses, and the chance to transform fully from student to scientist. I had been called, and I was answering.

June 2017. Cambridge, Massachusetts. Last week at NIBR, Libère looking over the research towers that had been his office for nearly two years.

Part Six

TRANSCENDENT HORIZONS

"Science knows no country, because knowledge belongs to humanity, and is the torch which illuminates the world."

— LOUIS PASTEUR

Chapter 18

THE HYPOTHESIS OF A LIFETIME

The dry heat hit me like a wall as I exited the terminal at Los Angeles International Airport, so different from Boston's humid summers. On the way to my new home, the salty scent carried by Pacific winds mixed with the sound of Los Angeles traffic, creating a symphonic experience that would become the soundtrack of my doctoral years.

That Monday, I was scheduled to report to the Health Sciences Campus (HSC) at the Keck School of Medicine of the University of Southern California to begin my first rotation. I would be working on research in stem cell biology to understand the root causes of leukemia. I was completing a summer rotation before the rest of the students arrived. During this time, I also read extensively from cell biology and biochemistry textbooks in preparation for the upcoming coursework. I had been out of school for a while and wanted time to readjust.

When the rest of the cohort arrived in August, we met during orientation. It was immediately apparent that many of them came from significantly more privileged backgrounds than I did. Still, I was there, among them. I had great confidence in my intellect and even more confidence in my work ethic. No one in that room knew how to work under a scorching sun in farm fields in Burundi. And, it was unlikely that anyone had sold peanuts on the streets of Muyinga in the midst of a civil war.

As part of orientation, we visited the University Park Campus (UPC). Like the Sather Tower at Berkeley and the Crouse College Tower at Syracuse, USC's Webb Tower stood tall and imposing at the center of campus. I had learned that clock towers are a defining feature of university campus architecture across America. They serve as visual and historical landmarks that symbolize the grandeur of academic pursuits. I once believed their primary purpose was display, but I came to appreciate their role in timekeeping and spatial orientation, especially for new students. To me, they became familiar monuments, reminding me that new knowledge lay ahead.

Classes began, and formal rotations followed. The coursework was more challenging than I had anticipated. Being away from school for two years had not helped. I struggled with some specialized topics in molecular biology and, much like the French students I had studied alongside at Ohlone College, I relied on tutoring sessions with senior PhD students to catch up quickly. I also joined group study sessions with classmates, some of whom would later become lifelong friends.

In my research interests, I was primarily drawn to diseases of the immune system, particularly autoimmune disorders. I had long been curious about rheumatoid arthritis, as it runs in my family on my mother's side. My mother had lived with joint pain for as long as I could remember. On evenings when she returned home after long days working on the farm, she would describe pain in her knees, feet, and hands, which were often swollen. Before I understood the inflammatory nature of autoimmune diseases, I believed it was simply the result of physical wear and tear from a lifetime of demanding labor. To my younger mind, it seemed obvious that such repetitive work could produce those symptoms.

However, she would also recount the hereditary nature of the condition; *nyokuru* Sophia had it, and so did some of her cousins and uncles. By this point in my first year of graduate school, I already knew that rheumatoid arthritis is genetically inherited in nearly 60 percent of cases. The obvious realization was that I might have inherited the condition and that my future children were also predisposed. Genetic predisposition is a frightening reality to live with. I had already spent time reading about the disease and reviewing the medications that were currently available.

On one hand, I wondered whether I could purchase medications to send home to my mother. On the other hand, I was interested in pursuing research in this area to help discover new treatments. I learned that the disease is not curable, but that medications exist to manage symptoms and slow its progression. These include pain relievers and anti-inflammatory drugs such as ibuprofen, methotrexate, and prednisone. There were not many faculty members working on autoimmune disorders. In the U.S., cancer research and cardiovascular diseases tend to receive the largest share of research funding.

After rotating in a leukemia lab, followed by a stem cell engineering lab, and a translational genomics group, it was the fourth rotation that would determine the next four years of my doctoral training. When I first contacted Professor Mitchell, he responded quickly on a Sunday afternoon, which suggested an advisor who was readily available to students. We scheduled a meeting for Wednesday afternoon. I took the intercampus university shuttle from the Health Sciences Campus to the University Park Campus. The shuttle's air conditioning struggled against the afternoon heat, creating a microclimate in which the windows frequently fogged due to the temperature difference.

As I entered Professor Mitchell's office, the Los Angeles sun streamed through the windows, casting geometric shadows across the glass plaques on the walls. Each plaque displayed a journal cover publication, representing a hypothesis tested, a question answered, and a step forward in human knowledge. The research group, recently recruited from another university, was focused on a single mission: developing technologies to detect circulating tumor cells in cancer patients. While waiting for a new research tower to be completed, the team had been conducting its work in temporary laboratory and office spaces.

"Hello, I'm Sam. Welcome to our lab," he said, greeting me with an energy that matched the sharp, vibrant colors of the microscopy images displayed on the journal covers.

"Libère, it's great to meet you."

"Hello, I'm Don. Great to meet you." The other advisor in the research group, Professor Anderson, had joined the meeting to introduce himself.

My first impression was that Professor Mitchell, young and energetic, complemented Professor Anderson, who was much older and carried a visibly seasoned demeanor.

"So, what do you want to do when you grow up?" he asked immediately. It was a question I had not been asked before, a philosophical variation of the familiar inquiry about long-term professional goals often posed in job interviews. His voice carried the rhythm of someone who had asked the question countless times, yet still listened to each response as though hearing it for the first time.

"I want to make medicines. That has always been my vocation."

"What diseases are of interest for therapeutic development?"

"I'm fascinated by autoimmune disorders. There is a lot we don't know about what causes our own cells to revolt against us. We still don't know how to control faults in immune recognition mechanisms for therapeutic utility. The complexity of it all is intellectually captivating to me."

They both listened carefully as I described my family's predisposition to rheumatoid arthritis as an example of how the cells at the center of our immune defense mechanism can malfunction and lead to various maladies. Taking turns, they noted the technical and scientific challenges of studying autoimmunity and discussed how one might approach solving those challenges.

"Did you know that cancer is a disorder of the immune system?" Professor Dr Mitchell asked, sitting back in his chair like a wise man imparting wisdom to a young scholar. The leather chair creaked slightly as he leaned back, a sound that would forever be associated with moments of revelation in my mind.

I paused.

"I never thought about it that way," I replied. "It's obvious for cancers of the immune system, like leukemia and lymphomas. But what about carcinomas?" Carcinomas are the cancers commonly known as solid tumors, whose cells of origin are not immune cells.

The air in the office seemed to shift, charged with the electricity of a new understanding forming. At a high level, I already knew the answer to my own question. I had studied the process of oncogenesis in cell biology and had read oncology literature.

Before he could begin explaining the intricacies of the relationship between carcinomas and the immune system, I had already made the connections in my mind. Cancer arises as a result of accumulated mutations. Immune cells are constantly searching for and destroying cells that accumulate dangerous mutations. This process is known as immune surveillance; even in carcinomas, progression to a disease state results from the immune system's failure to eliminate cancerous cells.

He went on to describe how cancer cells develop sophisticated ways to evade the immune system, either by altering the proteins on their surfaces or by finding favorable locations and creating environments that are toxic to immune cells. Much like soldiers in an imperial war, they seek conditions where they can hide from immune defenses and establish new territory in the form of metastatic tumors.

He also shared that he had transitioned from physics to cancer research after his mother was diagnosed with breast cancer. This experience inspired him to develop early cancer detection technologies. This story resonated deeply with me, given my own connection to rheumatoid arthritis and autoimmunity.

The research team, a collection of scientists from various backgrounds, was developing technologies to capture and study tumor cells in the bloodstream of patients with cancer. With such technology, cancer can be detected earlier, treated more effectively, and more people can live cancer free.

In this brief interaction, I had switched camps. Preventing cancer felt like an even more impactful mission than developing medicines for those already afflicted.

"Also, we just secured funding for a new research program in multiple myeloma," Professor Dr Mitchell added, noting that myeloma is a disease of mature lymphocytes, the same cells responsible for autoimmunity. I was to lead the development of blood-based cancer detection technology for myeloma.

Unsaid was the fact that a newly funded project was also appealing, because it meant I would not have to worry about funding the research for a few years.

"Excellent, I'm up to the challenge."

On my way out, I looked around and imagined what it would be like once I had joined. The temporary lab space was made of wood and other non-permanent materials, and the whole structure was suspended in the air, as I could feel the hollow space beneath the bouncy floor. Each step created a slight vibration that traveled through the structure, a reminder of its temporary nature. It was rugged, nomadic, and transient, just the way I liked to live. I selected the lab for my final rotation and started the following week.

THE MIX OF INITIATING new projects, commuting between my classes at HSC and the lab at UPC, and getting to know everyone made the spring pass quickly. The team was a group of sharp scientists from different countries and scientific backgrounds. They moved between the lab and offices for experiments and scientific meetings as if the lives of patients whose samples we analyzed depended on their work. In the lab, the −80°C freezers emitted a low, constant drone, punctuated by the occasional whoosh of their defrost cycles, creating a mechanical heartbeat that could be heard from outside the makeshift labs.

On weekends, I explored the sights and scenes of Los Angeles. Some days were spent at the beach, others wandering through different neighborhoods and trying different eateries. The city revealed itself in layers during those explorations. Los Angeles was not just palm trees and sunshine. It was the smell of jasmine blooming in February, the sound of multiple languages mixing at Grand Central Market, and the way the light shifted from harsh noon brilliance to a golden hour that made even concrete look beautiful. Each neighborhood had its own microclimate, its own rhythm, its own colors, and its own particular way the fog rolled in from the ocean.

Beach days became my favorite. At sunset, the water was painted in hues of amber and crimson, as if the earth itself were trying to tell a story too vast for words. The salt air mixed with the scent of sunscreen and freedom, so different from the sterile Cambridge air I had been breathing for months.

I spent most weekdays in coffee shops, developing my research questions and studying for exams. Each café had its own personality. Mantra Coffee in Azusa, where the aroma of coffee mingled with desert air and old books; Copa Vida in Pasadena, where the baristas knew my order before I spoke and the exposed brick carried the scent of dark roast; and MCO in Koreatown, where the espresso machine's hiss and the flicker of neon lights provided a rhythmic backdrop to typing.

At the end of the rotation in May 2018, I officially joined the lab as the first year of graduate school came to an end. This meant I had formalized my PhD. I would file the paperwork to join the Medical Biophysics track, select my doctoral qualifying exam committee, and begin preparing for the qualifying exam before advancing to PhD candidacy. I had found my scientific home, a place where my questions about immune systems and cancer would find fertile ground. The hypothesis of a lifetime was taking shape, not only in the research I would pursue, but in the life I was building around biomedical research as a vocation.

The qualifying exam was due the following January, so I had a few months to synthesize a detailed proposal for my dissertation. What new knowledge would this work bring to the field of oncology and the broader biomedical sciences? How would my PhD research make an impact on patients' lives? These were the questions I needed to address during the qualification process. I consumed the relevant literature voraciously to expand my foundational knowledge, establish what was known and unknown, and determine which questions could be reasonably pursued within the timeline of a doctoral program. While the generation of new ideas relied on my own intellect, there was an entire support system to guide the process. This included PhD advisors and committees who challenged, molded, and stewarded my progress.

I now understand that science is a team sport. Beyond the larger research group, I sought to build a small team around our research in myeloma. I wanted to develop leadership skills and serve as a team lead. In our lab, it was common for doctoral students to mentor undergraduates. During the summer and throughout the fall, I progressively formed what came to be known as the M&M Team. Not because we consumed the famed Mars and Murrie candies, but because we were the Multiple Myeloma team, separate from other groups focused on various carcinomas.

On the M&M team, there was Rachel, a senior human biology major who had been with the lab for a few years and was excited about building new diagnostic assays, and who also came up with the M&M name. Jessica, a sophomore global health major, and Alexander, a freshman quantitative biology major, were fascinated by building predictive algorithms using biomedical data to improve patient outcomes. Ryan, a junior in mathematics, and Madison, a sophomore in quantitative biology, would join later, bringing an equally fierce drive to make an impact in oncology research. Just as I had been mentored many years before graduate school, I was now the senior PhD mentor for the M&M team.

We were generating preliminary observations for my proposed scientific hypothesis. We took turns imaging on the microscope and building preliminary prediction models. The cancer cell detection technology in the lab was based on the principle that cells could be plated on a glass slide, treated with a cocktail of protein antibodies that bind to specific cell types, and, under a microscope, these antibodies would light up in different colors. From these colors, combined with the respective physical characteristics of cells, we could identify which cells were cancerous and which were normal. In our assays, cancer cells were expected to appear bright red, while normal cells would look green. The first results from the assay to detect circulating tumor cells in myeloma came in.

One afternoon, Rachel sent a brief message with one microscopy image.

"The assay works!"

I ran to the microscope to examine the data. Like a marigold in full bloom among a field of green, large red cells were visible among small green cells. I took a few minutes to stare at the red cells; they were the myeloma plasma cells. In addition to the red stain, they displayed the characteristic eccentric nucleus and a perinuclear halo. I had been reading about these cellular features in the literature and describing in my proposal how our technology would detect them. After a few minutes marveling at the fact that this result alone represented significant progress, I replied:

"Excellent. Before we pop champagne, let's stain a few more slides to make sure this is reproducible."

Hearing myself, I realized it echoed a discussion I had with Andrew in Hilgard ten years earlier, only now the roles were reversed. I was the senior PhD student, the mentor. I had grown to enjoy guiding my team, celebrating small wins, and sharing life lessons. Like a secret vault opening to reveal hidden treasures, I shared the lessons I had learned from my mentors over years of scientific research: repeat the experiment. Cells are finicky. Read the figure caption. The devil is in the details. I had come to understand that transmitting knowledge and wisdom might be the only thing that truly transcends our existence.

Along with the results from the mathematical prediction work, I had generated preliminary data to support the claims in my proposal. I wrote a detailed version and, after reading it over and over again, carefully adding the last dots on the i's and strokes on the t's, I submitted it to the PhD program committee for review on Sunday, January 6, 2019.

In early March, I heard back about the proposal. My score fell below the immediate pass threshold. Reviewers had requested revisions. Most students in my cohort had revisions as well. There was even a rumor that the program had decided not to pass most candidates because they felt that previous cohorts had begun taking the qualifying exam less seriously. I read the email several times and thought, *this does not sound like failing.* We submitted a proposal, and they requested revisions, which seemed fair to me. Perhaps I had underestimated my own resilience.

As I prepared to respond to the reviewers' comments, I went to consult with my program advisor for guidance on revision strategy. I emailed the chair, who asked me to come to his office to go over the comments and help me understand what was expected. We sat at his office desk, the same one where I had first met him during the interview weekend, and he pulled up my proposal along with the committee's comments.

"It seems like the committee is mostly concerned that your proposal is too ambitious for the scope of work of a five-year PhD."

"Oh, are there specific aspects that made it too ambitious?" I asked, remembering that this is a common mistake in research proposals. We had learned in the grant writing class the year prior that everyone proposes a research question, but it has to be reasonably achievable within the candidate's environment.

"The number of samples and experiments is quite large, considering the steps required to acquire, process, and analyze them."

I realized that I had not explicitly explained in the proposal how our research group, a huge institute, operated. I described to him that parts of the sample handling and data analysis did not require developing new processes, methodologies, or infrastructure since they already existed within the institute and were at my disposal to support my proposed research.

"That makes sense. In your revision, make sure to include a section explaining which parts of the experiments are performed by you, which are performed by the technical team, which processes and systems are already built, and which ones will be developed as part of the proposed research."

"I will add that," I replied, quickly taking notes. "Anything else you recommend I address?"

"No, the rest of the proposal is really strong and impactful. We are all excited to see this work come to fruition in a few years."

"Excellent, thank you very much for your time and guidance." I left feeling confident that I would submit a stellar revision. I returned to the lab and incorporated the suggested edits. I reviewed the entire proposal several more times and added the additional preliminary results we had obtained between January and March. I wanted to send it back to the review committee that night but decided to sleep on it and submit it the next day.

La nuit porte conseil, as the old French adage goes, *the night brings counsel*.

The next day, I checked for typos, corrected the colors in the figures, and sent the resubmission. About five days later, I received an email confirming that I had passed and was ready for the oral examination.

On the morning of May 7, in a closed-door session in front of the five-faculty candidacy committee, I passed my oral qualifying exam after a grueling two hours of research presentation, questioning, and scientific discussions designed to challenge my proposal, my intellectual capacity, and my preparedness for PhD candidacy.

"Congratulations, that was very well done," the committee chair announced, marking my formal advancement to candidacy.

As was custom in the lab, a bottle of champagne and cake followed, surrounded by supportive lab mates who made me forget that I needed a nap after weeks of sleepless nights. The following two years continued with the rhythm of gathering data, analyzing results, writing manuscripts, publishing papers, and eventually graduating.

May 15, 2019. Los Angeles, California. Libère next to the screen monitor after passing the PhD qualifying exam. Photo © Jeremy Mason

Chapter 19

CITIZEN OF MANY WORLDS

A s I analyzed cells under the microscope from the newly stained patient samples, my phone rang. I stood up, took off my gloves, and stepped out of the cold, dark microscopy room to answer.

"Hello, Libère speaking."

"Hi, my name is Medina. I'm calling from the USC Gould Law office. How are you today?"

"Hi Medina, I'm well. I didn't recognize the number at first, but I remember you," I replied, walking toward my desk in the shared office space on the third floor of the USC Michelson Center for Convergent Biosciences, where our lab had recently moved.

"Yes, I'm calling with good news. We finished putting together your N-400 application, and we wanted to ask if you want to change your name as part of this process."

"Change my name? I wasn't planning to, but is that common?" I asked, sitting down. I had expected her to confirm some information for my citizenship application and was ready to open my computer to respond. I had not expected a conversation about changing my name.

"It's not required, but we've seen immigrants sometimes use this application to add an English name they would like to be called by."

"Can I add a middle name?"

"Absolutely. Do you know what name you would like to add?"

I paused. I had never considered changing my name, but I wanted a middle name to honor someone I considered instrumentally crucial in my life. I thought about using my dad's name, but when I wrote it down and said it aloud, it didn't feel right.

"I'm ready when you are. We just wanted to make sure you take this chance to make the change."

"Jensen. Use Jensen. J-e-n-s-e-n," I replied without hesitation.

When I couldn't use my dad's name, an immediate and obvious answer popped into my head: honor the person who had been my father figure in my dad's absence. My uncle, Jeans-Berchmans, was someone I had looked up to all my life. I was "son of John." However, "Johnson" sounded too familiar, almost clichéd for a naturalized American, and carried associations I did not want. I explored variations in other languages, and Jensen, the Scandinavian equivalent, fit perfectly. I had no particular connection to the region or culture, but it worked seamlessly as a middle name.

"Okay, your new full legal government name will be *Libère Jensen Ndacayisaba*. That's how it will appear on your Certificate of Citizenship and your U.S. passport."

"Confirmed, thank you."

"Great. We will send your application package to USCIS, and you will hear from them in a few weeks regarding the progress and status of your Naturalization application."

"Excellent, thank you very much, Medina. I appreciate the support from your office."

"It's our pleasure, and we wish you well in the next step. Do update us when you officially become a US citizen; we like to celebrate folks who use our services."

IT WAS IN APRIL 2019, eleven years after I had arrived in the United States, and after becoming a PhD candidate, that I applied for citizenship. The main advantages of citizenship over a green card are the ability to vote, run for office, and hold an American passport.

Until then, I had been too busy trying to survive to make time for the application. While I missed home, I didn't have the finances to travel to Africa whenever I wanted. At this stage, however, I felt secure enough in my life in America to take the step. The PhD stipend of around $33,000 a year in Los Angeles was not a lot, but it was enough that, after saving some money, I could plan a trip to see my family.

The application process was straightforward. Much like the asylum office at EBSC in Berkeley, I learned that the university offered free legal services to students. I provided all the required information for the N-400 application, and the office submitted my paperwork. I could hardly believe my luck. Once again, I did not have to pay thousands in legal fees. I thanked my lucky stars, more stars than those on the American flag.

A few weeks later, after receiving confirmation that my application had been accepted and all checks cleared, I began preparing for the in-person interview with a DHS officer. The interview would test my knowledge of U.S. history and government, as well as my ability to read, write, and speak English. These were tests I had been preparing for during my entire time in America. For several months leading up to the appointment, my lab mates quizzed me almost daily on U.S. history. There was a handbook of questions to study, and we carefully checked off each one as I mastered it.

My interview was scheduled for 9 a.m. Like the embassy interview in 2008 on Avenue des États-Unis and the 2008 asylum interview at the USCIS office in San Francisco, I woke up early, dressed in my best suit, and made my way to the Los Angeles field office.

The words "Federal Building" were emblazoned on the front of the multistory USCIS Field Office at 300 N Los Angeles Street in downtown Los Angeles. I arrived two hours early to avoid traffic and to give myself time to park and grab coffee. In the hallways, the solemnity was discernible, reinforced by the American flags, security checkpoints, and federal agents standing guard. Unlike at the Bujumbura embassy, I was not worried about my English, and these visits had become routine. Unlike the asylum interview in San Francisco, I did not need an attorney, and my immigration status was secure. After living in multiple U.S.

cities and now as a PhD candidate at a well-known university, I know the history of this country well.

"Good morning, Libère," the officer greeted me.

"Good morning, how are you?" I replied.

"I'm well. Please have a seat," she said in a gentle, welcoming voice, making it feel as though we were about to discuss simple business rather than a life-changing milestone.

As I sat down, I glanced at her monitor while she scrolled through my file. Photos of myself from 2008 and 2009 appeared. *They really know everything about me.* I briefly marveled at the technological advancements compared to Burundi, where even my birth certificate had been handwritten and required a personal visit to the provincial office to sign.

"Welcome to your citizenship interview. I will explain the procedure, and then we start. Does that sound good?"

"That sounds good to me," I replied.

"I will verify some information in your application, and I will also ask you up to ten civic questions. You need to answer six correctly to pass."

"Noted," I said, making a mental note to count questions as they came until I was certain I had passed.

"What year did you move to the United States?"

"What is the supreme law of the land?"

"When did you get your green card?"

The questions ranged from American history to civics, along with personal and professional questions to cross-check my file.

"Wait, may I ask how many more history questions are left? I lost track," I inquired

"I mixed the citizenship questions with the administrative checks. There are two or three more questions. Don't worry—you're a scientist, and I can tell you've prepared. You've answered everything correctly so far," she reassured me.

"Thank you," I said.

A few more questions followed, and just like the consulate officer in Bujumbura years earlier, she concluded with, "Congratulations! You passed."

This time, I was fully present, every sense alert. She explained that the next ceremony would be in December and that I would receive a formal invitation.

"You're an American now. Take your civic duties to heart."

"Yes, ma'am. Thank you," I replied, standing to shake her hand before gathering my folder and walking out.

I texted Isidore to share the news. "I passed. Ceremony in December," I wrote.

"I'll be there, rain or shine," he responded. "You have finally made it!"

The invitation arrived in September, confirming the details. On a crisp Thursday morning, December 19, 2019, I donned my suit once again. This time, a red-hued tie over a light blue shirt symbolized the colors of the American flag. Hundreds of us lined up at the Los Angeles Convention Center. Joy and relief were visible across the faces of the young and old, all shaped by the immigrant experience. Even amid the solemnity, the diversity was clear. Different languages echoed through the processional line, multinational stories converging in one place.

When the ceremony began, the federal judge welcomed us as new U.S. citizens, explained the importance of democracy, and administered the United States Oath of Allegiance.

I raised my right hand and declared:

"I hereby declare, on oath, that I absolutely and entirely renounce and abjure all allegiance and fidelity to any foreign prince, potentate, state, or sovereignty, of whom or which I have heretofore been a subject or citizen; that I will support and defend the Constitution and laws of the United States of America against all enemies, foreign and domestic; that I will bear true faith and allegiance to the same; that I will bear arms on behalf of the United States when required by the law; that I will perform noncombatant service in the Armed Forces of the United States when required by the law; that I will perform work of national importance under civilian direction when required by the law; and that I take this obligation freely, without any mental reservation or purpose of evasion; so help me God."

Almost like in a religious anointment ceremony, you feel the weight of the transition. In some ways, the old gives way to the new—the sense of belonging amplified. In other ways, you are still the same person; the nation of origin shaped the individual who is now an American. It is a dual identity, carrying new civic duties alongside the roots of the past.

As I looked around at my fellow new citizens, a sense of kinship and shared triumph filled the air. We had all fought for our place in this country, overcome obstacles, and carved our paths. Together, we were living embodiments of the American dream. The call of ambition seemed louder as I walked out of the ceremony, holding an American flag. There were more dreams to chase. I had inscribed my story into the broader narrative of American history and was ready to embrace my new home. The Burundian village boy belonged among skyscrapers, after all.

At the end of the ceremony, I descended the stairs of the LA Convention Center with my fellow newly minted Americans. Isidore, along with friends who had come to support me, waited below. His pride was unmistakable as he waved an American flag among the thousands gathered to celebrate their loved ones. His smile was ten times larger than when I had seen him sixteen years earlier at SFO. We took commemorative photos and then walked to the passport booth to submit my paperwork for a U.S. passport.

On January 9, 2020, my passport arrived in the mail, and I immediately laid it side by side with my Burundian passport.

The Burundian passport was older, rugged, and full of history. Its edges were worn and soft, like an old prayer book. Faintly, it still carried the scent of red dust. The scratches on the lion's head of the coat of arms whispered of the struggles I had endured before this moment. The inscription *Unité, Travail, Progrès*, visible at the base of the three spires, felt like an ancestral reminder: hard work leads to progress.

The U.S. passport was shiny, new, and blank, carrying the antiseptic scent of government offices. The gold seal of the United States gleamed in the center of the cover, with *E Pluribus Unum* inscribed above the bald eagle—a symbol of courage and freedom, reflecting the anchoring spirit that brought me to this milestone. Unlike the Burundian passport, which bore text in Kirundi, French, and English, the U.S. passport felt pristine, formal, and aspirational.

Almost like time traveling, the two documents represented the span of my life in America. They were a merger of identities: born Burundian, naturalized American. A dual citizen, a citizen of many worlds.

THE FIRST ORDER OF business was clear: I would visit my family, whom I had not seen in twelve years. They no longer lived in Gasorwe camp, where they were when I left. They were no longer in Burundi at all. In 2015, political unrest forced them to flee when then-President Nkurunziza was re-elected to a third term, despite the Constitution limiting terms to two.

The fear-filled survivors of Burundi's 1993 post-election violence, particularly Tutsi who had endured the political turmoil, chose to leave the country as a preventive measure, fearing new political prosecutions. My family was among them; they fled to Rwanda, where they felt safer. With my U.S. passport in hand, traveling to Rwanda was easy. The country offered a visa-on-arrival for U.S. citizens, and I was eager to take advantage of it.

Since late 2019, however, the COVID-19 pandemic has been sweeping across the globe. News of a rapidly spreading infectious disease didn't alarm me. I had grown up in regions accustomed to episodic bacterial and viral outbreaks, and I understood that public health mitigation efforts could contain a disease. Tropical countries had experience managing this. When the lab shut down, I went home without worry, expecting perhaps two and a half weeks before resuming the daily research routine.

I needed my research data to finish manuscripts for publication and complete my PhD. There was no way a temporary closure would derail my plans. Little did I know we would be stuck at home for over a year. Only essential workers—the lab's technical staff whose roles directly impacted patient samples—were allowed access initially. Over time, the lab organized a sparse, controlled schedule so that urgent experiments could continue. Fortunately, I had already generated a substantial amount of data, allowing me to pivot and focus on writing publications.

By summer 2020, Rwanda had contained the virus and began reopening its borders to tourists. I booked my trip, rented an Airbnb, and prepared for a seven-day quarantine upon arrival in Kigali. The KLM flight felt almost spiritual. I had not traveled internationally since that first trip from Bujumbura to San Francisco twelve years prior. I was about to touch African soil again. I barely slept as the plane crossed the Atlantic, this time in reverse. My transit was through Amsterdam Schiphol, not Brussels.

Customs and border protection were enforced as usual, but traveling with an American passport felt different, more straightforward, smoother, almost effortless. By now, the Brussels Airport smell incident was only a distant, amusing memory. At Schiphol, I navigated the airport with ease, interacting comfortably with KLM staff.

Most of my thoughts, however, were on my family. *How much had my younger siblings grown? Would my mother recognize me? Had they been managing well as refugees?*

We left Schiphol in the late afternoon on a direct flight to Kigali, with a quasi-usual stop in Kampala to pick up more passengers heading to Rwanda and Tanzania. Even during departure, I was surrounded by Rwandese travelers. Their language and mannerisms stirred memories of my homeland, Burundi, triggering a deep, ancestral nostalgia.

"Ladies and gentlemen, this is your captain speaking. We have crossed over the Red Sea and are now entering Africa's airspace. If you look out on the left side, that's Alexandria, Egypt, and you'll see the mesmerizing sunrise over the Mediterranean Sea."

The call repeated in Dutch.

I wasn't in a window seat, but I pictured the sunrises I had seen as a child in Burundi. The bright reds fractured across the morning clouds, spreading into golden yellows and amber over the prairies. The night's silence, broken by the songs of waking birds and roosters, seemed to echo in my memory.

By the time the captain spoke again, we had landed in Kampala. After a brief stop, we were in Kigali within the hour. As I stepped off the plane, the thick tropical air hit my nostrils with a familiar, almost ancestral greeting. I could almost smell the trees and banana leaves from the Kigali suburbs nearby. Without thinking, I dropped to my knees and kissed the ground. I hadn't planned to do that. I wasn't even in Burundi, yet the pull of home, the connection to the land where I had walked as a child, overwhelmed me. It felt as if all the souls connected to these soils were welcoming me back.

I proceeded to the security checkpoint and cleared my documents. Once shown where I would serve my mandatory quarantine, I gathered my belongings and boarded the hotel shuttle waiting outside. During the 48 hours quarantine, I coordinated with my family to wait until my COVID-19 test results came back. I also rented a car with a driver who could take us around during my stay. The next day, after receiving a negative test, I called the driver to take me to my family's residence. We would first stop at the Airbnb in Kabeza, Kigali, just a five-minute drive from the airport, a safe and convenient base for my week in Rwanda.

The four-bedroom house was modern and comfortable, with cozy beds, fridges, electricity, a TV, and nicely arranged living spaces. It felt more like a vacation home than a return to the old Gasorwe refugee camp or the familiar Bujumbura city. I put my belongings in one of the rooms and we drove to the countryside near the Burundian border, where my family had been living as refugees. The green hillsides, dotted with tea and coffee farms, reminded me of my childhood home. The unpaved roads, painted in brown-red and yellow-cream hues, mirrored the routes I had taken as a child in Bihogo. It became clear why both Burundi and Rwanda are often called *Pays à mille collines*—land of a thousand hills.

WHEN WE ARRIVED, the car rolled onto a narrow, single-lane street that saw little traffic. Just as in my childhood, village children gathered around, curious to see who had arrived. Some adults peeked from their homes, wondering about the commotion. The mud houses were surrounded by banana trees, just like those we had growing up. I realized my family had chosen this place for its resemblance to our old home.

The southwest of Rwanda and northeast Burundi are almost indistinguishable; any village here could have felt like home.

"That's the house," the driver said, pointing.

"They are here! They are here!" one of the children screamed, running toward the house.

I stepped out of the car, letting the wind greet me as my feet pressed against the dusty red soil. The little mud house looked just like our childhood home in Bihogo. The fence, made of short and neatly trimmed *minyari*–green pencil cactus trees, still carried the protective aura of the corner where Nkurikiye and I had hidden during long nights.

"Mom! Mom, they are here!" the child shouted again as he ran through the front door. I realized quickly this was my nephew, five years old, too shy to introduce himself, but his energy, bursting across the yard, reminded me of myself at that age.

I walked toward the house, my footsteps silent on the soft, dusty ground. The aroma of onions and tomato sauce drifted from inside, weaving through the air and grounding me to the moment. For a fleeting second, I wished I could take off my shoes to feel the earth beneath my feet. I recognized the rhythm of my mother's steps before I even reached the door.

"*Ewe mana yanje, waje wahashitse n'amahoro! Imana ishimwe!*" (My dear God, you're here, you arrived safely, praise the Lord!), she exclaimed, throwing herself into my arms with the longest, strongest hug, her arms moving up and down my back in that familiar, comforting tempo.

"I am here," I whispered, hugging her even tighter.

She paused briefly to look at my face, as if trying to reconcile the voice, the body, and the presence she had longed to see. One hug with my head on the right, another on the left, like a genetically encoded ritual, every molecule of my being recognized the greeting. Overcome with joy, she burst into song, the same hymns I had heard countless times growing up.

Violette, drawn by the commotion, ran into the house laughing at Mom's singing. It wasn't mockery; it was joy overflowing. I recognized her energy instantly, it was familiar, a living echo of the sister I had known.

Bovin, my shy nephew, peeked from behind the door, watching with wide-eyed curiosity. I called him over, but he stayed hidden, unsure of this strange yet familiar presence.

Elysé and Télesphore were in Congo; Elysé would join us later that night.

My mother looked almost the same, her fierce energy as commanding as ever, but there was a fatigue in her eyes that betrayed the years of raising five children amidst constant turmoil and displacement. My sister, once a skinny fourth grader when I left, had grown into a woman, now a mother herself.

I thought about all the events, milestones, and daily moments I had missed. A lump formed in my throat. I wanted to hear every story, every detail, but I realized it was impossible for them to recount twelve years of life in one afternoon.

"Where is the food? It's lunchtime," I asked, almost as if my subconscious were nudging me to stay present, to savor the moment with them.

They all laughed, taking in the sight of the same middle child showing up and making demands.

"Here comes the same old orders from the Bigombos," Mom joked, recalling how, aside from gaining a little weight, I hadn't changed. My body felt transported to my first semester break from Lycée when I returned home.

It also hit me, life here moved differently. Cooking took hours. Unlike fast food in America, you didn't just ask and have it ready.

"Okay, fine. I'll help cook. Where's the kitchen?" I said.

"Take a seat. Guests don't cook in this house," Violette replied, her tone firm but affectionate. In that single sentence, I felt the maturity she had gained during the years apart.

She knew I wasn't joking. She knew I'd probably sneak into the kitchen if allowed. I longed to cook as we used to, to touch every memory, to immerse myself in the smells, textures, and rhythms of home. But customs dictated otherwise, so I accepted my position as a guest and sat in the small living room of their two-bedroom house.

Violette returned to the kitchen, Mom went to bring drinks, and I took a moment to absorb my surroundings. The mud walls smelled like our childhood home, but the clean cement floor, the electricity, and the small comforts made it feel safer, warmer, and better cared for. Outside, a small gate enclosed the front yard. Chickens foraged among banana and cassava trees in the backyard. For the $30 monthly rent I regularly sent, this was more than decent. I felt relief knowing they were living in more comfort than I anticipated.

Mom brought out the traditional sorghum beer in a brown calabash, the exact drink I had been craving. I took a sip and let out a groan of satisfaction. Every cell in my body transported me back to childhood celebrations, holidays, and milestones. Sorghum wasn't too strong, so we drank it from a young age.

"You don't have to hug the calabash and chug it; we have more!" Mom teased, poking fun at me for not sharing after the first sip, as is customary.

After a few more sips, I passed it to the driver, who had been quietly observing the reunion and taking photos. As I had expected, Mom had invited neighbors to meet me. One by one, they came in, offering courteous handshakes followed by slight bows, a gesture of respect traditionally reserved for those of high status. I felt slightly awkward, but reminded myself that this was customary.

When the food was ready, they served me beans, cassava, potatoes, and beef in tomato sauce. Having cassava and potatoes on the same plate was unusual, but they had gone all out to let me taste everything I had missed. My soul felt nourished. Midway through the plate, Violette pointed out additional dishes: cooked cassava leaves, amaranth, and plantains. I groaned with happiness, overwhelmed by the flavors, the memories, and the sense of home.

"Can I swap the potatoes for plantains?" I asked.

"Whatever you like. Or I can make a separate plate," Violette replied.

"Better yet, pack everything—we're bringing it back to Kigali," I said, as if this were the last meal we'd ever eat and it could never be recreated.

As we ate, the familiar chatter unfolded. They asked about life in

America, commenting on news stories they had seen on TV or social media.

"Do you really have self-driving cars?" a young man asked.

"It's still in development, but yes—some cities have prototypes on the road," I replied. Their wide eyes and gasps reflected a mix of amazement and disbelief.

Questions came fast—about religion, food, race, and life in a foreign land. I asked about their children, family members, the weather, the seasons, and how the harvest had been that year.

By 4 p.m., after one last look around the homestead, we loaded into the car and headed back to Kigali—a two-to-three-hour drive along rugged, winding roads.

"Are we going to his house?" Bovin whispered to his grandmother, curious if I actually lived in Kigali. I smiled like a patient uncle, explaining Airbnb and where I stayed. He listened with wide-eyed curiosity.

We reached Kigali around 7 p.m. Elysé would arrive later, around 8 p.m., after six hours traveling from the Kivu region of the DRC. When he finally appeared, I barely recognized him. He had been in first grade when I left. Now, he stood taller than me, his voice deeper than both Isidore and Télesphore. Even the patch of tinea capitis that once marked the top of his head had vanished. Only his smile remained familiar.

That evening, we gathered for dinner as a family for the first time in years. Drinks in hand, we exchanged stories—old tales from Burundi and new ones from America. I shared my early years abroad, the homesickness I endured, and how I had adapted.

Curious about my American life, they asked about food. I joked, insisting it wasn't that good. Elysé, pointing out the nearby KFC and several pizza places, asked if we could try some. I was thrilled to share a piece of my experience with them.

The next day, we ordered pizza and KFC for takeout, since the pandemic made dining out unsafe.

"People eat this as a meal?" Mom asked, her voice tinged with disgust at both the amount of meat and the lack of vegetables. We all laughed. Violette took one bite and quickly abandoned both the fried chicken and the pepperoni pizza.

"It tastes like oil on plastic," she muttered, retreating to the kitchen to prepare something more familiar.

I mostly sat there, enjoying the fact that I had similar reactions to these dishes the first time I had them in the US. The KFC meals in Rwanda were more pleasant than the American version. They were made from organic, farm-raised chicken, and you could tell they were well fried. Elysé was having a party. He loved the excessive meat, and with a nice cold beer in hand, he looked to be thoroughly enjoying it. Bovin had mixed feelings. The cheese on the pizza was too much for him, and he preferred the fried chicken. As much as the quality was better, I also wanted more cassava leaves and maybe some quality plantains. I was just happy that they now had a sense of what American food tastes like.

One key item on my itinerary was to get us all matching tailored clothing in traditional fabrics. The vivid prints and colorful designs are somewhat spiritual, serving as a connection to the culture. One afternoon, we went to the market, which was now entirely outdoors, took measurements, and bought the fabric. The tailoring typically takes multiple days, so I paid extra to expedite the process. As a family custom, when we get together, we dress up in this attire and take photos. I made sure this would be arranged within the time I was visiting, and after a few days of waiting, they arrived. Mom and Violette had their robes tailored to their specifications, and the same was done for the boys. We spent an entire day taking photos in different areas inside and around our stay. Despite not being able to wear them and go out on the town, the photo sessions were sufficient to immortalize the reunion, almost exactly as we had done at the July 2007 graduation and farewell ceremonies in Gasorwe.

As my vacation ended, I insisted that I would return more frequently. *Was I reassuring them or reminding myself?* On the morning of my departure, my sister cried so much that she refused to accompany me to the airport. With words left unsaid, we all understood that she carried sad memories from January 2008, when I left and did not return for more than a decade. As much as I wanted her to come see me off with everyone else, it was a pain I could understand. Almost as if attempting to telekinetically send a consoling goodbye, I hugged her son a little tighter before entering the airport.

On my return flight, reconnecting with my ancestral roots renewed my African identity. Yet I was once again crossing hemispheres, feeling eternally bound to both. I was ready to return to the lab, complete the final stages of my PhD, graduate, and secure a lucrative job for future family reunions.

December 19, 2019. Los Angeles, CA. Libère after the naturalization ceremony at the Los Angeles Convention Center. © Isidore Niyongabo

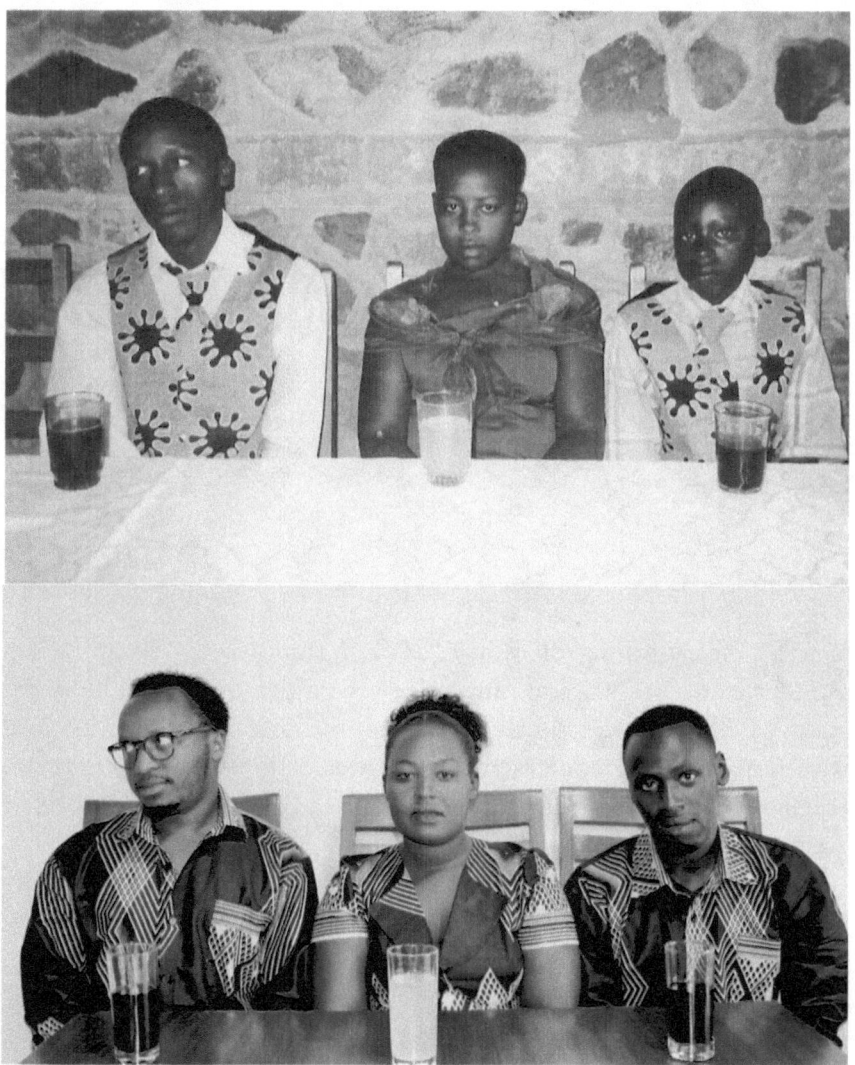

Top: July 2007. Gasorwe, Burundi. Libère, Violette, Elysé. Bottom: October 2020. Kigali, Rwanda. Libère, Violette, Elysé.

Chapter 20

THE IMPROBABLE DOCTOR

On the morning of May 7, 2022, I stood in the empty Galen Center at 7:05 a.m., my voice echoing through 10,000 vacant seats as I rehearsed my speech. In two hours, those seats would be filled with hundreds of graduates and thousands of loved ones gathered to celebrate. But in that quiet moment, it was just me, and the ghosts of everyone who had carried me to this point.

I had woken up at 5 a.m. to practice my speech in the university basketball arena. Instead of my usual classical music, I played Kanye West's *Graduation* album during the drive. The bass thumped through the car speakers, vibrating through the steering wheel and into my palms.

The lyrics matched the weight of the moment. More than that, they pulled me back to where it all began. *Graduation* was released in September 2007, right in the middle of my F-1 visa application to come to the United States for college. The songs were everywhere in Bujumbura, but back then, I barely understood what Kanye West was talking about. That morning, though, he was singing directly about the day ahead.

This day marked the culmination of five years of doctoral training in Medical Biophysics. After first-year rotations, I spent four years developing technologies to detect cancer cells in the blood, building methods to measure and quantify how the nature and state of these cells correlate with cancer progression. My PhD dissertation, *Multimodal Single-Cell Biology and Machine Learning to Characterize Plasma Cell Neoplasms*, documented coauthored, peer-reviewed publications and manuscripts. I knew that, from my first scientific paper to the discoveries still ahead, I wasn't simply adding to human knowledge, I was pushing its boundaries, contributing something that would outlast me.

IN THE WEEKS LEADING to graduation, the Keck School of Medicine of USC selected me as the PhD student speaker. I spent days reflecting on what it had taken to reach this milestone and on the nomadic life that shaped me, from refugee camps and boarding school to the Bay Area, the Syracuse snow, Boston, and five grueling years of doctoral training. Fifteen years later, the cringeworthy email I once sent to Elena had turned into reality. Unlike that evening in Brussels, my cologne, wood sage and sea salt, now carried confidence in its scent. And unlike the long nights of 2008 and 2009, I had secured a job offer before graduation. I had plenty I could brag about in a commencement speech. But each time I wrote the speech, I realized bragging could wait, because the day itself was not mine.

It belonged to Mom and her resilient spirit. It belonged to Nkurikiye and Domitila.

It belonged to Papa Chris.

It belonged to my fifth-grade teacher and other early educators who inspired me.

It belonged to the kind woman who guided me through O'Hare Airport.

It belonged to my mentors and role models.

It belonged to Isidore, who had seen it all unfold since my birth and was there to tell the tales.

It belonged to the strangers who became friends and family during my days in America.

It belonged to victims of wars across the globe.

It belonged to those who have experienced life without a home, whether in refugee camps, in slums and shantytowns on the outskirts of the world's wealthiest cities, or on the paved streets of America's metropolises.

It belonged to the souls in these places, often forgotten and often depicted as the refuse of human civilization.

In my transition from banana leaves to skyscrapers, I recognized that I was a product of this often forgotten corner of humanity. I had learned that diseases know no borders and that suffering requires no visa. I wanted my speech to reflect this reality.

WHEN I ARRIVED AT GALEN, I checked in at the entrance. The early morning air carried the scent of fresh-cut grass from the campus lawns, mixed with the industrial smell of the arena's cleaning products. I walked up to the stage. I had not yet dressed in my full commencement attire. I sat on the chair on the far left and practiced the speech on my phone for a few minutes before standing at the pulpit.

Emotions kicked in. I wished my mother were there. I wished Télesphore, Violette, and Elysé were there. I wished my whole village were there. I knew my father was looking down from above. I thought about all the sacrifices I had made, the friends I left behind at every turn of relocation, and all the sadness I had endured, often alone in the depths of the night. I thought about all the people who doubted me or openly discriminated against me. With a lump in my throat, I struggled to swallow. But I also counted my transient anchors.

Soon it was time to stand on stage, and I stood up to run my practice. I carefully read through my speech, pausing to look across the audience and project as I had practiced. My voice echoed through the empty seats and across the walls of the grand stadium. The acoustics transformed my words into something larger, as if the building itself were amplifying not just sound but significance. When the practice was done, I went backstage to get dressed and prepare for the procession. Like the Syracuse graduation, this marked the last day of a week-long commencement festivities. But this was the main event.

I put on my outfit: a heavy doctoral hood in cardinal red and gold, a doctoral cap, and a bright gold medal symbolizing my induction into the Order of Arête, the highest honor the university bestows on its most outstanding graduating students with advanced degrees, topped with a decorated sash bearing the flag of the United States on my right and that of Burundi on my left. I had decorated the classic academic attire to symbolize my life. A dual citizen, Burundian by birth and American by choice. More importantly, that day summarized the multicolored dual life I had lived. The two flags seemed to flutter slightly that morning, as if in conversation. We lined up, and the usual graduation day procession toward the stage began.

From the front row of the stage, the sea of faces from more than 3,000 attendees filled the Galen Center on a sunny May morning as I listened to Professor Mitchell deliver my introduction before my speech. Morning light streamed through the high ceilings, creating diagonal columns of golden dust motes that danced above the crowd. The ambiance briefly recalled my first meeting with him at the temporary lab building. *Did you know that cancer is a disease of the immune system?* This time, my mind nodded. *I do now. I very much do.*

Friends had come to offer support. Isidore, who had attended every one of my graduation ceremonies and major events, was in town again, this time with his wife, Diane, and my niece, Nasia. Although Nasia was only two years old, I knew she would be somewhere in the large audience and would recognize me on the stage. I imagined her seeing me on the big screen and pointing her little finger, saying, "Hey, it's my uncle." I hoped I would be a beacon in her life, a role model, so that someday she might shine, knowing that anything is achievable.

STEPPING FORWARD TO THE PODIUM, the sound of my steps mimicked the rhythm of my heartbeat as I imagined my words echoing across the vast audience. The first page fell from my folder. The paper fluttered down like a white butterfly, landing silently on the middle shelf of the podium. I picked it up and calmly placed it back on the lectern. I positioned my stance, carefully measuring the microphone's height. Chin up, I addressed the graduating class of 2022 at the USC Keck School of Medicine's 163rd Commencement Ceremony for PhD and master's degrees:

"Dean Meltzer,
Distinguished members of the faculty,
Beloved families,
Honored guests,
and the graduating class of 2022.
Today is an exciting day!
Before we are crowned for our scientific and intellectual achievements, let's first thank those who supported us!
Thank you to the teachers, from first grade to today's grade, who cultivated in us a sense of wonder and curiosity!
Thank you to the USC community, that served as an intellectual home for us to flourish.
Thank you to parents, families, and loved ones who were there for us through the good and bad days.
Personally, I'd like to thank my mom!
After losing my dad during the 1993 civil war in Burundi, my mom raised me and my four siblings as refugees.
Despite the fact that she never attended school and cannot read or write, she somehow understood the value of education and provided everything for us to follow our dreams.
From her, I learned the importance of hard work, resilience, courage, and humility.
Core values that have guided me along my path to this day!
So, thank you to our support systems that made sacrifices to make this day happen!
Let's give them a round of applause! Today is a day of celebration!
Because every one of us had to overcome many challenges to become the scholars and leaders that we are, right now!
I started school as a barefooted little boy in sub-Saharan Africa. Selling peanuts on the streets of northern Burundi.
Twice, I was hospitalized with malaria, and thanks to the scientists who developed chloroquine,

I am here today.
In 2008, I came to the United States to pursue higher education.
I landed in San Francisco, overwhelmed, as everything was big and life
moved fast.
Experiencing both homelessness and homesickness,
I quickly learned to navigate my new life.
Truth be told, there were moments when I wanted to give up.
But in the midst of all the obstacles,
The excitement of doing science and learning how medicines are made
kept me going.
Realizing that, one step at a time, my childhood dreams of becoming a
scientist started to seem attainable.
Perhaps someday, I thought to myself.
So, as I stand on this stage today, I am humbled, and I celebrate that what
was once a dream has been achieved.
As we rejoice on this extraordinary day,
let's take a moment to reflect,
not just on the exciting times and events that fueled our passion,
but also, on the tough days that challenged us
to push even harder and grow.
Perhaps it was the long and tireless nights in the lab,
writing a paper, studying for an exam,
or the disappointment from a failed experiment,
or COVID pandemic days we spent on never-ending Zoom calls,
or perhaps just the train track noise behind Currie Hall.
Whatever the challenges you faced,
Class of 2022, You did it!
So, allow yourself to feel,
feel the distance of how far You have come,
feel the heights of what You have achieved,
feel the weight of Your accomplishments,
and most importantly, feel the promise of what lies ahead!
Tomorrow, we begin anew!
And today I ask of you,
What will you do with your degree?

We are privileged to have been educated at one of the finest universities on this planet,
trained in basic science and clinical research by exceptional talent at the Keck School of Medicine of USC
One may ask, for what purpose then?
How will your intellectual prowess and scientific discoveries solve health-care disparities and enable access to medicines,
Not just for diabetic patients in LA's underserved communities who cannot afford their next dose of insulin, but also, for the children in South Sudan afflicted by measles.
How will your USC education and research contribute, not just to fight against anti-science trends in the United States, but also to reduce the gender education gap for girls kept out of school in Guatemala?
How will your research talents and innovations alleviate suffering, not just for wealthy executives but also, for the homeless on Skid Row strug-gling with mental health?
These are the grand challenges of our generation and we have been called for this vocation.
We are the pioneers of medical science, the guardians of human health.
USC trained us to unravel the complexities of human disease,
Let's also make sure that our impact in research and healthcare is acces-sible to all.
Congratulations, and Fight On!"

The sound of hands clapping filled the stadium. The applause rolled through the arena like thunder, wave after wave of sound that seemed to lift me off my feet. In the front right, one graduate wiped away her tears. I hoped they were tears of joy. I folded my speech folder and sat down in the front row among deans, vice deans, chairs of programs, and mentors whose mentees were being celebrated and hooded that day for completing their doctoral education. The weight of the moment settled around me like a familiar cloak.

When all the speakers were finished, we were hooded and the degrees conferred. The doctoral hood felt heavier, its velvet border soft against my neck, the weight of centuries of academic tradition resting on my shoulders.

OUTSIDE THE STADIUM AFTER the ceremonies, the California sun was bright after the dim arena lighting, making everyone squint as phone cameras clicked. Strangers stopped me in my tracks to say hello, congratulate me, and take selfies.

"Amazing speech!"

"That was an inspiring speech!"

"Can you take a photo with us?"

In the midst of all the English shouts, I heard a message in French.

"C'est lui, c'est lui!" (it's him, it's him). I turned. The familiar French accent felt like a warm embrace after hours of English.

"Le Docteur! Félicitations, mon fils!" (the doctor! Congratulations, my son!) said the dad, who, as I could tell, was in town for his daughter's graduation.

"Merci beaucoup", I replied, trying to check if I knew who they were.

"They are my parents. They flew in from Cameroon. We loved your speech, especially the part about malaria," continued the young daughter.

"Can we take a photo with you?"

"Of course!"

A few more groups stopped me to take photos. In proper Los Angeles fashion, I was a star for a few minutes. The improbable doctor.

For a brief moment, it felt like the village was there. Although they looked different, their pride in me filled the void imposed by the hemispheric distance between Los Angeles and Gasorwe.

In the midst of the commotion, I could see Isidore, Diane, and Nasia in the distance and made my way to them. As we hugged and I took in the moment's significance, I found myself briefly looking into my niece's eyes. I recounted the suffering inherited through our bloodline. Tracing from the Ntare ancestry during colonial times, to my grandparents' time, experiencing the Burundian independence and the wars that followed, to my mother's time, where women were deprived of education, and to my childhood and the war times that followed October 1993, and now, there was my brother's daughter tugging on my

PhD tassel. Her tiny fingers wrapped around the gold threads, pulling gently as if testing their reality. Amid all the achievements, I hoped my success was an intergenerational triumph that served as medicine for our intergenerational trauma. PhD, after all, is not what you accomplish, but the person you become.

I HAD A ONE-WAY Los Angeles-to-Boston flight booked for the next morning. I was returning to start my new job as a computational biologist at a small biotechnology company developing RNA-based medicines..

That evening, I held a farewell gathering with friends. The bar smelled of crisp drinks and celebration, glasses clinking with toasts that tried to capture five years in a few words. Friends came and went, congratulating me and saying their goodbyes. After all the times I had moved around and said farewells to friends, classmates, and colleagues I never reunited with, one might think it had gotten easier. I tried to hide it, but deep down I was filled with sorrow. Was this a final goodbye, again? These were the friends I cherished the most. Five years in LA, after Bihogo and San Francisco, was the longest I had ever lived in one place. These were strong connections I had made, and once again, I was packed up and ready to leave.

I went home and made sure my two suitcases were packed. The familiar ritual of folding life into portable containers, each item a memory compressed into fabric and necessity. In the quiet night, I sat on the balcony of my little room one last time and watched the hills of East Los Angeles. The night was warm, the neighborhood lights twinkling like earthbound stars. Somewhere beyond the lights were the laboratories where I had spent countless hours, the coffee shops where I had written my dissertation, the mountains and beaches where I had found peace between experiments.

Tomorrow, Boston awaited with its own promises. But tonight, in this liminal space between achievements and adventures, I was simply Libère: the barefoot boy who sold peanuts, the student who couldn't afford textbooks, the scientist who pushed the boundaries of knowledge, all existing simultaneously in one story. I closed the windows and slid into the bed sheets one last time. As my eyes grew heavy in the silence of the night, I quietly recited the immortal words of Bilbo Baggins: *"I think I'm quite ready for another adventure."*

May 7, 2022 at 7 am. Los Angeles, California. Libère, alone on the podium at Galen Center reviewing his speech. Photo © Sayuri Pacheco

May 7, 2022. Los Angeles California. Diane, Libère, Nasia, and Isidore after the commencement ceremony. Photo © Sara Ma

EPILOGUE

Shores of Tomorrow

I write these final notes in September 2025 from my home in Los Angeles. Outside the windows, palm trees sway in the winds from the Pacific Ocean. The Southern California sunlight pierces the cool marine air, carrying a golden quality found nowhere else, not the harsh brilliance of African noon, nor the watery light of Syracuse or Boston winters, but something in between, something I'm learning to call home. On my desk sits a photo from my PhD graduation at USC in 2022. Next to it, a family photo from Gasorwe camp in spring 2000, our tent house visible behind the cassava trees and green bean leaves. In the desk drawer lie my U.S. and Burundian passports, pages filled with stamps marking travels between worlds.

The manuscript I set out to write was meant to share humbling lessons from my pursuits, to catalog achievements and learnings. Instead, it became an excavation, each memory revealing not just what happened, but who I became. What the neocortex preserved were the anchors: people, moments, and lessons that held me steady while everything else shifted throughout my nomadic life.

Mom has finally stopped working and is settled in Rwanda. Between proudly showing off the land Isidore bought for her and thanking God that she no longer needs to pay rent as a refugee in a foreign land, she recites the rosary every waking hour and passes on the discipline she raised us with to Bovin, who started seventh grade this fall. In 2023, Isidore, Diane, Nasia, and I flew to Rwanda to celebrate her seventieth birthday. The sound of her laughter that day–unrestrained and musical–was the same as when Dad used to dance with her in our mud house in Bihogo.

Isidore, after graduating from the University of San Diego with a master's degree in Social Work and Economic Development, is now an executive at a global nonprofit organization, continuing his lifelong philanthropic devotion. He was Ohlone College's 2016 commencement speaker. As Nasia starts kindergarten this fall, we regularly reminisce about the stories we have lived and how to better our lives, the lives of our loved ones, and humanity in general. His book, *Happy at Zero*, is upcoming.

Télesphore married in August 2023. I flew into Bujumbura for the first time since my January 2008 maiden voyage for his wedding. The smell of eucalyptus along the airport road hit me like time travel; suddenly I was seven again, walking home from Mukoni Primary School. In the reception hall, I gave a speech in Kirundi to welcome the bride to the family. My accent had shifted, consonants softened by years of English, and when I said, *"twarera inkoko n'impene"*–we used to take care of chickens and goats, not realizing that *kurera* means *raising children*–and is not used for animals, the whole hall erupted in laughter at my American-accented Kirundi. In that shared laugh, I felt the beautiful absurdity of my journey: a PhD in my head, but the farm boy's tongue was still in my mouth. It was a humbling reminder of just how far, and yet how little, I had truly traveled.

Violette runs a small beauty business, a passion she recently discovered, in which I am an investor. We now call her Mabuja, or "boss lady," her phone constantly buzzing with clients, the same determined energy she had as a child, demanding, *"Ene, Libe, ene!"* She gets married in December, and the whole family will reunite once more to celebrate. Mom recently joked that she had already told her in-laws that I would be the one showing up to collect the dowry. *"For all those years you carried her on your back,"* she said, her eyes crinkling with both humor and mischief.

Elysé just graduated from university in August with a bachelor's degree in Information Technology from Cavendish University in Uganda. I flew into Kampala for the ceremony, and Mom, sitting beside me in the vast auditorium that smelled of fresh paint and ambition, wore what looked like the happiest expression of her life. As the speeches droned on in English she couldn't understand, I leaned close and translated, almost the same way I used to read letters in Gasorwe camp, watching her face light up with each *"with honors"* and *"distinguished achievement."*

For me, the twenty-five to thirty-hour flights from the U.S. West Coast to East Africa have become a pilgrimage. My body rebels against the time zones, the recycled air, the impossibility of sleep. But when I land in Kigali, Bujumbura, or Entebbe, that first breath of thick tropical air, carrying the scent of red earth and wood smoke, recalibrates something ancestral within me. In the birdsong, I hear the voices of ancestors. In the street hustle, I feel the resilience of my people. In the morning prayer calls, the embraces of loved ones, and the nourishment of home-cooked meals, I find root to my soul. Often, when I miss home, I play *Mà Vlast* at full blast, close my eyes, and imagine the thousand hills of my childhood. I am grateful for the mountains and seas whose fresh air mends my wounds, and for the generosity of human connection that softens my scars.

My past continues to drive me forward. Through biomedical innovation that still captivates my curiosity and social impact ventures that improve lives, I dream of changing the world, bringing health to the sick and education to the marginalized.

Soon I'll drive to the laboratory where my team awaits. The -80°C freezers will hum their familiar drone, reagents and samples arranged in tiny vials like a library of human hope. It is work that connects my past to my purpose, from the child who survived malaria to the scientist who hopes to help others survive their maladies.

To those navigating their own passages between worlds, refugees, immigrants, and anyone in transit to their next adventure, your accent isn't broken English; it is fluent resilience. The food that tastes like home but looks strange to others, that is not nostalgia, it is navigation. Your hyphenated identity is not division, but multiplication. The village wisdom and urban knowledge coexist in the same mind, in the same breath.

To those who offer anchors to others through policies, programs, and personal kindness: you are the lighthouse that illuminates the world, your humanity guiding lives as they turn toward their true course.

And to all the people, named or unnamed, whose paths I have crossed and who anchored me through life, you are written in the permanent record of the lives your grace and kindness have changed. To classmates and colleagues who became friends, and friends who became family, your permanence in my life deserves its own book.

As the California sun sets into the Pacific, it serves as a daily reminder that stability doesn't require stillness, that endings are also arrivals. Tomorrow brings another sunrise, another chance to be both anchor and voyage. The hands that sold peanuts on RN6 and bagged groceries at Safeway now pipette cells in research towers. The altar boy who recited prayers now sits in boardrooms. The village lives in these city towers. Every self remains present, forever anchored in the adventure itself.

"Seek to make your life long and its purpose in the service of your people."

— TECUMSEH

ACKNOWLEDGMENTS

First and foremost, I thank my writing coach, Karen Putz, for motivating me to begin this book project and for her extensive guidance on the scope of the content. Though she initially suggested writing a self-help or business fable, I am immensely grateful for her patience, wisdom, and trust during the early stages of this project. Perhaps I will write that self-help book in the near future.

Special thanks to Sara Ma, Jess C., and Kristin K., who bravely engaged with the first drafts and provided invaluable feedback. Your honest critiques and encouragement during the most critical stage of writing gave me the confidence to continue. I hope you enjoy reading the final version.

Many thanks to Lauren Putz for her early feedback on content structure and development. Her insights helped shape the narrative arc and thematic elements that became central to this book.

This work would not have been possible without the unwavering support of my family, who walked with me through memories that were sometimes painful, sometimes joyful, but always met with grace and understanding. My deepest gratitude goes to my Mom, who sat through long calls to help cross-check facts from my childhood.

Additional thanks to Violette, Elysé, and Télesphore for fact-checking stories from the camps, and to Isidore for reviewing nearly every chapter, from my early years to the present. Your collective memory and willingness to revisit difficult times made this narrative authentic.

Thanks also to Chris Nsabiyumva for reviewing some of the critical sociopolitical and historical elements of Burundi.

For her relentlessly enthusiastic critiques and for braving multiple versions of a nonfiction memoir despite her preference for fiction, I thank Rachel Utama. Her precision strengthened both the prose and the pacing of the narrative. As promised, my next manuscript headed her way will be a work of fiction.

I am also indebted to Aidan Moriarty for her meticulous proofreading, whose sharp attention to detail polished this work into its final form.

For the striking cover art, I thank the team at DesignDusk and Arslan for capturing the essence of this story in visual form.

I would also like to acknowledge the broader community of readers, writers, and storytellers. By creating space for narratives like mine, your support of diverse voices serves as an anchor for modern literature.

To everyone who has played a part in the journeys mapped across these pages: I am because you are.

To all who made this work of artistic expression possible, I am forever indebted. And to you, the reader, for holding this book and experiencing life through my lens, thank you.

May your days be anchored.

ABOUT THE AUTHOR

Libère J. Ndacayisaba is a Burundian American scientist and author of *Transient Anchors: From Refugee Tents to Research Towers*. He was six years old when the turmoil of the 1993 Burundian genocide shattered his peaceful childhood in the red-soiled mountains of Burundi. From years of displacement as a refugee and seminary education, he forged an unlikely path from village life to the forefront of biomedical science in the United States of America.

He earned his PhD in Medical Biophysics from the University of Southern California, where his research focused on myeloma, a cancer of the immune system. He has authored numerous peer-reviewed research publications in oncology and is a co-founder of an early-stage startup developing immunomodulation technologies, translating discoveries into therapies that extend lives.

Libère is an avid advocate for access to innovative healthcare and education through his philanthropic venture, the Tetradenia Foundation, named after a medicinal flower native to the Burundi highlands, delivering healthcare to remote and rural communities across the globe. He serves as a board director at SaCoDé—a nonprofit fighting period poverty in Burundi—and advises other social impact enterprises.

Science taught him to observe. Writing taught him to remember.

With a voice shaped by resilience and discovery, Libère writes to honor his country, humanity, and the journeys of countless lives whose stories remain untold. He speaks Kirundi, French, English, and some Swahili. *Transient Anchors* is his first book.

When not in the laboratory or at his desk, he can be found running on the trails and beaches of Southern California, attempting to cook Burundian dishes, traveling the world, or searching for the perfect cup of coffee.

He resides in Los Angeles, California—still learning how to stay.

www.ingramcontent.com/pod-product-compliance
Lightning Source LLC
Chambersburg PA
CBHW021222130626
46554CB00004B/1323